LEADING A
COMPETENCY-BASED
SECONDARY
SCHOOL

Robert J.
MARZANO

Patrick B.
HARDY

MARZANO
Resources

Visit **MarzanoResources.com/reproducibles** to download
the free reproducibles in this book.

555 North Morton Street
Bloomington, IN 47404
888.849.0851
FAX: 866.801.1447

email: info@MarzanoResources.com
MarzanoResources.com

Visit **MarzanoResources.com/reproducibles** to download the free reproducibles in this book.

Printed in the United States of America

Library of Congress Control Number: 2022033317
ISBN: 978-1-943360-45-1 (paperback)

Production Team
President and Publisher: Douglas M. Rife
Associate Publisher: Sarah Payne-Mills
Managing Production Editor: Kendra Slayton
Editorial Director: Todd Brakke
Art Director: Rian Anderson
Copy Chief: Jessi Finn
Senior Production Editor: Laurel Hecker
Content Development Specialist: Amy Rubenstein
Acquisitions Editor: Sarah Jubar
Copy Editor: Mark Hain
Proofreader: Jessi Finn
Text and Cover Designer: Abby Bowen
Associate Editor: Sarah Ludwig
Editorial Assistants: Charlotte Jones and Elijah Oates

TABLE OF CONTENTS

CHAPTER 3

CHAPTER 4

CHAPTER 5

ABOUT THE AUTHORS

Robert J. Marzano, PhD, is cofounder and chief academic officer of Marzano Resources in Denver, Colorado. During his fifty years in the field of education, he has worked with educators as a speaker and trainer and has authored more than fifty books and two hundred articles on topics such as instruction, assessment, writing and implementing standards, cognition, effective leadership, and school intervention. His books include *The New Art and Science of Teaching,* *Leaders of Learning, Making Classroom Assessments Reliable and Valid,* *The Classroom Strategies Series, Managing the Inner World of Teaching,* *A Handbook for High Reliability Schools, A Handbook for Personalized Competency-Based Education,* and *The Highly Engaged Classroom.* His practical translations of the most current research and theory into classroom strategies are known internationally and are widely practiced by both teachers and administrators.

Dr. Marzano received a bachelor's degree from Iona College in New Rochelle, New York, a master's degree from Seattle University, and a doctorate from the University of Washington.

To learn more about Dr. Marzano, visit www.marzanoresources.com.

Patrick B. Hardy, PhD, DMin, has enjoyed a distinguished twenty-six-year career in education. He was recently named principal at Hinsdale South High School in Darien, Illinois. Previously, he served as the executive director of equity and student success at Oak Park and River Forest High School District 200 in Oak Park, Illinois. Before assuming his role in District 200, Dr. Hardy was principal of Proviso East High School in Maywood, Illinois, which became the first certified secondary Marzano Academy in the United States. Additionally, Dr. Hardy served as a leadership coach with the University of Chicago's Network for College Success; principal and assistant superintendent in Freeport, Illinois; and principal and chief academic officer in Rockford, Illinois. As a district and school leader, consultant, and speaker, Dr. Hardy has focused his work, presentations, and keynotes on school transformation and innovation, leadership development and coaching, equitable education, and personalized competency-based education.

Dr. Hardy is a longtime member of Phi Beta Sigma Fraternity Inc., the Illinois Principals Association, and the Association for Supervision and Curriculum Development. Dr. Hardy's successful leadership has garnered recognition from a variety of organizations. In 2021, K–12 Dive recognized him as a Rising District Leader, and the National Teachers Hall of Fame acknowledged him as an Educator Who Makes a Difference based on nominations from community members. In addition, Dr. Hardy received the 2019 Service to Humanity Award from the Rockford Chapter of Phi Beta Sigma Fraternity Inc. In 2018, the West Cook Region of the Illinois Principals Association recognized Dr. Hardy as Principal of the Year, and Northern Illinois University's College of Education named him a Marguerite F. Key Fellow.

Dr. Hardy holds a bachelor of arts degree in history and secondary education from Xavier University of Louisiana, a master of education degree from Harvard University's Graduate School of Education, and a second master of education degree specializing in school administration from Cambridge College in Boston. In addition, he earned a doctorate of ministry specializing in pastoral studies from Andersonville Theological Seminary in Camilla, Georgia. He also holds a doctorate of philosophy in education from Capella University, where he graduated with distinction.

Introduction

This book is about leadership in secondary schools. Of course, there are many books with a similar focus. The secondary school leadership addressed in this book, however, focuses on a particular type of school that we refer to as a *Marzano Academy* or simply as the *academy model*. While this book is certainly designed for schools that are pursuing the official process of becoming a Marzano Academy, it is also intended for schools that do not wish to pursue that process but do wish to implement some of the components of the Marzano Academies model within their current system. Schools that wish to go through the formal process should contact MarzanoAcademies.org.

Traditionally, the term *academy* has been used to describe secondary schools, but it is now used across the K–12 continuum. Regardless of the grade level referenced, educators frequently use the term to describe a school designed to produce students who have mastered specific areas of knowledge and skill, such as an academy for the arts, an academy for science, an academy for literature, and so on. By convention, then, in the United States, the term academy generally means that a school has a primary and somewhat narrow focus. The academy model we describe here is, to a certain extent, the antithesis of the traditional approach to academies. Instead of having a primary, narrow academic focus, it is designed to develop a wide and interconnected array of knowledge and skills that allows students to pursue any endeavor they so choose and to succeed in that pursuit. We believe that this approach is particularly well suited to the substantial challenges of transforming secondary educational systems.

Moving the Mountain of Secondary Education

Calls to change education have been persistent and varied, particularly at the secondary level. There are some who make the case that the U.S. educational system has consistently failed to provide equal opportunities for all students, despite the elimination of some unjust social structures such as segregation (Harrison & Clark, 2016). Others go so far as to assert that the current education system inherently perpetuates inequality of opportunity (McGee & Hostetler, 2014). While most criticisms of the system are more centrist in nature, one fact that seems self-evident is that the public education system struggles to address the growing diversity of its students. Schools are enrolling more and more students of color, many of whom are also impoverished (Kondor, Owusu-Ansah, & Keyne-Michaels, 2019). In urban schools specifically, many students reside in neighborhoods of concentrated poverty and are being taught in a language other than their native tongue—four hundred different first languages are represented among English learners in the United States (Chen, 2021; Diem & Carpenter, 2012). Since the turn of the millennium, the percentage of school-age White children has decreased from 62 percent to 51 percent (de Brey et al., 2019). In 2020,

54 percent of K–12 public school students in the United States were students of color or multi-racial and 53 percent of secondary students identified as nonwhite, which means public schools are already majority minority (Riser-Kositsky, 2022; ThinkImpact, 2022).

Contrasting the heterogeneity of the student population is the homogeneity of the teaching population, which is primarily comprised of White, monolingual women. Over the same period that the percentage of White students decreased more than 10 percent, the percentage of White teachers did not change much, hovering around 80 percent (National Center for Education Statistics, 2020; U.S. Department of Education, 2016). The contrast could hardly be sharper.

While most of these classroom teachers are excellent, dedicated educators, it is reasonable to assume that more diversity in the teaching profession would help adapt to the growing diversity in the student population. Conversely, it is unreasonable to assume that a homogeneous teacher workforce can fully address the difficulties a growing number of students face as they try to navigate the education system, particularly at the secondary level (Robertson & Guerra, 2016; Santamaría & Jean-Marie, 2014). Such challenges include identifying reasonable options available to secondary students from varying socioeconomic backgrounds and planning mitigation strategies for obstacles unique to students from low-income families. Further, most public school teachers are not directly trained to confront the various educational and social inequities that exist in America's public schools (Convertino, 2016; Möller, 2012; Robertson & Guerra, 2016). The net effect of these forces is that schools regularly face the monumental task of tackling topics like culture, race, economics, gender, sexual orientation, language, religion, and other distinguishing characteristics that define individual student differences (Lund, 2011; Salvador & Kelly-McHale, 2017).

The diversity that characterizes public education will most likely become even more pronounced over time. Teacher education scholars Phyllis Robertson and Patricia Guerra (2016) noted that the White, monolingual, English-speaking student population in public schools is steadily declining compared to the rapidly growing populations of students of color who are not fluent in English. There are also contentions that high teacher turnover and persistent low expectations are more typical in the educational experiences of African American students and other marginalized groups than they are in the experiences of the general student population (Esposito & Swain, 2009; Reed & Johnson, 2010). At the secondary level, high teacher turnover can affect teacher quality and the ability of schools to offer advanced courses.

The education system's inability to meet the ever-expanding needs of diverse students ultimately manifests as marginalized groups not performing well academically when compared with students from more advantaged backgrounds. Psychologist Gail Furman (2012) pointed out that the increased awareness of multiple achievement gaps and the deficit thinking present in school policies and practices designed to address those gaps herald the need for systemic reform. We believe that any reform efforts to alleviate these problems cannot focus on individual components in isolation. Rather, component parts of the cumulative problem must be addressed as a system (Gomez-Velez, 2013). The circuit-board metaphor can provide some insight into this dynamic.

The Circuit-Board Metaphor

Like other large and complex institutions, the public education system is a network of interconnected components working together. Instruction, finance, assessment, human resources, culture, climate, and professional development are but a few of the various components of any education system. Typical reform efforts and innovations focus on one or two of these components. For example, a school or district might consider a new reading program or a new response to intervention (RTI) program as a major reform intervention. Such one-dimensional efforts do not address the systemic nature of the issues facing schools and do not foster continuous improvement (West, 2012). Education researcher Victoria M. Young (2018) maintained that practices and policies that require coordinated cultural, structural, and political strategies must replace typical myopic, one-dimensional reform efforts. We refer to this multifront approach as the *circuit-board effect*.

A computer circuit board is a sheet of material onto which engineers mount microchips, conductive pathways, and other components. Each microchip has a number of inputs or prongs along its sides that send electrical pulses along paths to other chips. When a microchip receives an electrical impulse, it either responds by performing an operation or passes the information along to other microchips that reply in various ways. All these communications, mathematical calculations, and transactions occur in milliseconds and provide the user with an output.

A circuit board is emblematic of the interconnectedness of the education system. Truly transforming education requires a type of systemic change that will yield a product that better serves all students. How can we configure the various circuits in the typical school to make them produce results hitherto not produced? The first step is to identify the right circuits. The Marzano Academies model provides such a guide to an interconnected system.

The History and Foundations of the Marzano Academies Model

The Marzano Academies model, as described in this book, is the product of decades of inter-related efforts to translate research and theory into practice, starting with efforts in the 1980s to integrate direct instruction in thinking skills into the K–12 curriculum (for instance, Marzano et al., 1988). Such efforts have proceeded up to the present, with works that cover a wide variety of topics, including instruction, leadership, curriculum, assessment, vocabulary, standards, grading, high reliability organizations, professional learning communities, personalized competency-based education (PCBE), student motivation, social-emotional learning, teacher and leader evaluation, and taxonomies of knowledge and skill, to name a few.

The model of secondary schools presented here is the integration of numerous research and theory efforts over multiple decades, all of which were developed such that every piece is designed to fit with every other piece. This type of systematic planning is a unique aspect of the academy model in terms of school improvement. In contrast, in the name of school improvement, many secondary school leaders attempt to combine separate and sometimes disparate programs designed independently by different experts and organizations. While such efforts are well intended and have a certain intuitive appeal, they often fail because the selected initiatives might clash and cancel each other out, even though all are effective in their own right. For example, a high school leader might simultaneously try to implement a new online algebra tutorial program and a new online reading intervention without realizing that they both add a great deal of content to an already bloated curriculum. While each program could be useful independently, together—and without corresponding changes to make room in the curriculum—they add new requirements for content coverage that teachers simply can't meet.

Marzano Academies employs its sixteen school-level indicators, which have all been designed so as to be compatible with the other indicators, in a seamless system that produces consistent, high-quality education. This model is a departure from traditional structures of schooling in a number of ways. First, and perhaps foremost, it is a competency-based system. *Competency-based education* (CBE) refers to the practice of promoting students to the next level only when they have demonstrated mastery of the academic content at the previous level. Time is not a factor—a student can progress at an accelerated rate in one subject and take more time in another. For example, a middle school student might be working on sixth-grade English language arts (ELA) content and eighth-grade mathematics content, even though she is chronologically a seventh grader. Students are organized into classes and groups by their ability rather than by age, allowing teachers to provide more targeted, effective instruction. CBE ensures that students actually learn before advancing, so they master the content the school considers important at each level and are prepared for the next one.

Second, to articulate the content students are expected to learn at each level and in each subject area, the Marzano Academies model defines its academic program in a highly precise manner. For each topic that students must master, a *proficiency scale* delineates the progression of learning, from basic knowledge and skills, to the target level that students are expected to reach, to opportunities for advanced applications. A manageable set of proficiency scales for each content area at each level ensures consistency—students master the same content and skills no matter which teachers they learn from. The power of proficiency scales is that they show exactly what students need to know and how they will get there. Furthermore, teachers assess students, score work, and report grades based on proficiency scales. Feedback to students lets them know where on the scale their current level of knowledge falls, making it easy for them to see what they need to do to improve. When teachers report grades, those grades do not take the form of an omnibus percentage or letter grade, but rather a set of individual scores for each topic that the student is currently working on.

A third way that the Marzano Academies model differs from a typical traditional school is its recognition that effective education goes beyond academic content. The model includes directly teaching cognitive and metacognitive skills, such as analytical thinking, problem solving, impulse control, and collaboration. These skills are as essential to preparedness for life and career as academic content, so age-appropriate learning progressions for each skill are defined through proficiency scales. Students learn information and processes related to each skill and teachers give feedback on students' mastery thereof.

The Marzano Academies model also includes social-emotional components. The community of the school sets the environment for learning, and the quality of that community impacts the quality of students' education. The academy model emphasizes relationships and a sense of belonging among students, teachers, leaders, and other stakeholders. In addition to regular social-emotional learning on topics like mindfulness and empathy, students in a Marzano Academy participate in inspiring programs like those presented by Rachel's Challenge, an anti-bullying organization that focuses on kindness and compassion (www.rachelschallenge.org).

The final unique component we will mention here is the Marzano Academies approach to instruction. An *instructional model* defines in detail the practices associated with excellent teaching. The Marzano Academies instructional model includes forty-nine elements of effective instruction for CBE, ranging from content-delivery elements, like recording and representing content, to elements related to the classroom context, such as showing value and respect for all learners. With support from school leaders, teachers are expected to set goals and develop their abilities relative to the elements of the instructional model. Instruction in the Marzano Academies model also includes the systematic use of strategies known to improve students' retention of information, such as cumulative review.

While the Marzano Academies model may seem complex, its components form a coherent whole that drives toward a single goal: the highest-quality education for all learners. The structure that allows school leaders to manage these seemingly different initiatives in a cohesive, integrated fashion is the concept of a high reliability organization.

High Reliability Leadership

The academy model utilizes a high reliability approach to leadership. While there has been a great deal written about leadership in K–12 education, until recently there has been relatively little written about *high reliability* leadership in education. The high reliability process used in the academy model is outlined in the book *Leading a High Reliability School* (Marzano, Warrick, Rains, & DuFour, 2018).

At its core, a high reliability perspective involves monitoring the relationship between the actions that an organization takes to enhance its effectiveness and the extent to which these actions do, in fact, produce their desired effects. In the literature on high reliability organizations, those actions an organization takes are referred to as *leading indicators*, and the concrete results produced from monitoring the effects of the leading indicators are referred to as *lagging indicators*.

Leading and lagging indicators are the operational cornerstones of the high reliability process employed in the academy model. There are sixteen leading indicators that constitute the Marzano Academies model. We refer to them as *school-level indicators* (SLIs). Those sixteen leading indicators are as follows (Marzano Academies, n.d.).

SLI 1. **Safe, Orderly, and Supportive Environment:** The school has programs and practices in place that provide students, parents, and staff with a sense of safety, order, and support.

SLI 2. **Student Efficacy and Agency:** The school has programs and practices in place that help develop student efficacy and agency.

SLI 3. **Inspiration:** The school has programs and practices in place that are designed to inspire students by providing opportunities for self-actualization and connection to something greater than self.

SLI 4. **Personal Projects:** The school has programs and practices in place that allow students to engage in projects of their own design.

SLI 5. **Instruction and Teacher Development:** The school has a Marzano Academies–approved instructional model that it uses to provide feedback to teachers regarding their status and growth on specific pedagogical skills.

SLI 6. **Blended Instruction:** The school procures online resources and engages teachers in activities that help them develop online resources for score 2.0, 3.0, and 4.0 levels on proficiency scales.

SLI 7. **Cumulative Review:** The school has programs and practices in place that ensure students continually review and revise critical content and practice various forms of assessment relative to that content.

SLI 8. **Knowledge Maps:** The school ensures that students use knowledge maps as tools to comprehend and write various types of texts.

SLI 9. **Measurement Topics and Proficiency Scales:** The school has well-articulated measurement topics with accompanying proficiency scales for essential academic content.

SLI 10. **Cognitive and Metacognitive Skills:** The school has well-articulated measurement topics and accompanying proficiency scales for cognitive and metacognitive skills that are systematically taught and assessed throughout the curriculum.

SLI 11. **Vocabulary:** The school has programs and practices in place to ensure that all students have a working knowledge of tier one, tier two, and tier three vocabulary.

SLI 12. **Explicit Goals for Students' Status and Growth:** The school has explicit goals for students' status and growth at the individual student level and at the whole-school level.

SLI 13. **Classroom Assessment:** The school has an assessment system that ensures the use of reliable and valid classroom assessments that measure each student's status and growth on specific measurement topics.

SLI 14. **Reporting and Grading:** The school has a reporting and grading system that depicts both status and growth for individual students and allows for students to work at multiple levels across different subject areas.

SLI 15. **Collective Responsibility:** The school has programs and practices in place that ensure teachers collectively provide instruction, support, and assessments on measurement topics regardless of whose class students are primarily assigned to.

SLI 16. **Flexible Scheduling:** The school employs scheduling practices that allow students to receive instruction, support, and evaluation on measurement topics at any level in any subject area.

Note that each of the sixteen indicators references programs and practices. As previously described, this is the essence of a leading indicator. A school is executing some program or practice for distinct purposes. These sixteen leading indicators for the academy model represent non-negotiable interventions in which the school must engage. They also represent sixteen areas for which concrete data must be generated and monitored. These data are the basis for establishing lagging indicators. In effect, leading indicators are the starting place for implementing high reliability leadership and lagging indicators are the quantitative evidence that validates the efficacy of the leading indicators.

Secondary school leaders can employ the following five steps to navigate the relationship between leading and lagging indicators to achieve high reliability status in their schools using the academy model.

Step 1. Make sure there are explicit programs and practices in place for each of the sixteen leading indicators.

Step 2. Create lagging indicators for the sixteen academy leading indicators based on the desired effects implicit or explicit in the leading indicators and establish criterion levels for success.

Step 3. Collect data on the school's status regarding the lagging indicators.

Step 4. If the school has not met the minimum requirements for a lagging indicator, refocus attention and resources on the actions inherent in the associated leading indicator.

Step 5. Continually collect data on the lagging indicators and respond accordingly.

These steps are implicit in the scale an academy uses to judge its progress on each of the sixteen indicators. To determine the extent to which a school is operating as a high reliability organization, an academy leader uses a five-point scale that ranges from not using (0) to sustaining (4) to evaluate the performance of the school on each of the sixteen indicators. Consider figure I.1.

For each indicator, an academy leader examines the programs and practices in the school and determines the school's status using this scale. At the not using (0) level of the scale in figure I.1, a school has made no attempt to develop programs and practices that address the indicator. The school has not even begun to take step 1 of the high reliability process. At the beginning (1) level of the scale, the school has initiated step 1 by attempting to develop programs and practices that address the specific indicator but is doing so in an incomplete manner and still has work to do to

Level Descriptions	
4 **Sustaining**	The school exhibits all behaviors at the applying level and takes proper action to intervene when quick data indicate a potential problem.
3 **Applying**	The school employs programs and practices that address the academy school-level indicator and can provide lagging indicators to show the desired effects of these actions.
2 **Developing**	The school employs programs and practices that address the academy school-level indicator but cannot provide lagging indicators to show the desired effects of these actions.
1 **Beginning**	The school is in the beginning but incomplete stages of developing programs and practices that address the academy school-level indicator.
0 **Not Using**	The school does not attempt to develop programs and practices that address the academy school-level indicator.

Source: Adapted from Marzano et al., 2018.

FIGURE I.1: Generic scale for high reliability status in the academy model.

fully address the indicator. It is only at the developing (2) level where a school has completed step 1. The school has programs and practices in place that address the indicator. Those programs and practices are complete and executed without significant errors or omissions.

It is interesting to note that discussions of school effectiveness have traditionally stopped here, at the completion of step 1. This phenomenon is discussed at length in the book *Leading a High Reliability School* (Marzano et al., 2018). Briefly, though, during the 1980s there was a school-reform movement to identify those programs and practices that had substantial correlations with student achievement. Of course, the literature on high reliability organizations calls those programs and practices *leading indicators*. But the reform of the 1980s stopped at the execution of the identified programs and practices. To this extent, the high reliability movement in schools across the country can be thought of as an extension of those early efforts. This extension starts at the applying (3) level of the scale.

It is at the applying (3) level of the high reliability scale that a school can produce evidence as to the effectiveness of its leading indicators. This requires the execution of steps 2, 3, and 4 in the high reliability process. Step 2 involves the actual creation of the lagging indicator. This requires school leaders to identify the specific type of data they will collect along with the criteria for interpreting those data. In step 3 of the process, the school collects data, analyzes them, and compares them to the criterion for success. In step 4, if the school has not met the criterion scores it has established, it refocuses attention and resources on the actions inherent in the associated leading indicator.

At the highest level of the high reliability scale, sustaining (4), the school continues to collect data (referred to as *quick data* because they are designed to be quick and relatively easy to collect) to ensure that the school has embraced a continuous improvement process. This is the essence of step 5 in the high reliability process. When a school reaches this level of operation, it is functioning as a high reliability organization. When a secondary school is operating at the applying (3) or sustaining (4) level on all sixteen school-level indicators, it is effectively manifesting the circuit-board effect.

For each of the sixteen school-level indicators, the high reliability scale is the school leader's guide as to where the organization is relative to becoming a Marzano Academy and what it must do to achieve or maintain the applying (3) or sustaining (4) levels. Each level of the scale represents a specific status relative to a specific indicator. To exemplify how a school leader would interpret and use the scale, consider school-level indicator 1, providing a safe, orderly, and supportive environment for all constituents. At the not using (0) level of the scale, the school leader would have no discernable evidence that the school has plans to implement programs that address the safety, order, and support of the school, or no evidence that individual teachers are using strategies and activities that address this area on their own even though there is not a schoolwide program in place.

At the beginning (1) level of the scale, the leader would have written plans regarding the implementation of programs and practices that address students' needs for safety, order, and support but there would be little or no evidence that these practices are happening schoolwide, or the school might have a written plan for the implementation of specific programs but no evidence that teachers are implementing these programs with fidelity.

To be scored at the developing (2) level of the high reliability scale, the school would have not only written plans for the implementation of programs and practices that address safety, order, and support, but also evidence that teachers are implementing those programs and practices (that is, the leading indicators) with fidelity.

At the applying (3) level of the scale, the school leader has identified the type of evidence that would indicate the school's programs and practices are working and the standards that evidence must meet. For example, the school leader might have implemented a specific program used each morning for students to get to know each other throughout the year. In addition, the leader has set the standard that 90 percent of students believe that their peers like them and know them well. Finally, the leader sets up a process to survey students to see if the school is meeting that goal.

Finally, at the sustaining (4) level of the high reliability scale, the leader ensures the school continues to maintain its standards by using focus group discussions and quick conversations with students, parents, and teachers. The leader might also collect information about safety, order, and support by systematically examining school-level reports on things like incidents of bullying.

Lagging Indicators

For each of the sixteen school-level indicators, leaders must select lagging indicators related to the specific programs and practices the school is implementing for that indicator. To illustrate, assume that for school-level indicator 1 (safe, orderly, and supportive environment), a school leader has focused on the following areas.

- The safety of the physical plant
- Access to communication devices
- Crisis and emergency procedures
- Systematic practice of safety and emergency procedures
- Programs and practices for belonging and esteem

To create lagging indicators, leaders would select a few of the programs and practices they are employing that they consider particularly timely and critical for their school. In this example, the school leader would have one or more specific programs and practices for each of the five focus areas to ensure that they address the specific needs of the school. The school leader could identify one or more lagging indicators for each of these areas. Figure I.2 lists some possible lagging indicators a school leader might construct.

Programs and Practices	Lagging Indicator Data	Potential Standard for High Reliability Status
Safety of the physical plant	Physical inspection report of areas critical to safety	100 percent of all critical areas of the physical plant meet safety standards
Access to and use of communication devices	Percentage of teachers and staff that have access to communication devices	90 percent of teachers and staff have access to communication devices and 100 percent of those use them as intended
Systematic practice of safety procedures	The frequency of practice sessions for safety procedures	Safety procedures are practiced bimonthly with 100 percent of practice procedures executed without significant errors or omissions
Schoolwide programs for students to get to know each other	The percentage of teachers using specific classroom strategies The percentage of teachers engaging in schoolwide programs	100 percent of teachers use specific classroom strategies that enhance students' sense of safety, order, and support 90 percent of teachers engage in the schoolwide program for students to get to know each other on a daily basis
Perceptions of students, teachers, and parents	Surveys of students, teachers, and parents	90 percent of students respond positively that they perceive the school as safe, orderly, and supportive 100 percent of teachers respond positively that they perceive the school as safe, orderly, and supportive 70 percent of parents and guardians respond positively that they perceive the school as safe, orderly, and supportive

Source: © 2022 by Robert J. Marzano.

FIGURE I.2: Potential lagging indicators and criteria for school-level indicator 1.

The first column in figure I.2 lists the programs and practices the school is implementing to address school-level indicator 1. The second column identifies the type of data that the school might collect to create a lagging indicator, and the third column describes the criteria the school leader might use to ascertain whether the school has achieved acceptable levels of performance.

It is important to note that the last row in figure I.2 addresses the perceptions of students, teachers, and parents. School staff can collect perceptual data for each of the sixteen school-level indicators using survey instruments. Although it is not necessary to have perceptual data for each school-level indicator, we highly recommend that leaders generate such data simply because of their timeliness and the utility of the information they provide.

When designing perceptual surveys, leaders must consider several factors. First, there need to be different surveys for students, for faculty and staff, and for parents. Each of these surveys should be specifically designed to understand how these individual stakeholders perceive the specific indicator. Survey questions like the following would be useful for gathering perceptual data on school-level indicator 1, for example.

- Is the school a safe place?
- Is the school an orderly place?
- Does the school have clear routines, procedures, and rules in place?

- Does the school have a crisis plan and are all stakeholders aware of this plan?
- Does the school communicate safety and order procedures?
- What types of decisions are made with community input?
- How are school safety and order data collected and communicated?

Regardless of questions used, the principal needs to determine the minimum acceptable thresholds for each lagging indicator. For example, if 70 percent of parents state the school has clear routines and procedures in place, is this enough? This criterion score might suffice for parents but not for students and teachers.

A principal should set minimum threshold expectations before administering the survey to ensure that the results don't influence what is considered acceptable. Next, the principal should decide how often to administer the surveys to the school community, and the preferred administrative methods to ensure high participation rates. The principal can easily request every faculty and staff member take the survey during designated planning time, or during an in-service day. If the principal considers these perceptual surveys a priority, devoting such time ensures they are completed with consistency and fidelity. This is also true for students. The principal can designate a particular day and time that all classrooms will dedicate to administering the survey to all students.

Getting 100 percent of parents to complete a school survey might not be realistic. Knowing this, a principal will need to determine an acceptable number of families to survey. Obviously, the greater the number of completed surveys, the more accurate the findings. One strategy to ensure higher participation rates among families is to include the survey as part of another school event. One example is to set up several computers with the survey preloaded in the main office during parent-teacher conferences. The school can then direct all parents through the main office as they arrive for their scheduled conferences and can ask parents to take the survey then or stop back by before leaving. Another time to capture the responses of a lot of parents is during school registration. Many schools have registration "assembly lines" with specific stations. A principal might include a registration station with computers ready for survey completion. Schools can also use events such as PTA or PTO events, music and theater performances, or awards ceremonies as survey opportunities. Finally, a principal might include the survey link in the monthly newsletter to parents, explaining the purpose of the survey and asking for parent input. These types of home-based survey administration methods, however, might not yield as high a participation rate as the school-based methods will.

Finally, we want to emphasize that the leaders using the academy model might focus on very different initiatives than those described in this section. Each school leader must identify initiatives that meet his or her school's immediate needs relative to each indicator. The ones we discuss in this book are only examples of the many possible initiatives on which a school might focus.

Trim Tab Indicators and Customized High Reliability Scales

Those who engage in boating, aviation, and other similar activities are familiar with the principle of trim tabbing. In boating and aviation, trim tab devices are mechanical systems that allow the pilot of the boat or the airplane to make small changes in the controls that have large effects on how the boat or the airplane maneuvers. At a very general and nonmechanical level, trim tabbing means focusing on small, specific actions that will have the biggest effect on whatever endeavor is being executed.

Trim tabbing within the context of high reliability leadership means selecting a relatively few lagging indicators that will have the biggest impact on the effectiveness of a school relative to the school-level indicator being addressed. Stated differently, it might be somewhat inefficient for a leader to focus on all the potential lagging indicators for an aspect of the model—all those described in figure I.2 (page 9), for example. Rather, a school leader should select a subset of lagging indicators that will operate as trim tabs for the school. Then, the leader can customize the high reliability scale introduced in figure I.1 (page 7) to reflect the specific ways the school is addressing and monitoring the indicator. To illustrate, assume that a school leader has selected the subset of lagging indicators depicted in figure I.3, which represents a customized high reliability scale for school-level indicator 1.

Evidence	
4 **Sustaining** **(quick data)**	Quick data like the following are systematically collected and reviewed: • Focus group data with students, parents, and teachers • Quick conversations with students, parents, and teachers • Regular reports on incidents of bullying, misbehavior, absenteeism, tardiness, and so on
3 **Applying** **(lagging)**	Performance goals with clear criteria for success like the following are in place: • 100 percent of all critical areas of the physical plant meet safety standards • 90 percent of students participate in the schoolwide program for students to get to know each other • 100 percent of teachers use specific classroom strategies that enhance students' sense of safety, order, and support • 90 percent of students respond positively that they perceive the school as safe, orderly, and supportive • 100 percent of teachers respond positively that they perceive the school as safe, orderly, and supportive • 70 percent of parents and guardians respond positively that they perceive the school as safe, orderly, and supportive
2 **Developing** **(leading)**	Concrete programs and practices are in place to develop a sense of safety, order, and support, such as: • The physical plant is designed to maximize student safety and support • Communication devices are available and used by staff and teachers to ensure the safety and comfort of students • Safety procedures are in place and routinely practiced by staff and students • Teachers are trained in the schoolwide program for students to get to know each other • Teachers are trained in specific strategies in their classrooms
1 **Beginning**	• The school has written plans regarding implementation of programs for safety, order, and support but these have not been implemented • Individual teachers employ strategies to foster a sense of safety, order, and support, but there is not a schoolwide emphasis
0 **Not Using**	• The school has no written plans for implementation of programs for safety, order, and support • There is no classroom implementation of strategies for safety, order, and support

Source: © 2020 by Marzano Academies, Inc. Adapted with permission.

FIGURE I.3: Customized high reliability scale for school-level indicator 1.

Also note that at the sustaining (4) level of the customized high reliability scale, school leadership has identified data they can collect relatively quickly regarding this indicator. Those types of data include conversations with various constituent groups, remarks made during focus group discussions, and systematic review of reports that are readily available relative to the school's safety, order, and supportiveness.

A Phased Approach to Implementation

Having discussed the high reliability leadership process with respect to individual school-level indicators, we now turn our attention to the process of implementing all sixteen. There are many ways to organize the sixteen school-level indicators in the Marzano Academies model. In the book *Leading a Competency-Based Elementary School*, Robert J. Marzano and Brian J. Kosena (2022) organized them into categories that involve similar outcomes. For the purposes of this book, we organize them into phases of implementation. A phased approach is particularly useful in secondary schools because of their departmentalized structure. Many large comprehensive middle schools and high schools have a history of working in departments that have little interaction with each other. In contrast, the Marzano Academies model operates on the assumption of extensive interaction between departments and shared responsibility for decisions about individual students. This shift does not happen in a single moment or a single year. Continuing the circuit-board analogy, we believe that secondary school leaders should switch on the sixteen circuits (that is, school-level indicators) in a specific order to avoid disrupting the system so much at the beginning that it creates resistance to the overall process. Figure I.4 depicts our recommended four-phase organization of the sixteen school-level indicators.

Phase 1	Phase 2	Phase 3	Phase 4
Safe, Orderly, and Supportive Environment (SLI 1)	Measurement Topics and Proficiency Scales (SLI 9)	Cognitive and Metacognitive Skills (SLI 10)	Personal Projects (SLI 4)
Student Efficacy and Agency (SLI 2)	Classroom Assessment (SLI 13)	Vocabulary (SLI 11)	Cumulative Review (SLI 7)
Inspiration (SLI 3)	Reporting and Grading (SLI 14)	Blended Instruction (SLI 6)	Knowledge Maps (SLI 8)
Flexible Scheduling (SLI 16)	Instruction and Teacher Development (SLI 5)	Explicit Goals for Students' Status and Growth (SLI 12)	Collective Responsibility (SLI 15)

FIGURE I.4: Four phases of implementation for the Marzano Academies school-level indicators.

Using this phased approach, leaders should have adequate time to train the faculty and staff and manage available funding and other resources effectively. Teachers will have time to concentrate on specific indicators rather than tackling the entire model at once. Finally, the school will have opportunities to celebrate smaller milestones along the way.

It is important to note that the phases are not necessarily equal in their duration. Stated differently, leaders should not assume that each phase requires an entire school year to fully implement the new indicators. While it is useful to think of each phase representing a single year, it might be the case that some phases take more than a year and other phases take less than a year. Also, phases can overlap. For example, a school leader does not have to completely implement the school-level indicators in phase 1 before beginning phase 2.

How This Book Is Organized

In this book, we organize the sixteen school-level indicators into four phases that constitute chapters 1 through 4. For each indicator, we explain key concepts and present strategies and decision points that secondary leaders can apply in their schools. In addition, the section for each school-level indicator includes suggested lagging indicators and a customized high reliability scale. Chapter 1 deals with the first recommended phase of implementation for secondary schools. It addresses the school-level indicators of safe, orderly, and supportive environment, student efficacy and agency, inspiration, and flexible scheduling. Chapter 2 addresses the second phase of implementation, focusing on the indicators of measurement topics and proficiency scales, assessment, reporting and grading, and instruction and teacher development. Chapter 3 covers the third phase, including cognitive and metacognitive skills, vocabulary, blended instruction, and explicit goals for students' status and growth. Chapter 4 details the fourth phase and the indicators of personal projects, cumulative review, knowledge maps, and collective responsibility. Finally, for secondary schools to move to a CBE system, school leaders must be aware of the fact that they are engaged in second-order change and must meet this challenge with transformational leadership. To this end, chapter 5 delineates four specific roles of transformational leaders.

Readers should note that secondary education encompasses grades 6–12, commonly divided into middle school (grades 6–8) and high school (grades 9–12). Thus, in this book we present examples from the full range of grades, though with an emphasis on high school.

CHAPTER 1

Phase 1: Laying the Foundations

To a great extent, every academy is a unique creation. This first phase allows secondary school leaders to lay a strong foundation but still affords flexibility when it comes to the design of the school. The purpose of the first phase of implementation is to develop the supportive context that allows a school to develop its own unique model and put in place four of the most foundational school-level indicators. However, even before implementing the first four indicators, the school leader should engage in some preparatory work that involves the following four components.

1. Developing a leadership team

2. Creating a shared vision

3. Assembling a vanguard team

4. Selecting a learning management system (LMS)

One of the first things secondary school leaders should do is identify a group of people within the school who will form the leadership team. In our experience, school leaders refer to such groups by many names: the leadership team, the guiding coalition, the mastermind group, or the leadership alliance, among others. In this book, we use the term *leadership team* to refer to this group. The constitution of the team is up to the school leader. Members should be people who are committed to changing the school for the better, are willing to dive deeply into the specifics of each component of the change, are willing to be brutally honest about the current reality of the school, and are quintessential problem solvers. There is no set number of people who should constitute the leadership team, but we recommend it should remain small enough that all members can easily share their ideas.

Second, to start the process of shifting to the Marzano Academies model, the leadership team should develop a shared vision. In *The Handbook for Personalized Competency-Based Education*, Robert J. Marzano, Jennifer S. Norford, Michelle Finn, and Douglas Finn (2017) discussed the importance of establishing a shared vision among various constituent groups. While there are many benefits to a shared vision, perhaps the most important is that it allows various constituent groups to be involved in the design of the school's future, thus providing a broad base of ownership in the endeavor. Additionally, that common vision of the future provides constituents with a rallying point to return to when details present obstacles. Secondary school leaders should begin by engaging stakeholders from diverse groups such as certified staff (teachers, media specialists, guidance counselors, and instructional coaches), classified staff (teacher aides and maintenance, custodial, cafeteria, transportation, health, and administration staff), students, parents and guardians, community members, and representatives from local businesses. Marzano, Norford, and colleagues (2017) suggest that all members of the various constituent groups involved in the process should answer a series of guiding questions like the following to elicit their beliefs and ideas.

- How are our students doing academically? What assessments are the most valid measures of our students' learning and to what extent do they support our conclusions?

- What happens to our students once they leave our system?

- What are the most important purposes of our school?

- What life skills do we want our students to learn?

- What are some personal characteristics we would want our students to cultivate?

- How should our school support its students?

- How should we ensure that students learn essential content before they leave our school?

- How should we ensure that students are moving at a pace that meets their specific needs?

One approach to gathering responses to these questions is to provide members of constituent groups with questionnaires where they can briefly record their answers. Designated leaders or representatives of constituent groups can then summarize the major trends in answers to each question. Another option is to employ *hosted conversations*, in which a leader invites a specific constituent group to meet with the leader at a specific time and place. A nice touch is for the leader to send personal invitations to specific group members asking them to attend. Ideally, each stakeholder group should participate in a separate meeting, with the caveat that meetings be conducted in a timely fashion. Staff or constituent representatives should take notes regarding the content of these conversations and summarize them for each group.

School leaders can synthesize the collected constituent answers into a concise shared vision. Consider the following examples.

> *Through the collaboration of students, parents, teachers, and community members, McCarthy Middle School will build a personalized competency-based system that allows students to master important academic content and pursue their personal goals and dreams.*

> *Students at Kappa High School will develop knowledge and skills for lifelong learning along with core academic knowledge and skill in an environment of challenge, self-efficacy, and support.*

Once the shared vision is constructed, leaders should communicate it to all stakeholders, from community members to students.

The third step is to assemble a *vanguard team*—a group of teachers and other related staff such as guidance counselors who begin to experiment with a CBE approach. Where the function of the leadership team is to guide conceptually, recommend decisions to the school leaders, and solve problems, the function of the vanguard team is to be on the leading edge of implementation regarding the sixteen school-level indicators. While the leadership team and the vanguard team are separate groups, it is very reasonable for some or all of the members of the leadership team to also be part of the vanguard team. To assemble this group, it is useful for the school leader to personally approach teachers and *invite* them to participate in the efforts of this initial group. For example, a high school leader might start by inviting teachers from each of the major departments within the school. In addition to invited teachers, any other teacher who applies should be a part of the group. For example, a mathematics teacher whom the leader did not specifically approach might hear about the endeavor and ask to be part of the team. It's important to include such volunteers, in part to send the message that the project is open to all members of the staff and the final outcome will be a collaborative creation. Additionally, we have found that teachers who volunteer to be in the vanguard group tend to be involved team members and bring a great deal of energy to the design process. Finally, there are no hard-and-fast rules governing the size of the vanguard team. It should contain enough members to be representative of the various departments within the school. Thus, large comprehensive middle and high schools might have fairly large vanguard teams. If such groups become so large that it is difficult to convene, then form subgroups, each of which would have one representative on a vanguard management team.

The vanguard team should stay ahead of the pace of the implementation in that the members should be piloting aspects of all sixteen school-level indicators—even those indicators slated for implementation much later in the process. For example, cumulative review is one of the indicators that are formally implemented in phase 4 of the implementation plan. However, the school leader should elicit members of the vanguard team to implement cumulative review in their classrooms right from the start. This is important to the vanguard team's role of field-testing programs and practices; it also allows leaders to set up demonstration classrooms for as many components of the model as possible. As the name indicates, a *demonstration classroom* is one that other teachers and interested members of various constituent groups can visit to observe the implementation of various components of the model the school is creating. Demonstration classrooms will produce valuable information the leadership team can use to inform the full rollout of the model.

With the school's local budget or in collaboration with district officials, the school leader can create a package of incentives for teachers participating in the vanguard team. It is important to choose incentives that will support their work, as opposed to providing a set of unrelated rewards. One possible incentive might be a classroom set of laptops to support differentiation, blended learning, and access to digital content in the learning management system. As another option, the school leader might consider upgrading vanguard classrooms with furniture that is mobile, is designed for flexible classroom layouts that accommodate grouping, and includes writing surfaces and open-front storage. Other incentives could include classroom supplies like sticky notes, chart paper, markers, filing systems, and other materials that will support CBE. Finally, the leader might provide reasonable stipends to compensate teachers for attending weekend and evening professional learning opportunities and collaborative sessions. This suggestion may be the most important since a school leader should include ongoing, job-embedded professional learning opportunities that most likely will not take place during the school day. Whatever the leader's decision, the idea is to incentivize teachers, honor their time, provide the needed resources, and demonstrate commitment to the project.

The final preparatory step school leaders can take is to select a learning management system. A learning management system is a software application that a school uses to enable blended learning and track information about the learning process for students on each aspect of the curriculum. CBE-friendly platforms are always evolving and improving, so leaders should research the available options. Marzano Academies uses and recommends the Empower Learning LMS (www.empowerlearning.net) because its systems were designed from inception with the competency-based approach in mind. Consequently, we use examples of the Empower LMS throughout this book. Those who elect to use other systems should ensure that they include specific features addressed in this book. When deciding on an LMS, leaders should consider how the platform will address issues like transcripts, CBE grading and reporting, and athletic eligibility, which are three hot-button items at the high school level. A school's LMS must be able to produce a competency-based transcript and calculate eligibility based on the state's or school's required formulas. Equally important is a platform's ability to communicate with the district's student management system. Often, state education agencies pull data directly from the district's student management program, and teachers will appreciate working with two systems that are easily compatible. Once the leadership team selects a platform, teachers on the vanguard team should deploy the LMS in their classrooms from the outset.

With these preparations in place, the leadership team should be ready to implement the four school-level indicators in the first phase.

1. Safe, orderly, and supportive environment (SLI 1)

2. Student efficacy and agency (SLI 2)

3. Inspiration (SLI 3)

4. Flexible scheduling (SLI 16)

We believe that these four indicators can involve the most teachers without changing the system in such a dramatic fashion as to cause discord.

Safe, Orderly, and Supportive Environment (SLI 1)

The school-level indicator of safe, orderly, and supportive environment is an obvious foundation for any significant change in schooling. Any effort to install a new system such as CBE will not get very far if the school lacks a safe, orderly, and supportive environment. Of course, there are many aspects of safety, order, and support that secondary school administrators commonly focus on even if they are not necessarily trying to transition to a CBE model. These include the following.

- Practices that ensure the safety of the physical plant

- Systematic practice of safety procedures

- Specific classroom strategies and procedures that enhance safety, order, and support

Secondary schools of all types commonly address these factors. Principals and other leaders secure entry points, schedule emergency drills, establish communication protocols, write crisis plans, vet campus visitors, and guide teachers to ensure students have their physiological and self-esteem needs met in the classroom. For each of these areas, principals should have plans and protocols in place, ensure adequate training for staff, and regularly practice the protocols. For example, every secondary school leader should have clear plans and protocols that ensure all entrances are secured at all times. New staff members should be trained in these protocols, perhaps with mentoring from staff members who have been at the school for some time. Periodically, the school leader would have all staff members practice key protocols such as ensuring that all doors into the building are locked. For a detailed description of how to address these issues within the academy model, see *Leading a Competency-Based Elementary School* (Marzano & Kosena, 2022). Although that book is designed for elementary schools, the programs and practices it describes for this particular school-level indicator also apply to the secondary level.

Within a CBE system at the secondary level, programs and practices that focus on student support are of particular importance. By definition, one of the hallmarks of a CBE system is that students are expected to demonstrate competence in the topics addressed in each course. Of course, this goes well beyond the expectations in a traditional system and requires more awareness on the part of students in terms of what they have already mastered and what they are still working on. Thus, a key component of a secondary school seeking to implement the Marzano Academies model is a strong student advisory program.

Student Advisory Programs

The overall logic behind a strong advisory program is that some secondary students, particularly in large high schools, feel insignificant and unconnected to others, resulting in their turning inward and isolating themselves. When a student feels and acts this way, success in a CBE system can be extremely difficult. This is because a CBE system requires students to interact with their teachers and their peers in ways that support their own learning and that of others. To counteract these perceptions, students need a personal connection with one or more adults they regard as their advocates, interested in their present and future success. A strong advisory program, in which all students have at least one adult whom they can turn to and whom they know supports them, provides this connection and advocacy. Students who participate in a strong advisory program experience connection to a caring adult, connection to peers, and growth in life skills that are useful in and outside of school (Vander Ark, 2015). Effective advisory programs are associated with a number of positive results, including lower dropout rates, higher four-year graduation rates, and continued academic pursuits after high school (Blum & Libbey, 2004; Croninger & Lee, 2001; GreatSchools Staff, 2021; Poliner & Lieber, 2004; Youth Transitions Task Force, 2006). Here we address some of the prominent features of a secondary advisory program.

Tom Vander Ark, founder of Getting Smart (www.gettingsmart.com), has consistently advocated for strong advisory programs at the secondary level. He explained that the goal of an advisory program is to help students figure out who they are, where they're headed, and how they're going to get there (Kulaas, Ryerse, & Vander Ark, 2017; Vander Ark, 2015). To accomplish this, an advisory system must ensure that each student has an adult who knows them and helps them navigate the various demands and obstacles of middle school and high school. Vander Ark contended that high school, in particular, can be a confusing time with increasing options for students. This is particularly true of secondary students in a CBE system. He recommends that advisory programs have goals for each student like the following (Kulaas et al., 2017).

- Provide emotional support and advocacy for each student.

- Help students identify and address their current academic needs.

- Prepare for student-led conferences.

- Help students identify personal issues and needs and help them connect with appropriate programs and agencies when needed.

- At the high school level particularly, help students plan for their post-secondary lives and provide them with guidance as to next steps to their desired goals.

- Expose students to community resources that might help them in their development.

- Directly teach students skills that enhance their sense of efficacy and agency.

Advisory groups can be organized in a variety of ways. The most obvious way is to use traditional grade levels. Another way is to create groups based on students' approximate readiness levels in ELA, mathematics, or science and ensure that the students stay together over several years. Still another option is to use mixed-age groups; however, high school leaders must ensure that graduating students have an advisor focused on graduation. At the middle school level, a leader might assign an advisor who attends to the needs of students who are working on high school content. Advisory groups are typically made up of fifteen to twenty-two students. To achieve smaller groups, secondary schools usually must expand the pool of adults who lead advisory sessions well beyond the teaching staff. Such additional adult advisory leaders might include administrators, support staff, counselors, behaviorists, and qualified members of the local community who are paid for or volunteer their services.

Scheduling is another important logistical aspect of establishing advisory groups. Marzano, Norford, and colleagues (2017) suggest the following options.

- Advisory is treated like any other course, with the same duration and frequency as academic and elective classes. An important distinction between this arrangement and the rest is that different students will have advisory at different times of day.

- Advisory occurs once a week as a longer block class (two or three hours).

- Advisory occurs twice a week in shorter sessions (one hour or one class period).

- Advisory replaces one class period each week, using a rotating schedule.

- Advisory occurs daily in short sessions, similar to a traditional homeroom (though not necessarily at the start of the day).

- Every day begins and ends with advisory, emphasizing setting daily goals and revisiting them at the end of the day.

- Advisory occurs only during transition times, such as the beginning and end of the quarter or semester. In this arrangement, the school's master schedule would change for the first and last week or two of each quarter or semester; students would attend advisory daily to set goals and create their learning plans and then to review progress and wrap up the learning period.

In the Marzano Academies model, advisory programs should focus on activities specific to the model, such as the following.

- In the academy model, students' status and growth on measurement topics (SLI 9, chapter 2, page 41) are always available for students and faculty to see. One function of advisory is to ensure that all students know their own current status on the measurement topics in the courses they are taking and what they must do to increase that status.

- Given that students know their current status on each measurement topic in each course, they can use advisory to set specific goals for themselves on specific topics and make plans for accomplishing these goals. To this end, advisors should be ready to help students craft their goals and the plans that will allow them to accomplish their goals.

- An advisory period provides time for students to work in groups of two or three to accomplish common goals. Specifically, if two students have set goals related to the same measurement topic, they can work together on those goals during advisory period.

- Advisory can also be a vehicle for informing students about opportunities in and outside of school of which they might not be aware. For example, a high school advisor might make students aware of an upcoming opportunity to visit a nearby community college to learn about their offerings.

- Advisory represents a perfect opportunity to teach and reinforce important cognitive and metacognitive skills (SLI 10, chapter 3, page 88). Advisors can introduce these skills through focused lessons or reinforce skills that students have learned in other classes.

- Advisory is a forum for advisors to provide students with inspirational activities like bringing in guest speakers or watching short movie clips about people who have overcome great challenges in life (see SLI 3 later in this chapter, page 29).

Advisory programs also support teachers (Marzano, Norford, et al., 2017). For example, when teachers have questions about a particular student, they might go to that student's advisor to obtain a more detailed understanding of that student's wants and needs. In effect, a well-structured advisory provides a way to easily collect, store, and access information about each student.

High Reliability Leadership for School-Level Indicator 1

As described in the introduction, to determine the extent to which the school is operating as a high reliability organization, an academy leader uses a five-point scale that ranges from not using (0) to sustaining (4) to evaluate the performance of the school on each of the sixteen indicators. Specifically, school leaders would identify those programs and practices they use to establish a safe, orderly, and supportive environment (that is, their leading indicators) and establish lagging indicators for each. Figure 1.1 lists some potential lagging indicators for a safe, orderly, and supportive environment. Leaders would then select trim tab indicators to create a customized high reliability scale with which to assess their school's level of performance. Figure 1.2 (page 22) depicts a possible customized scale a school leader might design for school-level indicator 1, a safe, orderly, and supportive environment.

Programs and Practices	Lagging Indicator Data	Potential Standard for High Reliability Status
Safety of the physical plant	Reports from district-level reviews of procedures	100 percent of all critical areas of the physical plant meet safety standards
Systematic practice of safety procedures	Records of practice and drill sessions	100 percent of safety drills are conducted without error
Specific classroom strategies and procedures that enhance safety, order, and support	Data from classroom observations and teacher self-reports	100 percent of teachers use specific classroom strategies that enhance students' sense of safety, order, and support
Student advisory programs	Attendance records from advisory program	100 percent of students attend the advisory program and report it helps them do better in school
Perceptions of students, teachers, and parents	Surveys of students, teachers, and parents	90 percent of students respond positively that they perceive the school as safe, orderly, and supportive 100 percent of teachers respond positively that they perceive the school as safe, orderly, and supportive 70 percent of parents and guardians respond positively that they perceive the school as safe, orderly, and supportive

FIGURE 1.1: Potential lagging indicators and criteria for school-level indicator 1.

Evidence	
4 **Sustaining** **(quick data)**	Quick data like the following are systematically collected and reviewed: • Focus group data with students, parents, and teachers • Quick conversations with students, parents, and teachers • Regular reports on incidents of bullying, misbehavior, absenteeism, tardiness, and so on
3 **Applying** **(lagging)**	Performance goals with clear criteria for success like the following are in place: • 100 percent of students attend the advisory program and report it helps them do better in school • 100 percent of all critical areas of the physical plant meet safety standards • 100 percent of teachers use specific classroom strategies that enhance students' sense of safety, order, and support • 90 percent of students respond positively that they perceive the school as safe, orderly, and supportive • 100 percent of teachers respond positively that they perceive the school as safe, orderly, and supportive • 70 percent of parents and guardians respond positively that they perceive the school as safe, orderly, and supportive
2 **Developing** **(leading)**	Concrete programs and practices are in place to develop a sense of safety, order, and support, such as: • A comprehensive advisory program is in place • The physical plant is designed to maximize student safety and support • Teachers learn specific strategies in their classrooms
1 **Beginning**	• The school has written plans for a comprehensive advisory program but the plans have not been implemented • The school has written plans regarding implementation of programs for safety, order, and support but these have not been implemented • Individual teachers employ strategies to foster a sense of safety, order, and support, but there is not a schoolwide emphasis
0 **Not Using**	• The school has no written plans for implementation of programs for safety, order, and support • There is no classroom implementation of strategies for safety, order, and support

Source: © 2020 by Marzano Academies, Inc. Adapted with permission.

FIGURE 1.2: Customized high reliability scale for school-level indicator 1.

Student Efficacy and Agency (SLI 2)

Like a safe, orderly, and supportive environment, the school-level indicator of student efficacy and agency is foundational to the Marzano Academies model. Many educators use the terms *efficacy* and *agency*, with each having its own nuance. In the academy model, we consider efficacy and agency as two related but distinct constructs. *Efficacy* is a mindset grounded in the belief that, with proper focus and effort, an individual can accomplish a great deal, even in areas for which the individual does not believe he or she has natural talent. In the context of CBE, *agency* is most frequently discussed. According to education researchers Jenny Nagaoka, Camille Farrington, Stacy Ehrlich, and Ryan Heath (2015), agency is "the ability to make choices about and take an active role in one's life path, rather than being the product of one's circumstances" (p. 64). Where efficacy involves beliefs, agency involves actions. Students develop agency by explicit actions and decisions that have a direct and positive effect on their current circumstances.

Because efficacy is grounded in beliefs as opposed to actions, teaching students about efficacy and providing them with strategies to develop it is an abstract and nuanced endeavor. Additionally, before teachers start working with students in this domain, teachers should have a firm grasp of the nature of beliefs and how they affect efficacy. One of the more popular ways educators talk about the nature and function of beliefs is the concept of resilience. In a 1974 report focused on children who had overcome the effects of potentially traumatizing negative events, Norman Garmezy popularized the concept of resilience as it relates to education, noting educators should be aware of the phenomenon. In their book, *Resilience: The Science of Mastering Life's Greatest Challenges*, psychiatrists Steven M. Southwick and Dennis S. Charney (2012) defined resilient people as those who "bounce back" (p. 1) after trying events occur in their lives. They don't just survive these experiences but use them to gain awareness of the world and develop new skills. Bonnie Benard (2004), Tan Phan (2003), Lillian Rubin (1996), and others have also added to an understanding of the concept of resiliency, particularly as it relates to education.

More recently, the importance of teaching students about the nature and function of their beliefs has been linked to their general wellness, especially for students who have experienced trauma in their lives. In the book *The School Wellness Wheel*, Mike Ruyle, Libby Child, and Nancy Dome (2022) detailed the various ways in which beliefs can add to or detract from a person's mental health. Specifically, they noted that adverse childhood experiences (ACEs) can have a profound effect on how students think about the world. If students conclude that the world is an unsafe place for them, they will develop beliefs designed to protect from constant threats they perceive surround them. Making students aware of their own beliefs and how those beliefs affect their general outlook can help students develop efficacy and choose more positive ways of looking at the world.

There are a number of specific approaches to teaching secondary students about the power of beliefs and strategies to address beliefs. For the efficacy component of this indicator, we consider two specific approaches: learned optimism and growth mindset thinking. On the agency side of this indicator, strategies are quite concrete due to the nature of agency. CBE schools commonly focus on providing students with opportunities for voice and choice, both of which involve actions that give students some control over their educational experience. *Voice* involves creating opportunities for students to provide input into academic and cultural issues. *Choice* involves providing students with concrete alternatives in terms of academic and cultural activities. The following sections detail learned optimism, growth mindset thinking, voice, and choice.

Learned Optimism

Some of the earliest theories and recommendations regarding optimism come from the writings of Norman Vincent Peale. In 1952, Peale published *The Power of Positive Thinking*, which became quite popular over time and has sold over five million copies (Southwick & Charney, 2012). Southwick and Charney (2012) described Peale's recommendations:

- Make a true estimate of your ability and then raise it 10%.
- Formulate and stamp indelibly on your mind a mental picture of yourself as succeeding.

- Always picture success no matter how badly things seem to be going at the moment.

- Practice positive and peaceful thinking by making a list of positive and peaceful thoughts and pass them through your mind several times each day.

- Practice the technique of suggestive articulation, that is, repeat audibly some positive, success-oriented and peaceful words.

- Do not build up obstacles in your imagination.

- Adopt an "I don't believe in defeat" attitude.

- Start each day by affirming positive, successful, peaceful, and happy attitudes and your days will tend to be pleasant and successful. (p. 33)

Certainly, the type of optimism Peale promoted heavily emphasized thinking positively as often as possible and extinguishing any negative thinking. This is certainly a powerful idea in the abstract but hard to emulate in reality. In effect, it is perhaps unrealistic as a practical way of changing one's thinking. Indeed, in their book on resilience, Southwick and Charney (2012) qualified the concept of optimism with the adjective *realistic*:

> Contrary to popular belief, resilient optimists rarely ignore the negative in life by viewing the world through "rose-colored glasses." In their book *The Resilience Factor*, Karen Reivich and Andrew Shatté (2003) refer to this as "realistic optimism." Like pessimists, realistic optimists pay close attention to negative information that is relevant to the problems they face. However, unlike pessimists, they do not remain focused on the negative. They tend to disengage rapidly from problems that appear to be unsolvable. That is, they know when to cut their losses and turn their attention to problems that they believe they can solve. (p. 25)

Decades after Peale's initial work, Martin E. P. Seligman took a more clinical and balanced approach to optimism. His model was based on his now-famous 1965 study on *learned helplessness*. In that study he found that animals could be conditioned to act in a helpless manner. From this initial study he began working with human subjects to determine if people could train themselves to think optimistically in a realistic way. In *Learned Optimism*, Seligman (2006) explained that the inherent optimism or helplessness that people display in specific situations "is reflective of their *explanatory style*—how they explain positive and negative life events to themselves" (Marzano & Marzano, 2015, p. 68). As Seligman (2006) explained, in a five-year study of some four hundred third-grade students, he and his colleagues found a strong link between negative explanatory style and depression and poor performance. Conversely, they found a positive explanatory style enhanced students' abilities to deal with challenges in their lives. A positive explanatory style was also associated with enhanced academic achievement. Adults displayed similar patterns. A positive outlook in early adulthood was associated with increased health and happiness later in life.

Seligman (2006) further broke down explanatory style into three aspects to describe how optimists and pessimists view different types of events.

- **Permanence:** Is an event temporary or permanent? A pessimistic style views negative events as permanent and positive events as temporary, while an optimistic style thinks that negative events will soon pass and positive events are the usual state of things.

- **Pervasiveness:** Is an event isolated or pervasive? Pessimists let negative events affect how they respond in other parts of their lives, but do not diffuse positive feelings. Optimists take confidence and positivity from positive events and apply them to other areas, while isolating the effects of negative events.

- **Personalization:** Is an event caused by internal or external factors? A pessimistic style thinks that negative events are caused by personal failings and positive events are the result of external factors. An optimistic style internalizes positive events but not negative ones.

Table 1.1 describes variations in the aspects of permanence, pervasiveness, and personalization.

TABLE 1.1: Elements of Explanatory Styles

Aspect	Event Type	Optimistic	Pessimistic
Permanence	*Bad things*	Temporary: Temporary circumstances in my life cause the bad things that happen to me.	Permanent: Permanent elements of my life cause the bad things that happen to me.
	Good things	Permanent: Permanent elements of my life cause the good things that happen to me.	Temporary: Temporary circumstances in my life cause the good things that happen to me.
Pervasiveness	*Bad things*	Specific: When a bad thing happens in one area of my life, it doesn't negatively affect other parts of my life.	Universal: When a bad thing happens in one area of my life, it ruins my whole life.
	Good things	Universal: When a good thing happens in one area of my life, it makes my whole life better.	Specific: When a good thing happens in one area of my life, it doesn't positively affect other parts of my life.
Personalization	*Bad things*	External: A bad thing happened to me because of factors out of my control.	Internal: A bad thing happened to me because I didn't do something right.
	Good things	Internal: A good thing happened to me because I did something right.	External: A good thing happened to me because of factors out of my control.

Source: Marzano & Marzano, 2015, p. 70.

Seligman's model provides a quick reference for students to examine their tendencies toward optimism versus pessimism. Specifically, simply looking through the statements in table 1.1 and determining whether they relate to those in the optimistic column or the pessimistic column gives students a good sense of their tendency toward a positive (that is, optimistic) explanatory style versus a negative (that is, pessimistic) explanatory style.

Growth Mindset Thinking

Growth mindset thinking is one of the ten metacognitive skills that are part of the Marzano Academies model. We address these in depth in school-level indicator 10, cognitive and metacognitive skills (chapter 3, page 88). We consider growth mindset thinking here because it also serves as a general approach to helping students understand the importance of their beliefs and their thinking.

Popularized by Carol Dweck (2006), growth mindset thinking starts with the belief that effort is more important than talent when it comes to accomplishing complex goals. The antithesis of growth mindset thinking is fixed mindset thinking, which assumes that natural abilities are the prime determiners of success in accomplishing complex goals. Although Dweck popularized the term *growth mindset*, its roots stretch back to Seligman's (2006) work.

A very simple way to introduce growth mindset thinking is to communicate the "power of yet" to students. Marzano and Kosena (2022) explain that school leaders and teachers can encourage students to insert the word *yet* after any negative thought or statement about their ability, thus planting the seeds of a growth mindset. For example, if a student says, "I'm not good at biology," his teacher can respond by saying, "No, you're not good at biology *yet*."

Growth mindset thinking can also be a formal part of the curriculum. To make it so, the school would utilize a proficiency scale for this type of thinking, such as the one depicted in figure 1.3. As described in the introduction (page 1), a proficiency scale offers a detailed learning progression for a particular skill or piece of knowledge. We fully address the nature and function of proficiency scales in our discussion of school-level indicator 9, measurement topics and proficiency scales (chapter 2, page 41).

This proficiency scale elucidates the metacognitive skill of growth mindset thinking at a level appropriate for students in grades 6–8. Like all proficiency scales within the academy model, the growth mindset scale includes a progression of learning targets, key vocabulary terms, and success criteria. The 3.0 level of the scale represents proficiency. At the middle school level, the expectation is that students will recognize when they are not operating from a positive mindset and respond by executing a complex strategy involving self-analysis. The 2.0 level articulates the content that students will need to learn to reach proficiency and will be directly taught by teachers. In this case it includes some basic terminology like *challenges*, *improvement*, *persistence*, and *reframing*. It includes a five-step strategy that the teacher will explain, demonstrate, and guide students to practice. The 2.0 level also includes some basic facts about how a person might think and feel when executing growth mindset thinking. Finally, at the 4.0 level, the proficiency scale describes some specific applications of growth mindset thinking students should be able to demonstrate to be considered above proficient in this skill. In this example, students articulate specific situations (in school and outside of school) in which they should employ a growth mindset, set goals to do so, and evaluate progress.

Voice

Academy teachers foster voice by allowing students to have a say in the learning environment. For example, students can provide feedback on various academic issues including assessments and assignments that will demonstrate proficiency. There are a number of strategies teachers can use that provide students with opportunities to exercise their voice. The following is a short list of some of the voice tools commonly used in secondary schools.

- **Affinity diagrams:** These diagrams are useful anytime students generate a number of ideas or perspectives on a topic. After students have articulated their individual opinions or brainstormed ideas, they organize their statements into groups. The clusters of opinions or responses that share affinity represent the broad ideas that students have in common.

- **Digital platforms:** There are a wide variety of digital platforms (Padlet, Edmodo, and so on) available that teachers can use to allow students to express their opinions and concerns. For example, at the beginning of a class period, a teacher might ask students to state their

4.0	The student will:
	• Articulate specific situations (in school and outside of school) in which they should employ a growth mindset, set goals to do so, and evaluate progress.

3.5	In addition to score 3.0 performance, partial success at score 4.0 content

3.0	The student will:
	GMT1—Recognize when they are not operating from a positive mindset and respond by executing a complex strategy involving self-analysis.

2.5	No major errors or omissions regarding score 2.0 content, and partial success at score 3.0 content

2.0	**GMT1—**The student will recognize or recall vocabulary associated with self-analysis as it relates to growth mindset thinking (for example, *challenges, improvement, persistence, reframing*) and perform basic processes such as:
	• Describe a complex strategy involving self-analysis for growth mindset thinking (articulated by the class or the teacher in the form of a standard operating procedure [SOP]). For example, do the following. (1) Before you start a new task that seems challenging, relax, end what you were doing previously, and tell yourself you are going to give this task all your attention. (2) Notice your thinking about the task: Are you uninterested? Are you thinking the task is too difficult for you to accomplish? Are you thinking that the task will be boring? Are you thinking that you won't learn much from the task? (3) Try to reframe your negative thoughts in a positive way: "I'm going to find something interesting in this task." "I can do well on this task if I try hard enough." "I'm going to have fun doing this task." "I'm going to learn something from this task." (4) Make a commitment to giving this task your best effort. (5) Finally, when you've completed the task, identify some of the good things that you've accomplished by engaging in the task.
	• Understand what an individual might think and feel while operating from a positive mindset. For example, think, "I can do this if I try hard enough" or "I didn't do as well as I hoped on this task, but I know where I need to improve."

1.5	Partial success at score 2.0 content, and major errors or omissions regarding score 3.0 content

1.0	With help, partial success at score 2.0 content and score 3.0 content

0.5	With help, partial success at score 2.0 content but not at score 3.0 content

0.0	Even with help, no success

Source: © 2017 by Marzano Resources. Adapted with permission.

FIGURE 1.3: Growth mindset thinking proficiency scale, grades 6–8.

opinions about a poem they read as homework. Students enter their comments in the digital platform and then the whole class reviews the comments as instruction begins.

• **Parking lot:** The parking lot allows students to pose questions or issues that teachers can't address immediately in the classroom but will get to as soon as there is time. It can be employed with a simple piece of chart paper, on which students record questions or issues they want to bring up. When teachers have a break in the flow of classroom instruction, they go to the parking lot, read the questions or issues, and then address them with the whole class, a small group, or even an individual student as dictated by the question or issue. Another approach is to divide the piece of chart paper into four categories that help teachers address both general issues and issues with a focused purpose. Common categories are (1) things that are going well (symbolized by a plus sign), (2) opportunities for improvement (a delta or triangle symbol), (3) questions (a question mark), and (4) ideas (a lightbulb or lightning bolt).

- **Plus or delta:** With this activity, students record positive and negative input regarding what is currently going on in class. To use this strategy, teachers would occasionally pause instruction and ask students to react to what is occurring in class. A plus means things are going well and a delta means that things could be going better. Some secondary teachers employ hand signals like thumbs up as a symbol for plus and thumbs sideways as a symbol for delta. Teachers might also ask students for written comments on a piece of paper divided in half with plus comments on the left and delta comments on the right.

- **Exit slips:** Exit slips are short activities that students must complete before they leave the classroom. In effect, submitting an exit slip is a student's "ticket" to leave the class. Exit slips are commonly associated with academic content. For example, students might record their answers to a content question asked by the teacher on an exit slip. Just as easily, though, teachers might ask students to record their opinions about a particular topic or make recommendations as to what might be changed or added in class, thus making them vehicles for student voice.

- **Interactive notebooks:** Interactive notebooks provide students with opportunities to give teachers extended feedback. With this system, each student has a personal notebook to write in; the teacher can write in the notebook if invited by the student. For example, at the end of a class period, a particular student might place her notebook in a designated basket, cuing the teacher that the student wants the teacher to read the latest in the notebook. The teacher would read the entry, respond in writing in the notebook, and then return the notebook to the student, thus setting up a system of private interaction between the student and the teacher that allows for substantive and detailed feedback.

- **Class meetings:** Class meetings are a chance for teachers and students to gather and discuss problems and issues on a regular basis. They should occur on a routine schedule with a clear structure that promotes honest dialogue about current classroom issues. For example, a secondary teacher might establish a schedule that calls for a class meeting every other Friday for the last twenty minutes of the class period. Protocols would be in place to establish how students bring up issues and respond to others. For example, one protocol might emphasize that the group must complete a current discussion about a specific issue before group members can bring up another topic for discussion. Another protocol might state that no student can make comments about another student's intent for a specific action.

Choice

While voice is focused on creating opportunities for students to provide input into academic issues and cultural issues, choice is focused on providing students with concrete alternatives in terms of academic and cultural activities. As with voice, there are a number of tools that teachers can use to provide choice.

- **Power voting:** The operating principle underlying power voting is that students have multiple votes to cast so that they may weight their input according to their preferences. Typically, the term *vote* elicits visions of each individual casting a single vote for a single alternative.

However, power voting provides more options. For example, in one version of power voting called Spend a Dollar, the teacher gives students four votes, each worth $0.25. They might choose to spend their four votes all on one item of particular importance or spread their votes out among several items.

- **Choice boards:** Choice boards can take the form of any game board that visualizes choices available. Students pick from a variety of choices offered on the board regarding academic and cultural activities. Teachers can customize choice boards to meet a variety of needs, such as homework options, learning goals, types of assessments, and so on.

- **Choice menus:** Choice menus utilize the metaphor of a meal to provide opportunities for student choice. Each course of the meal represents a different type of choice for students. For example, "appetizers" might be choices regarding introductory content or vocabulary words. "Main course" offerings might be choices relevant to content in proficiency scales while "dessert" items can offer extra activities or extensions to help students extend learning to achieve a 4.0 scale score.

- **Must-do and may-do lists:** When teachers use this strategy, they present students with a set of activities, all of which appear on one of two lists. A must-do list covers the expectations all students must meet; the may-do list offers a variety of choices students may select after they have accomplished the expectations on the must-do list.

- **Task cards:** A task card lists tasks or learning activities for students to complete that are associated with score 2.0, 3.0, or 4.0 learning targets from a specific proficiency scale. A task card can simply provide short questions that require students to explain content they have learned or practice a skill or process. A teacher can provide a set of task cards for the learning targets that students are currently working on. Students pick a task card when they finish another task early or when they have independent work time.

Secondary teachers are typically quite adept at creating their own variations of these activities. Teachers should archive the activities they develop in a schoolwide repository. For example, teachers might make brief audio recordings describing the strategies they have developed for providing voice and choice. These recordings would be stored electronically so that all faculty and staff have access to them.

High Reliability Leadership for School-Level Indicator 2

Figure 1.4 (page 30) lists some potential lagging indicators for student efficacy and agency. From this list, the leader would then select trim tab indicators to create a customized high reliability scale. Figure 1.5 (page 30) depicts a possible customized scale a school leader might design for school-level indicator 2, student efficacy and agency.

Inspiration (SLI 3)

It's not much of a secret that many secondary students, especially those in high school, like to think of themselves as mature and cool, not prone to getting moved or excited by events and ideas. But secondary teachers and leaders know that this is just a façade. All one needs to see is the great lengths to which students will go to win a prize, get a sticker or a candy bar, earn a certificate, or receive an award. The fact of the matter is that secondary students want and need to be inspired.

Programs and Practices	Lagging Indicator Data	Potential Standard for High Reliability Status
Learned optimism	Observation data regarding teachers' use of specific classroom strategies	90 percent of students report that learned optimism strategies have helped them in school and in life
Growth mindset thinking	Observation data regarding teachers' use of specific classroom strategies	90 percent of students report that growth mindset thinking has helped in school and in life
Voice activities	Observation data regarding teachers' use of specific classroom strategies	90 percent of teachers can provide explicit evidence of their classroom voice activities
Choice activities	Observation data regarding teachers' use of specific classroom strategies	90 percent of teachers can provide explicit evidence of their classroom choice activities
Perceptions of students, teachers, and parents	Surveys of students, teachers, and parents	90 percent of students report that they have a better sense of efficacy and agency 70 percent of parents report that they see positive changes in their children's efficacy and agency

FIGURE 1.4: Potential lagging indicators and criteria for school-level indicator 2.

Evidence	
4 **Sustaining** **(quick data)**	Quick data like the following are systematically collected and reviewed: • Walkthrough observational data • Quick conversations with teachers and students • Quick conversations with parents
3 **Applying** **(lagging)**	Performance goals with clear criteria for success like the following are in place: • 90 percent of students report that learned optimism strategies have helped them in school and in life • 90 percent of students report that growth mindset thinking has helped in school and in life • 90 percent of teachers can provide explicit evidence of their classroom voice activities • 90 percent of teachers can provide explicit evidence of their classroom choice activities
2 **Developing** **(leading)**	• Teachers have explicit strategies for enhancing learned optimism • Teachers have explicit strategies for enhancing growth mindset thinking • Teachers have explicit strategies for enhancing students' voice and choice
1 **Beginning**	• The school has written plans for developing student efficacy and agency but there is no implementation of those plans • A few teachers execute their own strategies to develop student efficacy and agency but there is no schoolwide emphasis
0 **Not Using**	• The school has no written plans for developing student efficacy and agency • There is no implementation of efficacy and agency strategies at the classroom level

Source: © 2020 by Marzano Academies, Inc. Adapted with permission.

FIGURE 1.5: Customized high reliability scale for school-level indicator 2.

In the introduction (page 1), we defined this school-level indicator as a school having programs and practices in place that provide students with opportunities for self-actualization and connection to something greater than self. This is a reference to the hierarchy of needs and goals psychologist Abraham Maslow initially developed in the 1940s and 1950s (Maslow, 1943, 1954) and then further expanded over time (Koltko-Rivera, 2006; Maslow, 1969, 1979). Maslow's hierarchy includes six levels of human needs and goals, as shown in figure 1.6. Levels 1 through 4 of the hierarchy represent basic human needs. Levels 5 and 6 represent human aspirations that have the power to provide a sense of purpose. When humans engage in activities related to these top two levels of the hierarchy, they are operating in an environment ripe for inspiration. Many educators intuitively emphasize such activities without ever formally addressing the theory behind such actions.

Hamish Brewer (2019), also known as the Tattooed Skateboarding Principal, reminded teachers and leaders that they should encourage students to pursue their dreams, ideas, and aspirations and engage them through activities that seize their imagination. Whether they employ a traditional approach or CBE approach, schools should inject some form of inspiration into the school day. This is especially important in a CBE secondary school that requires students to demonstrate competency on specific measurement topics, demands that they try and retry, and challenges them to stretch. Students can sometimes perceive these added requirements as complex obstacles they must overcome. At these times, inspiration can help them discover that the challenges of a CBE system can represent opportunities as opposed to problems. It is also important for leaders to remember that adults in the building—faculty and staff—also need systematic doses of inspiration.

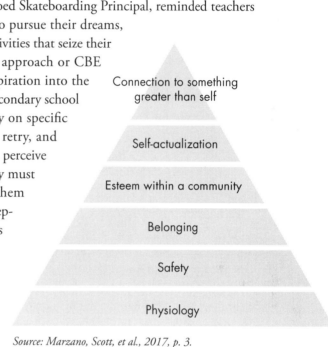

As is the case with efficacy and agency, if educators are to systematically address inspiration, they should understand what it entails.

Source: Marzano, Scott, et al., 2017, p. 3.

FIGURE 1.6: Maslow's hierarchy of needs and goals.

The Nature of Inspiration

If teachers are expected to provide inspiration, it is useful for them to study its nature and function. Fortunately, there is much guidance available to this end. As described by psychology scholars Todd M. Thrash, Andrew J. Elliot, Laura A. Maruskin, and Scott E. Cassidy (2010), inspiration is linked with transcendence. When people are inspired, they rise above their current circumstances. Even in the most dire and unpleasant situations, inspiration enables human beings to experience beauty and embrace possibility. Such experiences are sometimes referred to as *peak experiences* and are multifaceted:

> Many of the experiences that individuals find most fulfilling—peak experiences . . . creative insights . . . spiritual epiphanies . . . and emotions of awe and elevation . . . —cannot be controlled or directly acquired, because they involve the transcendence of one's current desires, values, or expectations. Indeed, life would likely seem bland if one's strivings were never interrupted and informed by such experiences. We propose that *inspiration*, which is central to each of the above experiences, is an important influence on well-being. (p. 488)

In effect, when a teacher does things that elicit inspiration in students, those students see their environment differently with fewer constraints and more opportunities.

A Three-Pronged Approach to Inspiration

When designing programs and practices for inspiration, we recommend a three-pronged approach that includes school, classroom, and community activities. We consider each briefly and then touch on the support that school leaders must dedicate to these inspirational programs.

School-Level Inspirational Activities

We begin with school-level inspirational activities because their presence sends the message that these activities are school priorities. School-level inspirational activities emanate from the school leader and commonly involve all students in the school. The following are examples of school-level inspirational activities.

- Celebratory assemblies that recognize students' achievements in academics, attendance, athletics, and service or awards such as teacher of the month

- Positive enrichment assemblies such as guest speakers, movies, and other external programming

- Morning announcements that include quotes, poems, and shout-outs or other informal recognitions of teachers and students

- Speeches or talks given by the principal or teachers

- Monthly small-group recognitions for students who meet certain criteria, such as engaging in acts of kindness, achieving learning targets, or improving their behavior

Perhaps the most visible type of school-level activity is an assembly program. Schools employing the Marzano Academies model commonly use the programs designed by Rachel's Challenge. Rachel's Challenge is an organization that has developed school-level programs and activities designed to inspire students and create a culture of kindness and compassion. The programs are based on the writings and life of seventeen-year-old Rachel Scott, who died at Columbine High School in 1999. Rachel was the first student to be killed in the first school shooting that brought the potential of catastrophic school violence to the attention of the general public—a tragedy that foreshadowed the dark future of violence in American schools. As of May 2022, the *Washington Post* reported that since Columbine over 185 students and educators have been killed in school shootings and over 310,000 students have directly experienced gun violence in 331 schools (Cox, Rich, Chiu, Muyskens, & Ulmanu, 2022). While Rachel's death could easily be a reminder of the many tragedies that have befallen us, her life has been an inspiration to literally millions of students.

In the book *Motivating and Inspiring Students*, Robert J. Marzano, Darrell Scott, Tina H. Boogren, and Ming Lee Newcomb (2017) explained that Rachel was a normal junior at Columbine High School. She was known for her kindness and enjoyed acting in school theater productions. While she experienced typical teenage struggles, she also displayed an exceptionally mature perspective. She was aware of how she could make a difference in others' lives and determined to have a positive impact. In a class essay, Rachel described her personal code of ethics: to be "honest, compassionate, and [look] for the best and beauty in everyone" (Scott, n.d.). She believed this outlook would be her legacy, that she would "start a chain reaction" (Scott, n.d.) and affect millions of people.

Over the years Rachel's prediction has proven to be true. Her story is now told to secondary students primarily in the form of an assembly program that has touched the lives of millions of students. Participants hear the inspiring story of how Rachel lived her life dedicated to making a positive difference in the lives of all people she met. Her life stands as a testament to the potential for good that results from personal commitment. Since 1999, the Rachel's Challenge assembly program and other related activities have been presented in about 1,200 schools per year involving some thirty million people to date. The effects of those programs are notable, with about 150 students each year reporting that after hearing Rachel's story, they decided not to attempt suicide (Rachel's Challenge, 2021).

While the Rachel's Challenge assembly program is recommended to secondary schools seeking certification as Marzano Academies, there are certainly other similar programs schools might use. What is critical is that if secondary schools are to stimulate inspiration, such programs should occur systematically and frequently.

Classroom-Level Inspirational Activities

While school-level activities involve all students simultaneously, classroom-level activities are conducted by classroom teachers with their specific students. Different activities occur at different times from classroom to classroom. Inspirational classroom activities are perfect for advisory periods since advisory teachers are commonly tasked with helping students better understand themselves and keeping them positive and motivated.

One straightforward way for teachers to stimulate inspiration in students is to use stories and anecdotes. Such stories can be from their own experiences in life, things they have done themselves or things they have heard of others doing. Additionally, inspirational stories can come from students themselves. To this end, teachers might begin class by telling students an inspirational story they have heard or asking students to relate inspirational stories. To illustrate, a teacher might begin a particular class period by relating a story she saw on the local news about community members helping a family whose house had been destroyed in a fire. The teacher might then invite students to relate stories they have heard that inspire them and then explain why the stories are inspirational to them.

Classroom teachers can also try to facilitate brief moments of transcendence. Recall that one of the outcomes of inspiration is that it helps people think beyond their current circumstances about things or possibilities that are uplifting to them. This can be done by using brief (under a minute) video clips from the internet. For example, at the beginning of class, a teacher might play a twenty-second clip of animals in the wild engaged in what looks like play. The teacher would simply play the video and ask students to talk about the thoughts or feelings it stimulates in them.

Quotations are another way teachers can stimulate inspiration in their students. A teacher might read or display a quote at the beginning of class and let students ponder its meaning. After students have had some time to think about a particular quotation, the teacher would engage them in a conversation about why the quotation does or does not inspire them. Teachers can also engage students in whole-class discussions about the implicit ideals they see in quotes. For example, consider the following quote commonly attributed to Mark Twain: "Anger is an acid that can do more to the vessel in which it is stored than to anything on which it is poured" (Goens, 2021, p. 37). The teacher might begin the discussion with a consideration of what Mark Twain probably meant by this metaphor likening anger to acid. The teacher might then share personal examples of the negative effects of anger. Next, students would be invited to share examples from their own lives. The intent of such a discussion is not only to help students better understand the nature and power of anger, but also (more importantly) for students to realize that all humans struggle with anger at times in their lives.

Finally, teachers might use scenes from movies that depict a specific ideal or ideals. For example, a teacher might play a scene from a popular movie or documentary that portrays an act of valor that saved the lives of innocent people. Again, students would watch the clip and then react by discussing how it did or did not inspire them.

The following are additional activities that provide inspiration at the classroom level.

- Recognitions for positive classroom contributions such as acts of kindness, service, empathy, cooperation, achievement, and improvement
- Projects that include serving others
- Teacher recognitions of the actions of individual students or groups of students

Community-Level Inspirational Activities

Community-level inspirational activities typically do not occur very frequently but can be very powerful motivators. For example, imagine an event at which some students from the school are recognized as stellar employees by a local company. A teacher might obtain a video recording of the event and play it to her class. One of the obvious benefits of such activities is that students viewing the event would know those being recognized since they are members of the class or school. Another teacher might play a local news segment honoring firefighters who recently saved the life of a young boy who had fallen through the ice on a frozen pond. As another example, a teacher might ask an elderly member of the community who was a member of the Freedom Riders in 1961 to speak to the class about her experiences of that era and that event. Prior to the visit from the guest speaker, students would study that particular historical event. On the day of the visit, students would listen to a presentation by their honored guest and then ask questions to further their understanding.

The following list includes other ideas for community-level inspirational events.

- Community awards
- Scholarship celebrations
- Recognitions for internships and apprenticeships
- School and classroom grants
- Employee recognition (such as student employee of the month or an excellence in teaching award)
- District-level student and teacher recognitions
- Community service recognitions

Support for Inspirational Programs

Teachers will need concrete support to design and implement many of the activities that stimulate inspiration. If possible, the school leader should create a line item in the budget or use discretionary funds to purchase necessary resources. When inspirational events are celebratory in nature, the school will need a supply of medals, medallions, certificates, pins, and other things that can be used to recognize and acknowledge accomplishments. A school leader might also consider seeking donations for some items. Restaurants and other businesses may be willing to offer gift cards and discounts as acknowledgments.

High Reliability Leadership for School-Level Indicator 3

Figure 1.7 lists some potential lagging indicators for inspiration. From this list, the leader would then select trim tab indicators to create a customized high reliability scale. Figure 1.8 depicts a possible customized scale a school leader might design for school-level indicator 3, inspiration.

Programs and Practices	Lagging Indicator Data	Potential Standard for High Reliability Status
Classroom discussions about quotes, movie clips, or stories	Observations of classroom activities	100 percent of teachers use inspirational movie clips, stories, or quotations
School-level inspirational activities	Records of school-level events	90 percent of students report that they like the inspirational events and activities
Community-level inspirational activities	Records of community-level events	80 percent of students report that they like the community-level inspirational events
Perceptions of students, teachers, and parents	Surveys of students, teachers, and parents	80 percent of students report that the school in general gives them a more positive attitude about their lives

FIGURE 1.7: Potential lagging indicators and criteria for school-level indicator 3.

Evidence	
4 **Sustaining** **(quick data)**	Quick data like the following are systematically collected and reviewed: • Classroom walkthrough data • Focus group data with students and parents • Quick conversations with students and parents
3 **Applying** **(lagging)**	Performance goals with clear criteria for success like the following are in place: • 100 percent of teachers use inspirational movie clips, stories, or quotations • 90 percent of students report that they like the inspirational events and activities • 80 percent of students report that the school in general gives them a more positive attitude about their lives
2 **Developing** **(leading)**	• Schoolwide events and activities that are designed to inspire students are implemented • Individual teachers systematically implement brief activities designed to inspire students • Community-level inspirational activities are implemented
1 **Beginning**	• The school has written plans for inspirational events and activities but there is little implementation • A few teachers independently employ inspirational activities and events but there is no schoolwide emphasis
0 **Not Using**	• The school has no written plans for the implementation of inspirational events and activities • There is no implementation of inspirational events and activities at the classroom level

Source: © 2020 by Marzano Academies, Inc. Adapted with permission.

FIGURE 1.8: Customized high reliability scale for school-level indicator 3.

Flexible Scheduling (SLI 16)

The fourth school-level indicator addressed in the initial phase of implementation is flexible scheduling. At the secondary level, particularly in high school, scheduling is one of the most notable changes that must occur when shifting to a competency-based system. The ultimate goal of a flexible schedule is for students to receive instruction, support, and feedback in each subject area on content that is appropriate to their current level of development. This means that students are not locked into a specific course with a specific teacher for the entire academic year. Rather, when they have mastered the content in a given course, they move on to another course in a timely fashion. The schedule is set up in such a way that students can exit and enter courses at multiple points in the school year. Such transitions might occur every six weeks, every quarter, every semester, or on whatever schedule works best for the school, students, and teachers. A flexible schedule also means that there are times within the daily schedule when students can work independently or in small groups on specific topics. Ultimately, a flexible schedule allows students to work on course material even outside of normal school hours, which means that teachers must develop online resources. In a sense, the phrase "anytime, anywhere education" might best describe the ultimate goal of a CBE schedule.

Such schedules do not manifest in a single year. It will typically take several years of changes and adjustments to find a schedule format that meets all teachers' and students' needs in a particular school. This is why we recommend that secondary leaders start making small but significant changes to the schedule during the first phase of implementation. In this section, we explore a few options: focused instructional time (FIT), content-area saturation, and tutoring and summer sessions.

FIT Block

One way to begin experimenting with schedule changes is to modify the length of class periods or the school day to add a *flex period*, during which students can seek support or enrichment on specific measurement topics. Flex periods can occur before, during, or after school. Our preference is that they are placed during the school day. If not, they should be mandated or credited. Otherwise, the leader will face an uphill battle convincing secondary school students to attend such sessions before or after school. Shortening class and lunch periods in a seven- or eight-period schedule by just five minutes can add a thirty- to forty-minute flex period during each school day.

At the middle school level, a popular approach to flex periods is a focused instructional time block. The FIT block is a scheduled class period that could occur from once per week to five times per week. During FIT block, students work on topics that they were previously exposed to but have not yet mastered. In effect, the FIT block can be used as a tutorial period. Alternatively, FIT block can be a time when students are free to explore topics of their own personal interest. For this reason, some schools refer to FIT block as "Genius Hour." In these situations, students can choose any topic, take on any project, or solve any problem that is important to them; the role of the teacher is to support these student-generated goals by providing guidance and resources. The offerings available to students during FIT block should change frequently. For example, during a particular two-week period in a middle school, some science teachers might decide to offer students instruction and support on two topics they've identified as problematic for students. The next two weeks those same teachers might identify two different topics on which they will offer support.

Although FIT blocks are most common at the middle school level, there is nothing prohibiting their use at the high school level. A powerful variation of FIT block in high schools is to establish content-area *bullpens*. This, of course, is a reference to the baseball convention of having pitchers who are not currently in the game warming up on the sidelines so that they are ready for action at any time. In a high school, different teachers would be scheduled in their content-area bullpen at different times. In a large comprehensive high school, then, there would be one or more mathematics teachers in the mathematics bullpen during every period. Consequently, students know that they can go to the mathematics bullpen at any time and there will be someone there to help them with whatever mathematics topics they need support on.

Figure 1.9 depicts a simple approach to scheduling FIT block. It involves offering FIT block during lunch period so that students can elect to use lunch hour as a time to get help. If a school has multiple lunch periods, each lunch period would include a FIT block.

First Bell	7:15 a.m.
Tardy Bell	7:20 a.m.
Period 1	7:20–8:10 a.m.
Period 2	8:15–9:05 a.m.
Period 3	9:10–10:00 a.m.
Period 4	10:05–10:55 a.m.
Lunch + FIT Block	10:55–11:55 a.m.
Period 5	11:55 a.m.–12:45 p.m.
Period 6	12:50–1:40 p.m.
Period 7	1:45–2:35 p.m.

FIGURE 1.9: FIT block schedule.

Content-Area Saturation

Another way to employ flexible scheduling during the first phase of implementation involves what we refer to as *content-area saturation*, which means offering multiple sections of the same course in the same period. Scheduling two or three Integrated Math 1, English 9, or chemistry courses in the same period provides teachers with increased options for differentiation and personalization. Instead of a single teacher needing to differentiate for the multiple learning levels of their students, a pair or group of teachers can exchange students based on need or pace, allowing each teacher to provide more focused instruction. There is no need to change a student's entire schedule to provide intervention or acceleration. Ideally, each major content area has multiple saturation periods each day so that all or most students can have their core classes scheduled during a saturation period while still having flexibility in the rest of their schedules. For example, a school might schedule three sections of English 9 during second period and three more during sixth period. Students who have a course schedule conflict during one of these saturation periods can be assigned to the other and still receive the robust experience that content-area saturation offers.

An experienced scheduler will tell you that content-area saturation can strain the school's master schedule in that it requires that multiple sections of a course be taught at the same time during the day. This makes it a complicated but not impossible strategy. As we allude to in the previous paragraph, this approach might only include core subject areas, which usually need to have multiple sections in the schedule.

Tutoring and Summer Sessions

Before-school, after-school, and lunchtime tutoring represents another option for flexible scheduling. Even though tutoring does not change the schedule, it provides more options for students to catch up on content that they have been previously introduced to but have not yet mastered. It's important to remember that all such tutoring should focus on specific measurement topics (see SLI 9, chapter 2, page 41). Instead of general content-area tutoring addressing the whole syllabus for the entire semester or year, offer topic-specific tutoring in four- to five-week cycles. For example, the mathematics department might offer a four-week cycle of tutoring on topics like rational exponential expressions and fractional exponents. The next four-week cycle would offer tutoring on different topics like polynomial expressions.

Another aspect of flexible scheduling is to think of the school year as being extended. Specifically, a school leader might think in terms of the fifth quarter—a different way of conceptualizing summer school. Traditionally, the concept of summer school at the high school level has been that summer session is a time for students who did not pass a particular course during the regular school year to retake the entire course. Thus, students in a summer school course typically review all the content and sometimes take the same exams. In a CBE system, summer school students would have to demonstrate competence only on those measurement topics for which they had not demonstrated mastery during the regular school year. If a particular student had mastered thirteen of the fifteen topics for a specific course during the regular school year, during the fifth quarter (that is, summer session) that student would only have to address the two remaining topics.

High Reliability Leadership for School-Level Indicator 16

To reiterate, it will take a few years for secondary leaders to develop and finalize a comprehensive flexible schedule, but they can begin in the first phase of implementation using strategies described here: FIT block, content-area saturation, and tutoring and summer sessions. For additional information on the logistics of scheduling in a competency-based system, readers should consult *Scheduling for Personalized Competency-Based Education* (Finn & Finn, 2021).

Figure 1.10 lists some potential lagging indicators for flexible scheduling. From this list, the leader would then select trim tab indicators to create a customized high reliability scale. Figure 1.11 depicts a possible customized scale a school leader might design for school-level indicator 16, flexible scheduling.

Programs and Practices	Lagging Indicator Data	Potential Standard for High Reliability Status
FIT block	Student attendance records for FIT blocks	100 percent of students participate in FIT block activities
Before-school programs	Records of before-school activities	Enrollment for before-school activities is 80 percent or higher
Content-area saturation	Teachers instructing sections of the same course at the same time exchange students	All protocols and procedures for communicating about grouping and regrouping are executed with fidelity
Perceptions of students, teachers, and parents	Surveys of students, teachers, and parents	90 percent of students report that the school schedule provides them with expanded opportunities to learn

FIGURE 1.10: Potential lagging indicators and criteria for school-level indicator 16.

Evidence	
4 **Sustaining** **(quick data)**	Quick data like the following are systematically collected and reviewed: • Scheduling records indicating the frequency with which students change groups • Quick conversations with teachers and students about flexible scheduling
3 **Applying** **(lagging)**	Performance goals with clear criteria for success like the following are in place: • 90 percent of students report that the school schedule provides them with expanded opportunities to learn • 100 percent of students participate in FIT block activities • All protocols and procedures for communicating about grouping and regrouping are executed with fidelity
2 **Developing** **(leading)**	• Before-school programs are in place that help students develop knowledge and skills specific to their individual needs • FIT block occurs on a daily basis • Protocols are in place for regrouping classes
1 **Beginning**	• The school has written plans to create a flexible schedule but they are not specific enough to be actionable • Some teachers informally work together to create their own versions of flexible scheduling
0 **Not Using**	• The school has no written plans for a flexible schedule • There is no informal implementation of flexible scheduling at the classroom level

Source: © 2020 by Marzano Academies, Inc. Adapted with permission.

FIGURE 1.11: Customized high reliability scale for school-level indicator 16.

Summary

This chapter addressed the first phase of implementing the Marzano Academies model at the secondary school level. As a precursor to introducing the school-level indicators, school leaders should convene a leadership team to guide key implementation decisions. The leadership team's first job is to gather input from key constituent groups to craft the school's shared vision. That vision should be based on constituents' beliefs about the current strengths and weaknesses of the school, and the future the school is preparing students to enter. The school's shared vision should be the guiding light for all decisions.

With a shared vision in place, school leaders should identify a vanguard team of classroom educators who will be the first to deploy the specifics of the model in their classrooms. This vanguard team will begin implementing strategies for each of the school-level indicators as soon as possible (even those indicators scheduled for later phases) so that they will be prepared to lead all others in becoming familiar with all aspects of the model.

The four indicators to officially implement in phase 1 are as follows.

1. **Safe, orderly, and supportive environment (SLI 1):** The school has programs and practices in place that provide students, parents, and staff with a sense of safety, order, and support.

2. **Student efficacy and agency (SLI 2):** The school has programs and practices in place that help develop student efficacy and agency.

3. **Inspiration (SLI 3):** The school has programs and practices in place that are designed to inspire students by providing opportunities for self-actualization and connection to something greater than self.

4. **Flexible scheduling (SLI 16):** The school employs scheduling practices that allow students to receive instruction, support, and evaluation on topics at any level and in any subject area.

These indicators provide a foundation for the remaining twelve indicators and fit logically and rather easily into the current systems of most secondary schools. Therefore, they provide a "soft start" to implementing the model.

Finally, during all phases of implementation, school leaders should ask the following five questions.

1. Do the changes in this phase suggest that we should address any school or district policies?

2. Do the changes in this phase suggest that we should address any board of education policies?

3. Do the changes in this phase suggest that we should address any state-level policies?

4. Do the changes in this phase suggest we should address any contractual policies?

5. Do the changes in this phase create or lessen any inequities?

When addressing these questions, the leadership team might determine that the indicator of flexible scheduling requires a discussion with the teachers union regarding the extra time and pay for those teachers who will be involved in before-school tutorials with students. The leadership team might also determine that it is a good idea to make a presentation to the school board regarding the types of activities that will be used to inspire students so that they are well informed about specific strategies and have time for questions and input.

CHAPTER 2

Phase 2: Implementing the Core of a Competency-Based System

During the second phase of implementation, the secondary school leader should implement the following four school-level indicators.

1. Measurement topics and proficiency scales (SLI 9)

2. Classroom assessment (SLI 13)

3. Reporting and grading (SLI 14)

4. Instruction and teacher development (SLI 5)

We think of the indicators in phase 2 as the core of a competency-based system because they change the very structure of the academic program in secondary schools. Specifically, these indicators change the way students interact with content, including instruction, assessment, and reporting. When implementing these indicators, school leaders have less latitude than they do with indicators in the other phases; these indicators must be executed in relatively precise ways. For example, when implementing school-level indicator 1 (chapter 1, page 18), school leaders have many options and many ways to ensure safety, order, and support. In contrast, when implementing school-level indicator 9, measurement topics and proficiency scales, the school leader must establish measurement topics schoolwide and ensure teachers employ a specific format and specific practices when it comes to proficiency scales.

Measurement Topics and Proficiency Scales (SLI 9)

Measurement topics and proficiency scales are the mechanisms that fuel the entire Marzano Academies model. A *measurement topic* is a specific topic within a subject area that teachers will teach, assess, and score students on; a *proficiency scale* articulates an explicit progression of knowledge for a single measurement topic. At their core, measurement topics and proficiency scales represent a new way of designing, communicating, and implementing secondary curricula.

Traditionally, the curriculum for each subject area in secondary schools is developed through a multistep process that begins far away from classroom teachers. State departments of education often provide comprehensive curriculum guides that serve as the anchor documents for school districts. State departments typically design these documents by convening a curriculum-development committee comprised of educators from multiple schools, who then identify key issues and topics in each content area, identify resources, and develop assessments. The curriculum documents or standards sets these committees generate are then disseminated to districts and schools. Unfortunately, educators at the school level may encounter some challenges when trying to use them.

State and district standards suffer from a problem that has plagued the standards movement from the outset. Standards documents at the national, state, and district levels commonly include so much content that it is virtually impossible for teachers to adequately address it all. To illustrate, Robert J. Marzano, David C. Yanoski, Jan K. Hoegh, and Julia A. Simms (2013) analyzed Common Core standards documents and identified seventy-three standards statements for eighth-grade ELA. They found that each statement had an average of five topics embedded in it, for a total of 365 topics that teachers are expected to cover and students are expected to learn in a single school academic year. This problem presents itself in all content areas and grade levels.

Such an overloaded curriculum violates the principle of a *guaranteed and viable curriculum* as established by Marzano (2003) in the book *What Works in Schools*. *Guaranteed* means that the school ensures every teacher addresses a consistent set of topics articulated in a course of study. *Viable* means that the curriculum is focused and streamlined enough that teachers have time in the school day and in the school year to adequately teach and reinforce the content. When a curriculum contains an unreasonable amount of content, teachers must make idiosyncratic choices about what topics they will devote class time to. A guaranteed and viable curriculum for a particular content area and grade level eliminates variability in what students in different classrooms learn.

Creating a guaranteed and viable curriculum requires a process that builds on state-level efforts. A secondary school leader should convene content-area teams to select measurement topics and develop proficiency scales based on state, provincial, or district standards. The first task of the content-area teams is to identify the topics in the standards documents that will be the focus of instruction in each course. This is a value-driven process. Working from the reality that there is not enough time in the school year to adequately teach all of the content articulated in standards documents, content-area teams must ask themselves which topics are so important that they will guarantee those topics will be thoroughly taught, adequately assessed, and reported on. In general, for a given course, curriculum teams identify anywhere between fifteen and thirty topics they will focus on. In the academy model, these topics are *measurement topics* since teachers will formally assess them and report students' scores.

Another option some districts and schools use is to start with a resource called the Critical Concepts and make changes, adaptations, and deletions to meet their local needs. Marzano Resources analysts created the Critical Concepts using a rigorous process of dissecting national and state standards (see Dodson, 2019; Simms, 2016). The result was a guaranteed and viable set of measurement topics and accompanying proficiency scales for core content areas in grades K–12. Table 2.1 depicts the number of measurement topics across the grade levels for mathematics, science, and ELA.

TABLE 2.1: Essential Topics in Mathematics, Science, and ELA

Subject	K	1	2	3	4	5	6	7	8	9	10	11	12	Total
Mathematics	10	9	14	14	15	14	16	15	16		64			187
Science	9	11	11	13	15	10		31			36			136
ELA	18	20	19	19	18	15	15	14	15		14		14	181

Source: Simms, 2016.

To illustrate the nature of the Critical Concepts, consider the fourteen measurement topics in ELA at the grades 11–12 level. As this list demonstrates, the Critical Concepts measurement topics are broad categories of knowledge and skill.

1. Applying text organization and structure

2. Analyzing ideas and thoughts

3. Analyzing claims, evidence, and reasoning

4. Analyzing narratives

5. Analyzing point of view and purpose

6. Analyzing style and tone

7. Comparing texts

8. Analyzing language

9. Generating text organization and structure

10. Generating claims, evidence, and reasoning

11. Sources and research

12. Generating narratives

13. Revision and style

14. Editing

Across these fourteen ELA measurement topics, there are thirty-nine individual learning targets on which students must demonstrate proficiency. Considering that these topics are for grades 11 *and* 12, it amounts to about twenty learning targets per grade level. Given a 180-day school year, ELA teachers and students certainly have time to adequately address twenty topics.

Once a school has a concise set of measurement topics for each course, the next step is to develop proficiency scales. Content-area teams can generate scales locally if desired (readers should consult Hoegh's [2020] *A Handbook for Developing and Using Proficiency Scales in the Classroom*). Here, we consider the characteristics of proficiency scales using Critical Concepts scales, which Marzano Academies and other schools can customize.

Each Critical Concepts measurement topic has an associated proficiency scale. For example, figure 2.1 (page 44) depicts the scale for the grades 11–12 ELA topic of analyzing claims, evidence, and reasoning. Note the format of this scale. The ELA content on which this scale focuses is explicit at three levels of the scale: 2.0, 3.0, and 4.0. Score 3.0 contains the *target content*: what students should know and be able to do to demonstrate proficiency. In the case of this multidimensional scale, to demonstrate proficiency, students must do three things: (1) evaluate the rhetorical aspects of an argument, (2) evaluate an argument's use of reasons and evidence, and (3) evaluate the reasoning in historical, political, and legal texts. The content at the 2.0 level represents knowledge and skill that are necessary for students to reach the 3.0 level. This scale details score 2.0 content separately for each of the three elements at the 3.0 level. Finally, the 4.0 level of the scale contains an example of a complex task that demonstrates students' ability to apply the knowledge and skill of the content at the 3.0 level.

The score 1.0 and score 0.0 levels do not contain explicit content. Score 1.0 signifies that a student cannot demonstrate knowledge and skill at the 2.0 and 3.0 levels independently, but with help demonstrates partial success with some of the content at both levels. The 0.0 level indicates that students cannot demonstrate any success with the content even with help. Finally, the half-point scores

4.0	The student will: • Compare how two texts with similar claims use rhetoric and evidence to assert their arguments and combat opposing arguments, using inferences drawn from the texts and context to explain why the two writers' approaches to their claims differ or if one's approach is more effective (for example, compare Elizabeth Cady Stanton's "Declaration of Sentiments and Resolutions" to Hillary Clinton's "Women's Rights Are Human Rights" and describe similarities and differences in the presentation of each text's argument as well as possible reasons for why these similarities or differences exist).
3.5	In addition to score 3.0 performance, partial success at score 4.0 content
3.0	The student will: **ACER1—Evaluate the rhetorical aspects of an argument** (for example, decide whether Frederick Douglass's use of rhetoric to draw listeners' attention to the issue of slavery in his speech "What to the Slave Is the Fourth of July?" is effective). **ACER2—Evaluate an argument's use of reasons and evidence** (for example, decide whether the logic and strength of the evidence given in the Declaration of Independence for the withdrawal of the United States from the British Crown is adequate). **ACER3—Evaluate the reasoning in historical, political, and legal texts** (for example, decide whether the reasoning in *New Jersey v. T.L.O.* is grounded in constitutional support).
2.5	No major errors or omissions regarding score 2.0 content, and partial success at score 3.0 content
2.0	**ACER1—**The student will recognize or recall specific vocabulary (for example, *connotation, ethos, logos, pathos, rhetoric*) and perform basic processes such as: • Describe pathos, logos, and ethos. • Annotate sections of a text that appeal to a reader's emotions (such as descriptive words with strong emotional connotations). • Annotate sections of a text that present facts, data, or other verifiable evidence. • Annotate sections of a text that strengthen a reader's perception of the author. • Count how many times (approximately) an author uses particular rhetorical strategies and note if one is used more frequently than others. • Describe reasons why an author might use a particular rhetorical strategy. **ACER2—**The student will recognize or recall specific vocabulary (for example, *argument, backing, claim, counterclaim, evidence, grounds, opposition, outline, qualifier*) and perform basic processes such as: • Describe types of materials and sources that can serve as appropriate evidence in a text. • Annotate the claims and evidence given in a text. • Describe the grounds, backing, and qualifiers given for a text's central claim. • Create an outline of the various claims in a text and evidence provided for each. • Summarize the argument in a text. • Annotate sections in a text where an opposing claim is addressed. • Describe the grounds, backing, and qualifiers given for an opposing claim in a text. **ACER3—**The student will recognize or recall specific vocabulary (for example, *argument, claim, constitutional, evidence, precedence, reasoning, structure*) and perform basic processes such as: • Annotate the claims and evidence given in a text. • Summarize the claims in a text and the evidence given for them. • Annotate evidence that links an argument to constitutional support (in legal texts). • Describe how precedence affects legal arguments. • Describe the conclusions made in a text. • Describe the context of a text. • Create an outline of the argument presented throughout a text.
1.5	Partial success at score 2.0 content, and major errors or omissions regarding score 3.0 content
1.0	With help, partial success at score 2.0 content and score 3.0 content
0.5	With help, partial success at score 2.0 content but not at score 3.0 content
0.0	Even with help, no success

Source: © 2016 by Marzano Resources. Used with permission.

FIGURE 2.1: Proficiency scale for analyzing claims, evidence, and reasoning, grades 11–12 ELA.

represent partial success. For example, the score of 2.5 indicates that students can demonstrate competence with the score 2.0 content independently, and some but not all of the score 3.0 content.

One obvious characteristic of the scale in figure 2.1 is that it contains a great deal of content at the score 2.0, 3.0, and 4.0 levels. Indeed, at the 3.0 level, there are three different topics listed. The Critical Concepts proficiency scales are purposefully designed as a starting place for districts and schools in their development of proficiency scales. Districts and schools should change, add, combine, and delete content as needed to ensure the proficiency scales they create address the local needs of the district or school.

One way to customize the Critical Concepts scales is to split them into multiple single-dimension scales, one for each of the elements at the score 3.0 level. For the scale in figure 2.1, which again has three score 3.0 learning targets, teachers can easily create three more focused proficiency scales. To illustrate, figure 2.2 is a single-dimension proficiency scale that focuses on evaluating an argument's use of reasons and evidence (ACER2), one of the three elements of proficiency from the original scale in figure 2.1. Note that in the single-dimension scale, teachers need to rewrite the score 4.0

4.0	The student will: • Compare how two texts with similar claims use reasoning and evidence to assert their arguments and combat opposing arguments (for example, compare Elizabeth Cady Stanton's "Declaration of Sentiments and Resolutions" to Hillary Clinton's "Women's Rights Are Human Rights" relative to their use of reason and evidence).
3.5	In addition to score 3.0 performance, partial success at score 4.0 content
3.0	The student will: **ACER2—Evaluate an argument's use of reasons and evidence** (for example, decide whether the logic and strength of the evidence given in the Declaration of Independence for the withdrawal of the United States from the British Crown is adequate).
2.5	No major errors or omissions regarding score 2.0 content, and partial success at score 3.0 content
2.0	**ACER2—**The student will recognize or recall specific vocabulary (for example, *argument, backing, claim, counterclaim, evidence, grounds, opposition, outline, qualifier*) and perform basic processes such as: • Describe types of materials and sources that can serve as appropriate evidence in a text. • Annotate the claims and evidence given in a text. • Describe the grounds, backing, and qualifiers given for a text's central claim. • Create an outline of the various claims in a text and evidence provided for each. • Summarize the argument in a text. • Annotate sections in a text where an opposing claim is addressed. • Describe the grounds, backing, and qualifiers given for an opposing claim in a text.
1.5	Partial success at score 2.0 content, and major errors or omissions regarding score 3.0 content
1.0	With help, partial success at score 2.0 content and score 3.0 content
0.5	With help, partial success at score 2.0 content but not at score 3.0 content
0.0	Even with help, no success

Source: © 2016 by Marzano Resources. Adapted with permission.

FIGURE 2.2: Proficiency scale for evaluating an argument's use of reasons and evidence, grades 11–12 ELA.

task to emphasize only the element on which this scale focuses, rather than all three elements in the original scale.

In sum, a guaranteed and viable set of measurement topics and proficiency scales defines what is taught, measured, and reported in the Marzano Academies model. While classroom teachers and students are the primary users of proficiency scales, school leaders have the responsibility of leading the schoolwide design process described in this section and ensuring teachers have the necessary professional learning and support, which we explore next.

Professional Learning and Support for Teachers

To accomplish this type of detailed curricular work, teachers must have appropriate support and professional development. Therefore, leaders cannot skimp on the necessary job-embedded and ongoing professional development for teachers. Topics for professional development should include the structure of a proficiency scale, how to unpack standards to identify measurement topics, how to introduce students to proficiency scales, how to plan instruction using proficiency scales, how to plan assessments using proficiency scales, and the like. Leaders should ensure that professional training includes a combination of *learning* from experts and *doing* the work. For example, leaders should not merely purchase proficiency scales from an external source and then implement them as is. This might be a temptation if a school utilizes the Critical Concepts. However, as described previously, the Critical Concepts are designed to be adapted for local needs. If teachers determine that they want to design their own measurement topics and proficiency scales from scratch, they will need even more time to do the work—leaders should set aside at least a full year for the design of the scales.

The process of designing proficiency scales should include opportunities for teachers to read the growing library of materials on proficiency scales and even review measurement topics and scales from other secondary schools. Learning from other secondary teachers and schools can be informative, thought-provoking, and inspiring. It is also important that leaders do not schedule professional learning opportunities and then disappear to their offices or other meetings. The school's leadership team should learn side by side with teachers whenever possible.

Support also includes providing resources that emphasize schoolwide consistency. All subject areas at all levels should use the same format for their proficiency scales. Of course, in the Marzano Academies model, we recommend the format exemplified by all the scales depicted in this book. To ensure continuity of design, it is useful to provide teachers with a template like that in figure 2.3.

This template helps teachers understand each level of the scale, as well as associated activities and assessment guidelines. As part of the design of a specific scale, the template has space to designate the course, measurement topic, school, and the state standard to which the scale is aligned. Note that we recommend that teachers doing this work should list their school at the top of the scale for ease of identification. Districts may share proficiency scales among schools or even with other districts, and courses, measurement topics, and standards may overlap or be similar. For example, many high schools might have a world civilizations measurement topic called "Culture and Diversity." Listing the school prevents confusion in situations where proficiency scales are shared or stored in a shared database.

The third column of the template, titled Activities, is where teachers fill in resources and particular instructional strategies they consider useful for the content at a specific level. For example, for the score 2.0 content, teachers might identify specific parts of a textbook that relate to the content, specific online resources, or even specific instructional strategies like comparison that would facilitate students' learning the content.

Course: _____   Measurement Topic: _____

School: _____   State Standard: _____

Score	Description	Activities	Assessment Ideas
Score 4.0 (Honors) Complex Content	This level is in addition to score 3.0 performance. The content at this level does not require explicit classroom instruction and the student demonstrates in-depth inferences and applications beyond what was taught in a variety of ways. Students must demonstrate this level of performance to receive honors credit.	Describe sample activities that require students to apply all score 3.0 learning targets.	Describe sample assessment tasks or ways for students to demonstrate they can go beyond what was taught.
Score 3.5	No major errors or omissions in 3.0 content, and partial mastery of 4.0 content		
Score 3.0 Target Content	This level articulates the expectation for all students at the level of the essential topics. Remember to limit the number of learning targets at this level to no more than three and that each learning target requires explicit classroom instruction.	Describe sample activities that guide students to reach proficiency with the target content.	Describe sample assessment tasks or ways for students to demonstrate proficiency with the target content.
Score 2.5	No major errors or omissions in 2.0 content, and partial mastery of 3.0 content		
Score 2.0 Simple Content	This level articulates the simple content, or the prerequisite knowledge and skill. It includes critical vocabulary terms (five to seven) related to the topic. Targets at score 3.0 typically have related targets at score 2.0 (but not required). Limit the number of targets at this level to no more than three, if possible, not including the vocabulary terms.	Describe sample activities that guide students to gain basic knowledge and practice basic skills.	Describe sample assessment tasks or ways for students to demonstrate understanding of vocabulary and basic knowledge and ability to perform basic skills.
Score 1.5	Partial success at score 2.0 content, and major errors or omissions regarding score 3.0 content		
Score 1.0	With help, partial success at score 2.0 content and score 3.0 content		
Score 0.5	With help, partial success at score 2.0 content but not at score 3.0 content		
Score 0.0	Even with help, no success		

FIGURE 2.3: Sample proficiency scale template.

*Visit **MarzanoResources.com/reproducibles** for a free reproducible version of this figure.*

The last column of the template asks teachers to provide guidelines for assessing the content at each level. This might include descriptions of ways students can demonstrate they know the content. It can also take the form of specific sample test items. A variation on this part of the template is to have teachers align the content with external assessments students take. Whether it is the SAT or ACT, a state-mandated test, or district benchmarks, the process of designing measurement topics and proficiency scales provides the school with opportunities to align what they teach and assess with what is assessed on interim tests, state tests, and national tests. Schools do not have to align *every* scale with external assessment blueprints. However, it is useful to create a document that identifies the connections between identified assessment priorities and the content within the curriculum. Note that only score 2.0, score 3.0, and score 4.0 include activities or assessments because the other scores refer to the content at those levels.

Writing proficiency scales offers an excellent opportunity to innovate curriculum, assessment, and instruction in a school, but teachers can also perceive it as an ominous learning experience and curricular responsibility. The school leader should make sure teachers are aware that proficiency scales do not have to be perfect on the first try—they will revisit the proficiency scales they are creating at the end of the year, at which time they can make changes and additions. To this end, the school leader should develop and implement a review process for measurement topics and proficiency scales where teachers within specific subject areas review each other's scales. Receiving input from teachers from different departments can also provide valuable insights. Together, these steps will equip leaders and teachers with the knowledge to engage in the ongoing cycle of writing, reviewing, monitoring, and revising.

To provide time for this cycle and the inevitable discussions, debates, and professional learning, school leaders may need to adjust their professional development budgets to compensate teachers for their time. Do not wait to be compelled by a bargaining unit contract, a grievance, or complaints. Plan and propose to pay teachers from the start. By doing so, the school leader will engender goodwill, honor a group of professionals who might often feel taken advantage of, and demonstrate commitment to the work. Based on the contractual hour rate, the school leader should set aside a pool of hours in the budget each year for writing and revising proficiency scales. Teachers, under the supervision of their department chairs or other direct managers, can request hours from the pool to develop or revise their measurement topics and proficiency scales. Whether teachers work from home, a library, a coffee shop, or the school, the school leader should trust them to complete the work and submit their required documentation.

Priority Measurement Topics

One of the biggest advantages of having proficiency scales is that it provides an opportunity for the school leader to establish priority measurement topics. A *priority measurement topic* is an area of learning that is of such great importance that the school should address it immediately. For example, in a high school that has several sections of an algebra course, educators might notice that most students across all sections have low proficiency scale scores for a specific measurement topic, such as balancing equations. This would be an indication that this measurement topic should be designated a priority. Teachers would then plan to determine the root cause of the problem and design expedient solutions. Analysis of the data from interim assessments will likely uncover a number of measurement topics and their related proficiency scales that should be placed on the priority list. At the high school level, educators can identify such topics at the department level or even the course level. On a systematic basis (for example, quarterly), department chairs and subject-matter experts should scan available data to identify those topics that require more emphasis or more detailed review. Then, they should communicate those topics to members of the department so teams can establish plans to increase students' learning in all priority areas.

High Reliability Leadership for School-Level Indicator 9

Figure 2.4 lists some potential lagging indicators for measurement topics and proficiency scales. From this list, the leader would then select trim tab indicators to create a customized high reliability scale. Figure 2.5 (page 50) depicts a possible customized scale a school leader might design for school-level indicator 9, measurement topics and proficiency scales.

Programs and Practices	Lagging Indicator Data	Potential Standard for High Reliability Status
Measurement topics and proficiency scales	Written documents with proficiency scales	100 percent of measurement topics and proficiency scales follow the prescribed format 100 percent of teachers selected for the design and development process actively participate
Guaranteed and viable curriculum	Estimates of the amount of time required to teach measurement topics and their accompanying proficiency scales	100 percent of measurement topics and proficiency scales adhere to the defining features of a guaranteed and viable curriculum
Professional learning and support for teachers	In-person and virtual professional development sessions	100 percent of teachers have engaged in professional development activities regarding measurement topics and proficiency scales
Priority measurement topics	Notes from schoolwide or districtwide efforts to identify priority measurement topics	Representatives from all academic subject areas participate in the identification of priority measurement topics
Perceptions of students, teachers, and parents	Surveys of students, teachers, and parents	90 percent of teachers perceive the measurement topics and proficiency scales as viable and useful

FIGURE 2.4: Potential lagging indicators and criteria for school-level indicator 9.

Classroom Assessment (SLI 13)

The approach to classroom assessment within the academy model represents a major paradigm shift for many secondary teachers. Traditionally, secondary educators have framed assessment as formative and summative *evaluations* of student performance. However, CBE reframes classroom assessment as part of an integrated system of assessments that provide feedback to students, teachers, and parents about individual students' status and growth (Marzano, Norford, & Ruyle, 2019). Some or many classroom teachers might need to re-examine their philosophies on assessment and their classroom assessment practices and adjust them to align with the new paradigm. School leaders must help teachers navigate this philosophical shift from assessment as evaluation to assessment as feedback. Education researchers Scott Marion, Maria Worthen, and Carla Evans (2020) argued that competency-based learning systems must integrate balanced assessment systems where different

Evidence	
4 **Sustaining** **(quick data)**	Quick data like the following are systematically collected and reviewed: • Reviews of teacher lesson plans and unit plans • Quick conversations with teachers and students • Examination of evidence scores in the LMS
3 **Applying** **(lagging)**	Performance goals with clear criteria for success like the following are in place: • 100 percent of measurement topics and proficiency scales follow the prescribed format • 100 percent of teachers selected for the design and development process actively participate • 100 percent of measurement topics and proficiency scales adhere to the defining features of a guaranteed and viable curriculum • 90 percent of teachers perceive the measurement topics and proficiency scales as viable and useful
2 **Developing** **(leading)**	• The format for proficiency scales has been articulated • Representative groups of teachers are involved in the design of measurement topics and proficiency scales • Guidelines are in place for a guaranteed and viable curriculum based on measurement topics and proficiency scales
1 **Beginning**	• The school has written plans for the articulation and implementation of proficiency scales and measurement topics for the major subject areas but there is little execution of the plans at the classroom level • Relatively few teachers implement instruction and assessment based on measurement topics and proficiency scales
0 **Not Using**	• The school has no written plan for instruction and assessment of measurement topics for the major subject areas • There is no implementation at the classroom level of instruction and assessment based on measurement topics for the major subject areas

Source: © 2020 by Marzano Academies, Inc. Adapted with permission.

FIGURE 2.5: Customized high reliability scale for school-level indicator 9.

types of assessments provide coordinated information that teachers can use to make instructional decisions about individual students. They also emphasized the fact that assessment systems must support decision making by providing students multiple opportunities and ways to demonstrate competence. Assessment systems should also continuously document students' progress over time.

A good place for a school leader to start with this school-level indicator is to consider how classroom assessment integrates with other assessments used by the school and district. As depicted in figure 2.6, the most frequent type of assessment data about student learning in the academy model comes from classroom assessments. They provide ongoing evidence of students' status and growth. Given that classroom assessments are designed around measurement topics and proficiency scales, they are at a very granular level.

The second most frequent source of assessment data is *interim assessments*, sometimes referred to as *benchmark assessments*. These are typically designed and administered by organizations outside of

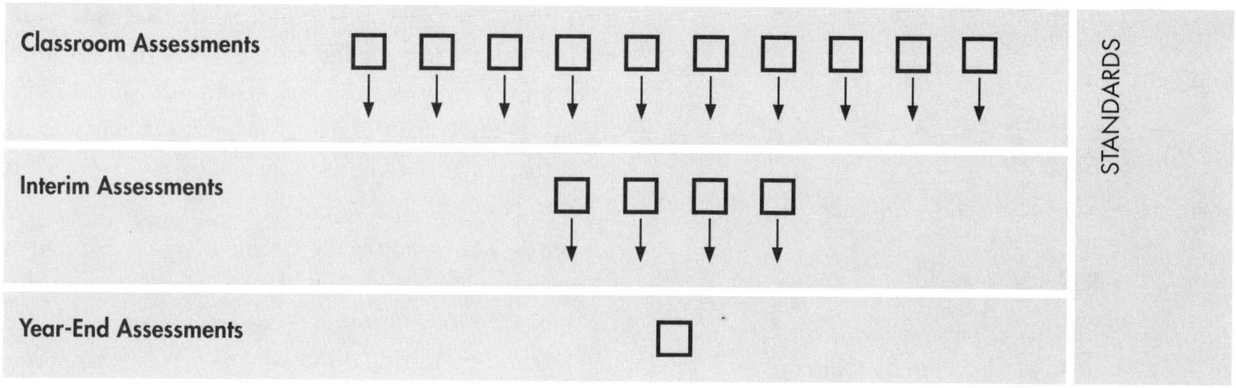

Source: Marzano, 2018, p. 6.

FIGURE 2.6: Academy assessment model.

the school or school system and are used to gauge student growth but not at the granularity level of classroom assessments.

The least frequent assessments employed in schools are year-end assessments such as state exams. Typically, states use year-end assessments to gauge how well schools and districts are performing with respect to state standards. These tests are designed to determine how well a school or district is performing as opposed to testing the performance of individual students within those systems.

This is only a brief overview of this model and its underlying rationale; a deeper discussion appears in two related books, *Making Classroom Assessments Reliable and Valid* (Marzano, 2018) and *The New Art and Science of Classroom Assessment* (Marzano et al., 2019). However, the main takeaway is that one of the most powerful structural changes a school can make is to use classroom assessments as the primary source of information for making decisions about the current status and growth of individual students. To be clear, academies still employ benchmark assessments and end-of-year assessments. However, they are used more for checks and balances at the school level. Accordingly, the remainder of this section reviews the classroom assessment practices that distinguish the academy model from traditional systems. These practices include the following.

- Types of classroom assessments

- Multiple scores for each student

- Current summative scores

- Supplemental topics

- Validation of scores from classroom assessments

- Changes to teachers' thinking about classroom assessments

We begin with types of classroom assessments.

Types of Classroom Assessments

The academy model for classroom assessment provides teachers with many options not available in the traditional classroom. Figure 2.7 (page 52) lists some of those options. The top box in figure 2.7 lists the various types of classroom assessments academy teachers can use to gather information about a student's current status on a particular proficiency scale. Notice that traditional tests are listed in figure 2.7. Certainly, academy teachers still use traditional tests, but they also have at

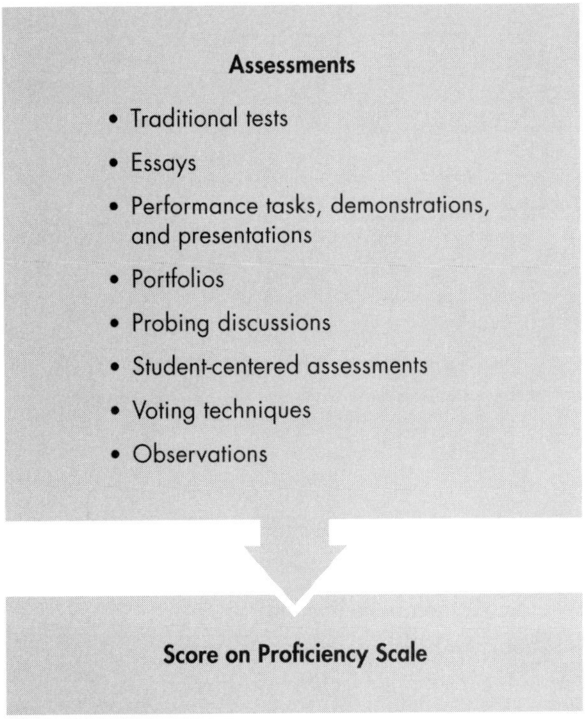

Assessments

- Traditional tests
- Essays
- Performance tasks, demonstrations, and presentations
- Portfolios
- Probing discussions
- Student-centered assessments
- Voting techniques
- Observations

Score on Proficiency Scale

Source: Adapted from Marzano, 2018.

FIGURE 2.7: Conceptual model for classroom assessment.

their disposal many other types. Some of these assessment types are not available to teachers in traditional classrooms simply because they require the use of proficiency scales. Stated differently, when proficiency scales exist, the types of activities that qualify as assessments increase dramatically.

Here we address two of the assessment types that cannot be used effectively without proficiency scales: probing discussions and student-centered assessments. For a detailed discussion of additional assessment types, see *Making Classroom Assessments Reliable and Valid* (Marzano, 2018), *The New Art and Science of Classroom Assessment* (Marzano et al., 2019), or *Teaching in a Competency-Based Secondary School* (Marzano, Aschoff, & Avila, 2022).

Probing Discussions

Probing discussions involve the teacher sitting down with a student, proficiency scale in hand, and asking a series of questions. It is the most flexible type of assessment within the academy model. To illustrate, assume that a teacher is working with high school students on a geography proficiency scale for the measurement topic of cultural convergence and divergence, shown in figure 2.8.

Using this proficiency scale, the teacher would structure questions to address the content at score 2.0, 3.0, and 4.0. For example, the teacher might design questions like the following.

- Score 2.0
  - Can you explain to me what cultural convergence means and what cultural divergence means?
  - Using the European countries we have been studying, can you describe an example of cultural convergence?
  - Can you identify a group that you consider representative of a specific culture and describe the defining characteristics of that culture?
- Score 3.0
  - Can you explain how advances in technology have affected the culture you've selected?
  - Can you explain how advances in communications have affected the culture you've selected?
  - Can you explain how globalization has affected the culture you've selected?
- Score 4.0
  - How do you think the culture you have selected will change over the next two decades?
  - What evidence can you provide for your predictions?

When engaged in the probing discussion, the teacher uses these preplanned questions, along with those he or she thinks up on the spot, to verbally examine an individual student's knowledge of the content one level at a time. Once the teacher is convinced that the student understands the score 2.0 content, he or she moves to score 3.0 queries. If the student responds accurately to some of the

4.0	In addition to score 3.0 performance, the student demonstrates in-depth inferences and applications that go beyond what was taught (for example, creates and defends a generalization about how culture will change over the next two decades).
3.5	In addition to score 3.0 performance, partial success at score 4.0 content
3.0	The student will: **CCD—Explain factors that contribute to cultural convergence or divergence** (for example, explain how advances in communication and transportation technologies and resulting globalization affect the pace of cultural change around the world and how these changes increase or decrease the differences between various cultures).
2.5	No major errors or omissions regarding score 2.0 content, and partial success at score 3.0 content
2.0	**CCD—**The student will recognize or recall specific vocabulary (for example, *cultural convergence*, *cultural divergence*) and perform basic processes such as: • Give examples of cultural convergence (for example, the overlap and interchange between Japanese and American cultures since World War II). • Give examples of cultural divergence (for example, increasing distinctions between Amish and mainstream American culture). • Describe characteristics that constitute a given cultural system (for example, describe the language, beliefs, cuisine, art, and traditions of the Māori). • Explain the effects of technological changes in communications and transportation systems on the speed and distances over which people, products, and ideas move.
1.5	Partial success at score 2.0 content, and major errors or omissions regarding score 3.0 content
1.0	With help, partial success at score 2.0 content and score 3.0 content
0.5	With help, partial success at score 2.0 content but not at score 3.0 content
0.0	Even with help, no success

Source: © 2019 by Marzano Resources. Adapted with permission.

FIGURE 2.8: Proficiency scale for cultural convergence and divergence, grades 9–12 geography.

3.0 questions but not all, the teacher would assign a score of 2.5 on the proficiency scale. Probably the most useful aspect of probing-discussion assessments is that the teacher can ask students to clarify their answers if the teacher needs more evidence to determine a student's current status as measured by the proficiency scale.

Student-Centered Assessments

Student-centered assessments are an extremely valuable practice within the Marzano Academies model. In 2009, education scholar John Hattie ranked 138 variables in terms of their correlation with student achievement. The variable ranked highest was what he referred to as *student self-reported grades*. The academy model employs the term *student-centered assessments*, but the two are analogous. In effect, Hattie reported that the activity most strongly associated with student achievement as measured by external assessments is students' self-reporting of their own achievement. In 2012, Hattie updated his research and added twelve variables, bringing the total to 150. The highest ranked variable in this updated review was titled *student self-reported grades/student expectations*. While student self-reported grades still held the highest position, Hattie changed his original description by adding that students should set goals about their own learning. Hattie (2012) explained the reason for this change in the following way: "Educating students to have high, challenging, appropriate expectations is among the most powerful influence in enhancing student achievement" (p. 54). Finally, in 2015 Hattie expanded his list to 195 variables. This time, the top-ranked variable was *teacher estimates of achievement*, and the third-ranked variable was student self-reported grades. (The second-ranked variable was collective efficacy, which we consider in our discussion of school-level indicator 15, collective responsibility; page 134.) If one considers this research in its entirety, it indicates that student-centered assessments along with teacher judgments about those assessments are at the top of the list in terms of what educators can do to enhance student achievement. In the academy model, there are two types of student-centered assessments: (1) student-generated assessments and (2) student self-assessments.

Student-generated assessments are those that students themselves design as evidence that they have reached a certain level of competence on a specific proficiency scale. For example, in a high school economics class, assume that at level 3.0, students are expected to demonstrate how to weigh the marginal costs, marginal benefits, and risks of alternative options to make the most effective decision. As a student-generated assessment, a student might record a verbal description of what she would do when presented with the option of purchasing a monthly bus pass for travel or making payments on a car. The student would describe the marginal benefits and costs of each option, identify possible risks, and identify the most effective choice. All of this would be part of the recording so the teacher could examine it at any time. The recording could be archived so that other students could listen to it later as an exemplar of what proficiency sounds like for this particular measurement topic.

Student self-assessment involves students asserting that they have attained a specific score on a specific proficiency scale and then backing up their assertion with concrete evidence. This form of assessment works best using personal tracking matrices. A personal tracking matrix resembles a proficiency scale in that it organizes content in a learning progression with the complex content at the top and the simpler content at the bottom. However, the personal tracking matrix uses student-friendly language to restate the learning targets within a proficiency scale as "I can" statements. Teachers can develop personal tracking matrices for students or work with them to develop their own matrices (Marzano, Norford, et al., 2017). To illustrate, figure 2.9 contains a personal tracking matrix that has been designed for a proficiency scale on the measurement topic of health and wellness.

Personal tracking matrices typically have a row dedicated to each piece of content, whereas a proficiency scale will combine them. For example, each vocabulary term has its own line in a personal tracking matrix, whereas vocabulary is listed together as score 2.0 content in a proficiency scale. The most important parts of the personal tracking matrix are the columns for students to rate themselves on each learning target, and the column to provide evidence of their learning. Specifically, when using a personal tracking matrix, students rate themselves using the following scale.

1. I'm still confused about this topic.

2. I've learned some but not all of the topic.

3. I've got this now.

Level	Indicator	My Rating			My Evidence
		I'm still confused about this topic.	I've learned some but not all of the topic.	I've got this now.	
4	I can show examples of different types of diets and explain how they might affect a person's body.				
3	I can explain what eating different types of foods might do to my body.				
2	I can explain foods that are in a balanced diet.				
2	I can read and explain a food label.				
2	I can give examples of fad diets and explain why they are not always healthy choices.				
2	I can give examples of unhealthy foods using the Dietary Guidelines for Americans.				
2	I can give examples of healthy foods using the Dietary Guidelines for Americans.				
2	I can explain the term *dietary guidelines*.				
2	I can explain the term *fad*.				
2	I can explain the term *additive*.				
2	I can explain the term *nutrition*.				
2	I can explain the term *calorie*.				
2	I can explain the term *protein*.				
2	I can explain the term *carbohydrate*.				
2	I can explain the term *sodium*.				

Source: Adapted from Marzano, 2017.

FIGURE 2.9: Personal tracking matrix for health and wellness proficiency scale.

*Visit **MarzanoResources.com/reproducibles** for a blank reproducible version of this figure.*

The last column of the personal tracking matrix is titled My Evidence. This is critical to the validity of a personal tracking matrix as a form of assessment. In this column, students record the evidence on which they are basing their evaluation of themselves. Such evidence might include a pen-and-paper assignment a student completed, a virtual assignment, a written explanation of content, and so on.

Multiple Scores for Each Student

One unique feature of classroom assessment in the academy model is that students receive multiple scores for each measurement topic. Additionally, not every student receives the same number of scores during a grading period. To illustrate how this might manifest, consider figure 2.10, which depicts the scores of five students over twenty days. Each column represents a specific day and each row represents a specific student. All scores relate to a specific measurement topic and its related proficiency scale.

Scores for: Atomic Structures 1

Student	Day																			
	1	2	3	4	5	6	7	8	9	10	11	12	13	14	15	16	17	18	19	20
Alex	1.0				1.5						2.0			2.0			2.5			2.5
Annie	1.5										3.0				3.0			3.5		3.5
Ben	2.0		2.0								3.0									4.0
Troy	1.0		1.5								2.5					3.0		3.5		3.5
Vaughan	2.0					2.5					2.5			3.0			3.5			4.0

Source: Adapted from Marzano, 2021a.

FIGURE 2.10: Varying number of assessments for different students.

On the first day of the unit, the teacher administered a pretest to all students and recorded each student's score. Thus, every student has a score entered on day 1. During the next nine days, the teacher assessed students individually. All students received scores but not all students were assessed on the same days. Ben and Troy received scores on day 3 but no one else did. Alex was the only one to receive a score on day 5 and Vaughan was the only one to receive a score on day 6. These individual assessments might have taken the forms of probing discussions, observations, student-generated assessment, and the like. On day 11, the teacher gave an assessment to the entire class and all students received scores. After that, assessments were again individual until the last day, when the teacher administered a posttest to the entire class and scores were assigned to each student.

A question that might immediately come to mind for many secondary teachers is, How do you determine which students should be assessed beyond the times all students are assessed? To answer this question, it's important to remember that sometimes students submit their own student-generated assessments or self-assessments. This in itself will result in more scores for some students. When determining which students require extra teacher-designed assessments, teachers can follow the general rule that the less sure they are about a student's scores, the more assessments they should use.

Current Summative Scores

Ultimately, each student must be assigned a current summative score for each measurement topic for the purposes of reporting and of examining learning trends. Notice the term *current summative score*. This is an important distinction within the academy model. Detailed and technical discussions of the concept of current summative scores are presented in the books *Formative Assessment and Standards-Based Grading* (Marzano, 2011), *Making Classroom Assessments Reliable and Valid* (Marzano, 2018), and *The New Art and Science of Classroom Assessment* (Marzano et al., 2019). Here we provide a brief discussion.

In brief, it is technically a misnomer to label a particular score *summative* when it comes to measuring student learning. The term *summative score* was first made popular within the field of project evaluation, where it was referred to as *summative evaluation*. When a project is complete, it is evaluated as to how well the final product meets the initial design specifications. For example, if a new schoolwide schedule were designed and gradually implemented over a semester, the summative evaluation would occur when the schedule was fully in place. This evaluation would focus on how well the implementation followed the original plan and the extent to which the schedule met its initial goals. As the schedule was gradually being implemented, it would be evaluated at significant benchmark points along the way. These evaluations would be considered *formative* because they address the project as it is still being implemented.

This concept became popular within the field of assessment because it made the important distinction that not all assessments are designed for the same purpose. However, over the years, some schools adopted the position that when measuring students on a specific topic, one assessment would be considered the summative assessment, rendering a summative score for all students. All of the assessments leading up to that summative assessment would be considered formative practice for the summative test. This makes little sense from a number of perspectives. First, when a student is learning a particular topic, it is inaccurate to think in terms of the student being done learning at some point. In contrast, with a concrete project like implementing a new schedule, there is a concrete endpoint. Learning does not adhere to this model. Another reason that this approach makes little sense is that it ignores a great deal of valuable information about each student that is contained in their responses to the items on the formative assessments.

The most egregious reason why the practice of administering a single summative assessment makes little sense is that it relies on the single score to provide an accurate estimate of a student's status. Psychometric theory (that is, the field of psychological testing and measurement) indicates that relying on a single score is precarious at best and highly inaccurate at worst. Table 2.2 provides a dramatic illustration of this important psychometric phenomenon. It depicts the amount of error one can expect in an individual student's score of 75 on a single test when one considers the reliability of the test. The precision of this single test is depicted across four levels of test reliability: 0.85, 0.75, 0.65, and 0.55. These quantities are referred to as *reliability coefficients*.

TABLE 2.2: 95 Percent Confidence Intervals for Observed Score of 75

Reliability Coefficient	Observed Score	Lowest Probable Score	Highest Probable Score	Range
0.85	75	69	81	12
0.75	75	67	83	16
0.65	75	65	85	20
0.55	75	64	86	22

Note: The standard deviation of this test was 8.33, and the upper and lower limits have been rounded.

Source: Adapted from Marzano, 2018.

This is a critical concept in educational assessment. Namely, the theory underlying all assessments is that the score a student obtains on any test, referred to as the *observed score*, is made up of two parts. One part is error and the other part is the student's *true score* on the particular test in question. Knowing the reliability of the test and a student's observed score allows one to compute a range of scores in which the student's true score probably falls. In this case, when the test has a reliability of 0.85, the range of scores in which the true score probably falls is between 69 and 81 for a range of 12 points. In contrast, if the reliability of the test was 0.55, the range of scores in which the true score probably falls would be between 64 and 86—a range of 22 points.

It is because of the inherent imprecision of an individual assessment that the Marzano Academies model promotes collecting multiple assessment scores for students on the measurement topics they are learning. In effect, teachers using the academy model do not use a single score from a single assessment to make decisions about the status of individual students. It's important to note that this does not mean that academy teachers should design and administer more traditional tests. Rather, a general rule is that teachers should assess students more but use fewer traditional tests. As depicted in figure 2.7 (page 52), there are a wide variety of classroom assessments available to teachers.

So how does an academy teacher assign a summative score for an individual student's series of scores on a specific measurement topic? To illustrate, assume that a particular student has the following six scores on a specific topic: 2.0, 2.0, 3.0, 2.5, 3.5, and 3.0. Traditionally, educators have averaged scores within a unit or course to assign a summative grade. The average of these scores is 2.67. However, an average assumes that no learning has occurred—the earliest score has the same weight as the latest. Therefore, we contend that the average is usually not a good candidate for the current summative score since it does not account for the fact that a student has increased their knowledge of the topic from the first score to the last.

One technique other than averaging teachers can use to assign a summative score is to simply examine that pattern of scores over time and assign the summative score that seems to represent the current summative score most accurately at the end of the grading period. The teacher starts by making an initial estimate of the summative score. For example, in this case (the scores 2.0, 2.0, 3.0, 2.5, 3.5, 3.0), this particular teacher might assign an initial summative score of 3.0. The teacher then asks himself how likely it is that this summative score is too high or too low given the pattern of observed scores. If the teacher concludes that the initial estimated summative score seems too high or too low based on the pattern of scores the student has exhibited, the teacher lowers or raises the tentative summative score by a quarter point or a half point. This is a new estimate of the student's summative score. The teacher repeats this process until the student reaches a point where the estimated score is a reasonable and defensible estimate of their current knowledge. In effect, this is an iterative approach in which a teacher assigns an initial summative score and adjusts it up or down based on how reasonable it is by examining the pattern of previous scores. Techniques for making such estimates as rigorous as possible appear in the books *Classroom Assessment and Grading That Work* (Marzano, 2006), *Formative Assessment and Standards-Based Grading* (Marzano, 2011), *Making Classroom Assessments Reliable and Valid* (Marzano, 2018), and *The New Art and Science of Classroom Assessment* (Marzano et al., 2019).

While examining the pattern of scores is a valid approach, there are also mathematical ways to compute a summative score that are more precise in nature. Employing mathematical models to aid in determining a student's current summative score at any point in time is one of the unique aspects of the Marzano Academies model. Formulas for these calculations are presented in the book *Making Classroom Assessments Reliable and Valid* (Marzano, 2018) and can be applied to any spreadsheet, like Excel. The formulas are also built into the Empower Learning LMS, which certified Marzano Academies employ. To illustrate, consider figure 2.11.

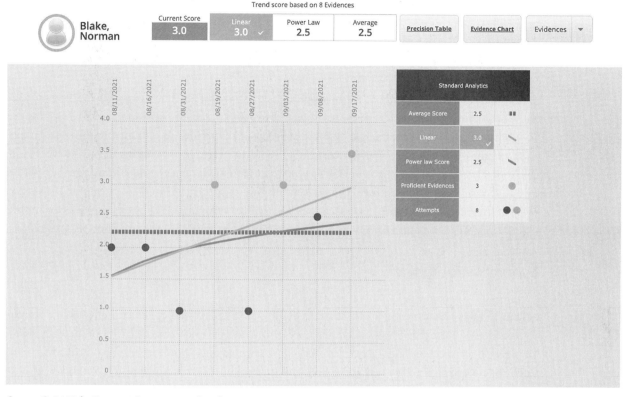

Source: © 2023 by Empower Learning. Used with permission.

FIGURE 2.11: Current summative score calculator in the Empower LMS.

The scores in figure 2.11 represent about a five-week period. The LMS refreshes this chart and recomputes the current summative score each time a teacher enters a new score for this specific student on this specific proficiency scale. Scores in the Empower LMS are referred to as *evidence scores* to emphasize that they are the evidence teachers will use to assign a current summative score.

The first score the student received was 2.0. The last score was 3.5. Altogether, the teacher has entered eight evidence scores during the five-week period. These scores came from the various types of assessments previously described, such as traditional tests, probing discussions, student-centered assessments, and so on. The teacher must now report a summative score that represents the student's final status.

The Empower LMS uses three mathematical models to compute the most probable summative score. One model is the average. As mentioned previously, this model gives equal weight to each evidence score, in effect assuming that little if any learning has occurred over the time the teacher scored assessments and entered the resulting evidence scores into the LMS. The average is depicted by the horizontal dotted line. A second mathematical model is the linear trend. The linear trend is computed under the assumption that students learn at a constant rate. It is the line that moves from lower left to upper right in a straight line. This means that students learn as much from week 1 to week 2 as they do from week 2 to week 3 and so on. The third mathematical model, the power-law trend, is depicted by the curved line that flattens out over time. It is computed under the assumption that students learn quickly in the beginning, but when they get to the more complex content at the higher levels of a proficiency scale, their rate of learning slows down or flattens out.

The LMS doesn't just compute these three analyses, it also identifies the mathematical model that has the least amount of error. In figure 2.11, this is indicated by the extended rectangle labeled *Linear* with the checkmark in it. In this case, the linear trend is the best model of the three. Thus, the mathematically recommended summative score of best fit is 3.0. The teacher uses this information to enter a summative score that appears in the box labeled *Current Score*. In this case, the teacher has opted to use the summative score recommended by the mathematical analysis, but it is important to note that the teacher can override the calculator if he or she has reason to believe that a different score better reflects the student's current level of knowledge or skill.

The Marzano Academies approach to assigning summative scores is obviously quite different from traditional assessment practices at the secondary level. At its core, the academy approach rejects the notion that a single score on a single test should be trusted as a measure of students' true status at any point in time. An interesting analogy regarding this practice is diagnostic testing during the COVID-19 pandemic. A single test might not be accepted as adequate evidence to determine whether people have the virus, due to the fact that the tests can produce false positives and false negatives. Taking at least two tests provides a more reliable conclusion. The same logic should be applied to determining a student's summative score on any given topic. A single test score is never enough.

Supplemental Topics

One issue that continually comes up in secondary schools is what to do about content that has no officially designed measurement topics with accompanying proficiency scales. Such content might be considered important by an individual teacher but not part of the mandatory proficiency scales for a specific subject area. For example, assume that a middle school geography teacher wishes to teach the following three topics: (1) causes and consequences of urbanization, (2) models of ecosystems, and (3) distribution of ecosystems and biomes. While the state's standards documents list these three topics, they are not included in the mandatory proficiency scales the district designed for the middle school level.

One way to address such situations is to include a supplemental topic category. The topics in the supplemental category are not related and do not have their own proficiency scales. Rather, a generic scale like that in figure 2.12 is used.

4.0	Advanced content
3.5	In addition to score 3.0 performance, partial success at score 4.0 content
3.0	Target content
2.5	No major errors regarding score 2.0 content and partial success at score 3.0 content
2.0	Simple foundational content
1.5	Partial success at score 2.0 content and major errors or omissions regarding score 3.0 content
1.0	With help, partial success at score 2.0 and score 3.0 content
0.5	With help, partial success at score 2.0 content but not at score 3.0
0.0	Even with help, no success

Source: Adapted from Marzano et al., 2019.

FIGURE 2.12: Generic scale for supplemental topics.

The most straightforward way to use this scale with supplemental content is to ensure that assessments for supplemental topics include items that address the foundational content (that is, score 2.0), items that address the target content (score 3.0), and items that address the advanced content (score 4.0). To illustrate, assume that a seventh-grade science teacher wanted to teach students supplemental content not addressed in the proficiency scale for the topic of light and vision. The teacher conducts lessons on the essential learning targets for light and vision, designs classroom assessments, and collects scores over time. However, for the supplemental content that is not in the official proficiency scale, the teacher would design a separate test only covering that supplemental content. The test would include items for the foundational content, target content, and advanced content for the supplemental topic. Each student's test would be scored. While the official topic of light and vision would have multiple scores for each student from the various assessments, the supplemental topic would have only one score for each student.

Over the course of a grading period (let's say nine weeks), the teacher might identify four supplemental topics that are not part of the official curriculum. The teacher would develop a single test for each of these four and enter a single score for each student on each topic. However, these scores would all be entered into the supplemental topic category. Since these four scores are on different topics that represent very different information and skills, the teacher would not examine the learning trend for individual students over time. However, the teacher could average these four different scores. In effect, the teacher can't generate a summative score for the supplemental topic, but the average score would communicate a student's central tendency across the four disparate topics.

Validation of Scores From Classroom Assessments

Classroom assessments, interim assessments, and end-of-year assessments should all work in concert. We have already noted that classroom assessments should be the first line of information when it comes to making determinations about students' status and growth on specific measurement topics. But educators should validate students' summative scores on classroom assessments periodically by comparing them to students' scores on interim and end-of-year assessments. To illustrate how this might be done, consider figure 2.13.

	Beginning-of-year benchmark assessment	Middle-of-year benchmark assessment	End-of-year benchmark assessment
ELA Teacher 1	Correlation: 0.89 Number of students: 31	Correlation: 0.82 Number of students: 31	Correlation: 0.78 Number of students: 31
ELA Teacher 2	Correlation: 0.77 Number of students: 25	Correlation: 0.65 Number of students: 25	Correlation: 0.81 Number of students: 25
ELA Teacher 3	Correlation: 0.56 Number of students: 18	Correlation: 0.74 Number of students: 18	Correlation: 0.75 Number of students: 18
ELA Teacher 4	Correlation: 0.43 Number of students: 24	Correlation: 0.56 Number of students: 24	Correlation: 0.61 Number of students: 24

FIGURE 2.13: Correlations between classroom and external assessments.

In this figure, students' summative scores derived from classroom assessments are correlated with the scores these students received on beginning-of-year, middle-of-year, and end-of-year exams. Leaders compute these correlations for each of the four teachers separately. If the correlations are high, then the scores assigned by classroom teachers can be considered valid. The correlations reported in figure 2.13 are analogous to actual correlations from academy schools and range from 0.43 (medium) to 0.89 (very large; see chapter 5, page 141, and Cohen, 1988).

This type of ongoing analysis is one of the most important leadership functions related to assessment. If correlations between students' scores on proficiency scales and their scores on benchmark and end-of-year external tests are high, then classroom assessment can be considered valid. If they are not, then leaders and teachers should explore changes in the proficiency scales, scoring practices, or both.

Changes to Teachers' Thinking About Classroom Assessments

The paradigm shift described in this section is significant. Confronting educators' mindsets related to classroom assessment will likely be an ongoing endeavor. For example, the notion of students being allowed multiple opportunities and ways to demonstrate competency and receiving multiple scores on a particular topic might be a significant struggle for some secondary teachers. Some secondary teachers might want to maintain the practice of giving a single end-of-unit test for all students simultaneously and then moving on to the next topic regardless of the results. These and other traditional mindsets may become challenges as the staff implement this school-level indicator. Still, the gradual impact of this transformative new philosophy is worth the initial uneasiness it may cause.

Secondary leaders should allow teachers some time and space, with support, to absorb and adapt to what may be a struggle for them. One method is to engage teachers in group readings and discussions on assessment practices to keep conversations going and the communication lines open. The school leader should also create opportunities for teachers to visit and learn from classrooms (within the school and in other schools) that are successfully implementing multiple types of assessment. Finally, the school leader should stress the fact that the academy model honors teachers by trusting them to use all assessment evidence available to discern the most accurate summative score for each student on each measurement topic.

High Reliability Leadership for School-Level Indicator 13

Figure 2.14 lists some potential lagging indicators for classroom assessment. From this list, the leader would then select trim tab indicators to create a customized high reliability scale. Figure 2.15 depicts a possible customized scale a school leader might design for school-level indicator 13, classroom assessment.

Reporting and Grading (SLI 14)

Reporting and grading within a CBE system involve several dramatic shifts away from the traditional model. The leader of a secondary academy must ensure that the school has a reporting and grading system that depicts status and growth on measurement topics and allows students to work at multiple levels across different content areas. We consider reporting and grading in a single indicator rather than as two separate items because these two elements are so intertwined that changes to one will likely have implications for the other.

Programs and Practices	Lagging Indicator Data	Potential Standard for High Reliability Status
Current summative scores	LMS records of teachers entering multiple evidence scores for students	100 percent of teachers use multiple evidence scores to compute current summative scores for students on measurement topics
Correlations between classroom assessments and external assessments	Summative scores from classroom assessments and scores from external assessments	Computed correlations between the percentages of students who demonstrate proficiency on measurement topics and state tests are 0.80 or greater
Types of classroom assessments	Teacher resources and training regarding the use of multiple types of classroom assessments	100 percent of teachers use multiple types of classroom assessments
Perceptions of students, teachers, and parents	Surveys of students, teachers, and parents	90 percent of students report that classroom assessments are accurate measures of what they know and are able to do

FIGURE 2.14: Potential lagging indicators and criteria for school-level indicator 13.

Evidence	
4 **Sustaining** **(quick data)**	Quick data like the following are systematically collected and reviewed: • Examination of reports in Empower depicting the number of teachers entering evidence scores • Quick conversations with teachers about how they determine current summative scores using patterns of evidence scores
3 **Applying** **(lagging)**	Performance goals with clear criteria for success like the following are in place: • 100 percent of teachers use multiple evidence scores to compute current summative scores for students on measurement topics • Computed correlations between the percentages of students who demonstrate proficiency on measurement topics and state tests are 0.80 or greater
2 **Developing** **(leading)**	• A comprehensive model of classroom assessment is in place that calls for a wide variety of assessment types • An assessment system is in place that requires teachers to use evidence scores to compute current summative scores
1 **Beginning**	• The school has written plans for an assessment system that employs evidence scores to compute current summative scores but there is no implementation of the system • A system is in place but only a few teachers use it
0 **Not Using**	• The school has no written plans for an assessment system that employs evidence scores to compute current summative scores • There is no implementation of evidence scores to compute current summative scores

Source: © 2020 by Marzano Academies, Inc. Adapted with permission.

FIGURE 2.15: Customized high reliability scale for school-level indicator 13.

Secondary leaders will find that grading in a CBE system is quite different from grading in a traditional system. Traditionally, students typically receive only an overall omnibus grade or percentage score. There is little or no information about how well students performed on specific topics covered in a course. Additionally, in a traditional system, students can commonly earn extra-credit points that have little or nothing to do with the content addressed in the course. CBE grading alleviates these issues.

Reporting and grading can take many different forms in a CBE system. First, we consider three major methods: (1) number of measurement topics mastered, (2) pace as a new metric for an overall grade, and (3) a standards-referenced approach. Then, we discuss additional important concepts for leaders to be aware of: students working at different levels within the same subject area, measurement topic recovery, and important decision points for reporting and grading.

Number of Measurement Topics Mastered

What might be called the purest form of CBE reporting is depicted in figure 2.16. This report card is for a middle school that includes grades 6, 7, and 8. One salient feature of this reporting method is the metric used to report a student's status in a given subject. That metric is simply to list how many of the total measurement topics for each course and level the student has mastered so far. For example, consider the column titled Literacy. The student is currently working at the eighth-grade level and has mastered twelve of twenty-one measurement topics. Further, the report card displays that the student has demonstrated competency in twenty-three of twenty-three measurement topics for seventh-grade literacy. This will always be the case in a competency-based system; students will have mastered all the measurement topics at the grade levels below where they are currently working in a given subject area.

Grade	Literacy	Technology	Mathematics	Art	Language Arts	Science	Social Studies	Physical Education
8	12 of 21			13 of 15			9 of 13	13 of 16
7	23 of 23	14 of 20		14 of 14	20 of 29	14 of 16	13 of 13	12 of 12
6	20 of 20	15 of 15	17 of 23	13 of 13	25 of 25	21 of 21	12 of 12	14 of 14

FIGURE 2.16: Competency-based reporting by number of measurement topics mastered.

Another feature of this report card is that it communicates the fact that at any point in time students will be working at different levels in different subjects. In this case, the student is working at the eighth-grade level in literacy but at the sixth-grade level in mathematics.

Another option for competency-based reporting at the high school level appears in figure 2.17. As is typical of high school offerings, the reporting system lists specific courses for various subject areas. In some subject areas, the courses have a clear progression from simple to complex. For example, in mathematics, students must learn the simpler content in Algebra I before they can enroll in Algebra II and so on. Of course, some departments may not have strict course sequences. For example, in the art department, painting is probably not a prerequisite for orchestra.

This format reports students' status for the courses they are currently taking using the metric of how many measurement topics they have mastered so far (compared to the total number in the course). In this example, the student has demonstrated proficiency in six of the twenty-two measurement topics in chemistry. In world history the student has mastered eleven of twenty-one measurement topics. In all courses, once students have demonstrated mastery (score 3.0 content) for all of the measurement topics, they receive credit for that course. Note that in the report card, completed courses have a label of proficient (3.0) or advanced (4.0). If students achieve a 4.0 on all (or the majority) of the measurement topics in a given course, they receive the score value of advanced as opposed to proficient. This is a simple convention that allows secondary schools to acknowledge students who have exceeded expectations or to differentiate student performance levels since, in a competency-based system, mastery is required and the lowest score a student can receive is a 3.0. While all students must achieve a 3.0 in each measurement topic to complete the course, some students will have 3.0s on all topics and others will have a mix of 3.0 scores and 4.0 scores.

Pace as a New Metric for an Overall Grade

The previous section explored a reporting system based on how many of the proficiency scales at a given grade level and subject area or within a given course the student has mastered within the time available. However, relative status can also be reported in terms of pace. Pace quantifies the extent to which students are moving through the measurement topics for a given year at a rate that ensures they will demonstrate proficiency on all of the scales by the end of the school year. The most straightforward way to report pace is to divide the school year into equal units based on the number of proficiency scales students must complete within a year.

Taking a high school sociology course as an example, assume students are expected to complete twenty proficiency scales by the end of the school year, which is thirty-six weeks in length. To accomplish this, they should demonstrate proficiency on one measurement topic once every 1.8 weeks (that is, 36 ÷ 20 = 1.8). Imagine that after eighteen weeks of the school year, a particular student has completed ten proficiency scales. That student would be considered on pace; the student has demonstrated competence on 50 percent of the proficiency scales in 50 percent of the school year. Conversely, a student who had demonstrated proficiency on only six measurement topics by mid-year would be considered behind pace since, with only 50 percent of the year left, the student would still have

Subject Area	Course	Score
Mathematics	Calculus	
	Geometry	
	Algebra II	12 of 24
	Algebra I	3.0 (proficient)
Science	AP Environmental Science	
	Physics	
	Chemistry	6 of 22
	Biology	3.0 (proficient)
Social Studies	Economics	
	World History	11 of 21
	U.S. History	4.0 (advanced)
	Geography	3.0 (proficient)
Language Arts	Shakespeare	
	Ancient Literature	13 of 22
	European Literature	3.0 (proficient)
	U.S. Literature	3.0 (proficient)
Art	Orchestra	
	Performing Arts	9 of 21
	Painting	3.0 (proficient)
Technology	Digital Graphics and Animation	
	Desktop Publishing	17 of 22
	Computer Science	4.0 (advanced)

Source: Marzano, 2010, p. 121.

FIGURE 2.17: Competency-based reporting with overall proficiency scale score in completed courses.

70 percent of the content to master. A school can establish a systematic reporting system depicting each student's current status relative to pace. To illustrate, consider figure 2.18.

Student	Expected Percentage of Proficient Measurement Topics	Observed Percentage of Proficient Measurement Topics	Pace
Brandon A.	50	45	Behind
Alex B.	50	50	On
Maria C.	50	60	Ahead
Mark D.	50	25	Behind
Ivan E.	50	50	On
Chris F.	50	70	Ahead
Sanjay G.	50	50	On
Cameron H.	50	50	On
Quamay I.	50	55	Ahead
Karla J.	50	50	On

FIGURE 2.18: Student pace report.

The example report in figure 2.18 is at the halfway point in the school year. The expectation at this point is that students would have demonstrated proficiency on 50 percent of the proficiency scales to be addressed during the year. The third column of the report depicts the actual percentage of measurement topics for which each student has demonstrated proficiency. The fourth column highlights whether each student is on pace, behind pace, or ahead of pace.

Pace is a very powerful way of determining status and can provide valuable information about how well individual students are performing. Reporting on students' pace can even stimulate interventions for those students who are lagging behind in their progress.

A Standards-Referenced Approach

While the two preceding methods of reporting avoid traditional grades, CBE is not incompatible with letter grades or percentage scores. There are certainly ways to maintain the integrity of a CBE system while reporting traditional grades, as some schools are required to do. Traditional grades may also alleviate the concerns some secondary educators, students, and parents have about the interpretability of CBE reporting for college entrance requirements.

To demonstrate, assume that it is the end of a nine-week grading period and a teacher has addressed seven measurement topics during that period. As described in our discussion of classroom assessment (SLI 13, page 49), each student would have a current summative score on each of these topics. One particular student might have the following set of summative scores: 2.5, 3.5, 3.0, 3.0, 2.5, 2.5, and 2.0. For the purposes of reporting an omnibus grade, these scores can be combined using an average. The unweighted average for this student's seven summative scores is 2.71 (that is, $19 \div 7 = 2.71$). This can be transformed into an overall grade using a conversion scale like that in table 2.3 (page 68).

Based on the conversion chart, this student's average score of 2.71 would translate to an overall grade of 84 percent or B. This represents the student's central tendency in terms of the seven measurement topics. One might say that the student's overall tendency for this particular nine-week grading period was to demonstrate solid understanding of the foundational knowledge at the score 2.0 level and high-partial understanding of the score 3.0 content. Once the student is able to demonstrate mastery on all seven measurement topics, he or she will have earned an overall grade of A as indicated by this conversion table.

It is important that secondary leaders understand the consequences of using this scheme to assign overall grades. If the cut score for the grade of A starts at an average score of 3.0, then ultimately, every student will obtain a letter grade of A by the time they finish a course. There is clearly nothing wrong with this outcome. However, some secondary schools choose to establish different cut points for the traditional letter grades such that all students will not automatically receive an A when they have demonstrated proficiency on the scales. To illustrate, consider table 2.4 (page 70), in which the cut score for the grade of A starts at score 3.50 as opposed to 3.0. This means that to obtain a grade of A, students would have to receive a score of 4.0 on at least half of the measurement topics. The higher the cut score for a grade of A, the more scores of 4.0 are needed to achieve it. Accordingly, the cut score for the grade of B is also much higher, and so on.

Students Working at Different Levels Within the Same Subject Area

Another issue that can come up in CBE systems that use the standards-referenced approach is how to generate an overall grade when some students are working on measurement topics from different grade levels. This commonly occurs at the middle school level (that is, grades 6, 7, and 8) where students are still organized into grade levels on the basis of age but allowed to work on content above or below their age-based grade level. For example, a seventh-grade science student might be working on one or more eighth-grade topics. If all students were working on seventh-grade measurement topics only, then computing an overall grade would be rather straightforward. When students are working at multiple grade levels, educators must have a consistent method of combining scores on topics from different levels.

One method is the weighting scheme depicted in table 2.5 (page 72). This scheme weights scores based on how much above or below grade level a topic is. Scores on topics below grade level are adjusted to be lower, and scores on topics above grade level are shifted higher.

To illustrate how this system works, assume that a seventh-grade student is working on ten measurement topics during a grading period for science. Seven of those topics are at the seventh-grade level and three topics are at the eighth-grade level. At the end of the grading period, the student receives a current summative score for each of the ten measurement topics. Figure 2.19 depicts these scores.

For the seven seventh-grade topics, the student received relatively high scores: two scores of 4.0, three scores of 3.0, one score of 3.5, and one score of 2.5. However, on the three eighth-grade topics, the student received much lower scores: 1.5, 1.0, and 0.5. This makes sense because the student has recently started working on these more difficult, higher-level topics. The unweighted average for these ten scores is 2.6, which translates to a grade of B using the first conversion table in table 2.3 (page 68). However, the fourth column of figure 2.19 lists the weighted scores. Note that the student's scores for the seventh-grade topics stay the same, but the scores for eighth-grade topics are weighted to account for the fact that they are above the student's chronological grade level. The weighted average using this scheme is 3.5, which translates to a letter grade of A.

Measurement Topic	Grade Level	Unweighted Score	Weighted Score
Topic 1	7	3	3
Topic 2	7	3.5	3.5
Topic 3	7	4	4
Topic 4	7	3	3
Topic 5	7	2.5	2.5
Topic 6	7	3	3
Topic 7	7	4	4
Topic 8	8	1.5	4.5
Topic 9	8	1.0	4
Topic 10	8	0.5	3.5
Total		26	35
Average		2.6	3.5

Source: © 2021 by Robert J. Marzano.

FIGURE 2.19: Example weighted scoring scenario.

TABLE 2.3: Converting Proficiency Scale Scores to Percentages and Letter Grades

Scale Score	Percentage	Grade	Scale Score	Percentage	Grade	Scale Score	Percentage	Grade	Scale Score	Percentage	Grade
4.00	100	A	2.30 to 2.34	76	C	1.30 to 1.31	50	F	0.73 to 0.75	25	F
3.90 to 3.99	99	A	2.25 to 2.29	75	C	1.28 to 1.29	49	F	0.70 to 0.72	24	F
3.80 to 3.89	98	A	2.20 to 2.24	74	C	1.26 to 1.27	48	F	0.67 to 0.69	23	F
3.70 to 3.79	97	A	2.15 to 2.19	73	C	1.24 to 1.25	47	F	0.64 to 0.66	22	F
3.60 to 3.69	96	A	2.10 to 2.14	72	C	1.22 to 1.23	46	F	0.61 to 0.63	21	F
3.50 to 3.59	95	A	2.05 to 2.09	71	C	1.20 to 1.21	45	F	0.58 to 0.60	20	F
3.40 to 3.49	94	A	2.00 to 2.04	70	C	1.18 to 1.19	44	F	0.55 to 0.57	19	F
3.30 to 3.39	93	A	1.95 to 1.99	69	D	1.16 to 1.17	43	F	0.52 to 0.54	18	F
3.20 to 3.29	92	A	1.90 to 1.94	68	D	1.14 to 1.15	42	F	0.49 to 0.51	17	F
3.10 to 3.19	91	A	1.85 to 1.89	67	D	1.12 to 1.13	41	F	0.46 to 0.48	16	F
3.00 to 3.09	90	A	1.80 to 1.84	66	D	1.10 to 1.11	40	F	0.43 to 0.45	15	F
2.95 to 2.99	89	B	1.75 to 1.79	65	D	1.08 to 1.09	39	F	0.40 to 0.42	14	F

Scale Score	%	Grade	Scale Score	%	Grade	Scale Score	%	Grade	Scale Score	%	Grade
2.90 to 2.94	88	B	1.70 to 1.74	64	D	1.06 to 1.07	38	F	0.37 to 0.39	13	F
2.85 to 2.89	87	B	1.65 to 1.69	63	D	1.04 to 1.05	37	F	0.34 to 0.36	12	F
2.80 to 2.84	86	B	1.60 to 1.64	62	D	1.02 to 1.03	36	F	0.31 to 0.33	11	F
2.75 to 2.79	85	B	1.55 to 1.59	61	D	1.00 to 1.01	35	F	0.28 to 0.30	10	F
2.70 to 2.74	84	B	1.50 to 1.54	60	D	0.98 to 0.99	34	F	0.25 to 0.27	9	F
2.65 to 2.69	83	B	1.48 to 1.49	59	F	0.96 to 0.97	33	F	0.22 to 0.24	8	F
2.60 to 2.64	82	B	1.46 to 1.47	58	F	0.94 to 0.95	32	F	0.19 to 0.21	7	F
2.55 to 2.59	81	B	1.44 to 1.45	57	F	0.91 to 0.93	31	F	0.16 to 0.18	6	F
2.50 to 2.54	80	B	1.42 to 1.43	56	F	0.88 to 0.90	30	F	0.13 to 0.15	5	F
2.45 to 2.49	79	C	1.40 to 1.41	55	F	0.85 to 0.87	29	F	0.10 to 0.12	4	F
2.40 to 2.44	78	C	1.38 to 1.39	54	F	0.82 to 0.84	28	F	0.07 to 0.09	3	F
2.35 to 2.39	77	C	1.36 to 1.37	53	F	0.79 to 0.81	27	F	0.04 to 0.06	2	F
			1.34 to 1.35	52	F	0.76 to 0.78	26	F	0.01 to 0.03	1	F
			1.32 to 1.33	51	F				0.00	0	F

Source: Marzano, 2018, pp. 100–101.

TABLE 2.4: Conversion Table With Different Cut Points for Letter Grades

Scale Score	Percentage	Grade	Scale Score	Percentage	Grade	Scale Score	Percentage	Grade	Scale Score	Percentage	Grade
4.00	100	A	2.30 to 2.34	76	C	1.30 to 1.31	50	F	0.73 to 0.75	25	F
3.90 to 3.99	99	A	2.25 to 2.29	75	C	1.28 to 1.29	49	F	0.70 to 0.72	24	F
3.80 to 3.89	98	A	2.20 to 2.24	74	C	1.26 to 1.27	48	F	0.67 to 0.69	23	F
3.70 to 3.79	97	A	2.15 to 2.19	73	C	1.24 to 1.25	47	F	0.64 to 0.66	22	F
3.60 to 3.69	96	A	2.10 to 2.14	72	C	1.22 to 1.23	46	F	0.61 to 0.63	21	F
3.50 to 3.59	95	A	2.05 to 2.09	71	C	1.20 to 1.21	45	F	0.58 to 0.60	20	F
3.40 to 3.49	94	B	2.00 to 2.04	70	C	1.18 to 1.19	44	F	0.55 to 0.57	19	F
3.30 to 3.39	93	B	1.95 to 1.99	69	D	1.16 to 1.17	43	F	0.52 to 0.54	18	F
3.20 to 3.29	92	B	1.90 to 1.94	68	D	1.14 to 1.15	42	F	0.49 to 0.51	17	F
3.10 to 3.19	91	B	1.85 to 1.89	67	D	1.12 to 1.13	41	F	0.46 to 0.48	16	F
3.00 to 3.09	90	B	1.80 to 1.84	66	D	1.10 to 1.11	40	F	0.43 to 0.45	15	F
2.95 to 2.99	89	B	1.75 to 1.79	65	D	1.08 to 1.09	39	F	0.40 to 0.42	14	F

Range	Score	Grade	Range	Score	Grade	Range	Score	Grade	Range	Score	Grade
2.90 to 2.94	88	B	1.70 to 1.74	64	D	1.06 to 1.07	38	F	0.37 to 0.39	13	F
2.85 to 2.89	87	B	1.65 to 1.69	63	D	1.04 to 1.05	37	F	0.34 to 0.36	12	F
2.80 to 2.84	86	B	1.60 to 1.64	62	D	1.02 to 1.03	36	F	0.31 to 0.33	11	F
2.75 to 2.79	85	B	1.55 to 1.59	61	D	1.00 to 1.01	35	F	0.28 to 0.30	10	F
2.70 to 2.74	84	C	1.50 to 1.54	60	D	0.98 to 0.99	34	F	0.25 to 0.27	9	F
2.65 to 2.69	83	C	1.48 to 1.49	59	F	0.96 to 0.97	33	F	0.22 to 0.24	8	F
2.60 to 2.64	82	C	1.46 to 1.47	58	F	0.94 to 0.95	32	F	0.19 to 0.21	7	F
2.55 to 2.59	81	C	1.44 to 1.45	57	F	0.91 to 0.93	31	F	0.16 to 0.18	6	F
2.50 to 2.54	80	C	1.42 to 1.43	56	F	0.88 to 0.90	30	F	0.13 to 0.15	5	F
2.45 to 2.49	79	C	1.40 to 1.41	55	F	0.85 to 0.87	29	F	0.10 to 0.12	4	F
2.40 to 2.44	78	C	1.38 to 1.39	54	F	0.82 to 0.84	28	F	0.07 to 0.09	3	F
2.35 to 2.39	77	C	1.36 to 1.37	53	F	0.79 to 0.81	27	F	0.04 to 0.06	2	F
			1.34 to 1.35	52	F	0.76 to 0.78	26	F	0.01 to 0.03	1	F
			1.32 to 1.33	51	F				0.00	0	

TABLE 2.5: Weighting Scheme for Students Working on Topics at Different Grade Levels

Measurement Topics Two Levels Below Grade Level		Measurement Topics One Level Below Grade Level		Measurement Topics One Level Above Grade Level		Measurement Topics Two Levels Above Grade Level	
Earned Score	Weighted Score	Earned Score	Weighted Score	Earned Score	Weighted Score	Earned Score	Weighted Score
4.0	1.0	4.0	2.0	4.0	7.0	4.0	8.0
3.5	0.5	3.5	1.5	3.5	6.5	3.5	7.5
3.0	0.0	3.0	1.0	3.0	6.0	3.0	7.0
2.5	0.0	2.5	0.5	2.5	5.5	2.5	6.5
2.0	0.0	2.0	0.0	2.0	5.0	2.0	6.0
1.5	0.0	1.5	0.0	1.5	4.5	1.5	5.5
1.0	0.0	1.0	0.0	1.0	4.0	1.0	5.0
0.5	0.0	0.5	0.0	0.5	3.5	0.5	4.5
0.0	0.0	0.0	0.0	0.0	3.0	0.0	4.0

Source: © 2021 by Robert J. Marzano.

Measurement Topic Recovery

One of the principles of CBE is that students demonstrate competency in the measurement topics in each course or grade-level subject area before progressing to the next course or level. A commonly asked question from secondary educators is, What happens if a student has not demonstrated proficiency in all the required measurement topics by the end of the school year? A viable answer is that secondary schools should provide students with opportunities for *measurement topic recovery*, sometimes known as *credit recovery*. Of course, this is particularly important at the high school level because high school graduation is typically predicated on the concept of earning credits for the successful completion of each course.

There are many ways that schools can offer measurement topic recovery. One option is to create an individualized learning plan (ILP) for each student that details the student's missing measurement topics. To guide the student to master these topics, the ILP would list learning resources for each one (see blended instruction, SLI 6, in chapter 3, page 106). The ILP should also provide a schedule for measurement topic recovery that ensures the student will be ready to matriculate or graduate. For example, in high school, ILPs should aim to have students recover all missing measurement topics prior to the start of their fourth year of enrollment (that is, the beginning of senior year).

A further option is to utilize tutoring programs. As described previously, tutoring in the academy model should focus on specific measurement topics, making it a useful venue for measurement topic recovery. A school leader might examine student data, determine which measurement topics have the largest numbers of students below score 3.0 or below grade level, and offer four- to five-week tutoring sessions during FIT block for those specific measurement topics. The leader then assigns students to tutoring according to their ILPs. The leader can take the same approach using before-school and after-school programming. Instead of students attending these programs to receive general support, tutoring staff should design the program to focus on specific measurement topics in three- to five-week cycles. School leaders can publicize which measurement topics the program will cover and at what point, and then assign or advise students to the program, backing it up by informing parents.

The same is also true of web-based credit recovery programs. Teachers may develop such programs internally and house them on the school's LMS. The school may also use pre-existing programs developed by external organizations. Leaders can review the content of such programs and align modules to specific measurement topics so that teachers, leaders, or staff charged to coordinate credit recovery can assign students to specific modules to recover their missing topics.

With measurement topic recovery systems in place, graduation becomes a true celebration of the fact that students have mastered the content. In effect, the school leader can certify that all students have met the requirements for graduation.

Important Decision Points for Reporting and Grading

Clearly the school-level indicator of reporting and grading provides leaders with a variety of options that range from a pure competency-based approach (that is, simply reporting how many measurement topics a student has mastered) to a standards-referenced approach that converts proficiency scale scores to traditional grades. It is important to note that there is no single best approach that schools should use at the secondary level. As the leadership team reviews the options, they will have to consider state reporting requirements, reports to parents, student reports, athletic eligibility requirements, and transcripts.

In some cases, leaders will find few guidelines from specific agencies in terms of the reporting requirements. Athletic eligibility is a classic example. Specifically, state athletic associations may not be very familiar with the differences between reporting in a traditional system and in a CBE system and provide only broad guidelines, such as students must *pass* a specific number of classes and eligibility reports for students must be filed weekly. Leaders must consider how well the selected reporting system meets current eligibility requirements and provide the state athletic association with alternatives when it does not. In all cases, reporting is usually focused on demonstrating that students are making adequate academic progress. Thus, it is the leader's job to translate students' status and growth as measured by CBE metrics into those that have historically been used in a traditional reporting system.

Regardless of the specific decisions about reporting and grading, school leaders should communicate early and often. These transitions will challenge not only teachers but also parents and students. It's not uncommon that parents want their children's schools to mirror the schools they attended, especially when it comes to reporting and grading. Nearly every educator has heard a parent begin discussions or debates about reporting and grading or other issues in education with statements like, "When I was in school . . ." Similarly, if students did not experience a competency-based system in elementary or middle school, they will also have questions and need support. Clear, proactive communication is an important way to face these challenges head-on. Involve stakeholders in the initial discussions, explain the changes repeatedly and plainly, offer training for parents, use school hours to educate students, and keep the focus on the reasons behind the transition—its benefits to students. The following is a list of possible ways to communicate with constituents.

- Create an explanatory document that accompanies all transcripts for students who transfer out of your school.

- Ensure the school's profile sufficiently explains grading for colleges, universities, and other post-secondary options that require transcripts.

- Create separate videos for parents and students that explain grading, and translate videos into languages other than English, if appropriate.

- Create separate videos for parents and students that explain how to access the LMS to view student progress.

- Create flyers, pamphlets, frequently-asked-questions pages, or other documents that include explanations of grading. Post versions of these documents on the school's website, mobile app, or other digital platforms. Stock print versions in the main office, parent center, and other spaces that parents and community members may frequent.

- Since competency-based report cards can be lengthy, consider sending a letter to parents at report card time that directs them to the learning management system to review student progress. That first letter should provide each parent with their login and password. Subsequent messages can advise parents about whom to contact if they have forgotten or lost their login information.

- Conduct town hall meetings, small-group discussions, coffee with the principal, and any other in-person events to discuss CBE inclusive of grading and reporting. Facilitate conversations frequently during the first and second phases of implementation and a minimum of twice per year every year after that.

High Reliability Leadership for School-Level Indicator 14

Figure 2.20 lists some potential lagging indicators for reporting and grading. From this list, the leader would then select trim tab indicators to create a customized high reliability scale. Figure 2.21 depicts a possible customized scale a school leader might design for school-level indicator 14, reporting and grading.

Instruction and Teacher Development (SLI 5)

Clearly, instruction in a competency-based secondary school where students might be working on different content at different paces will have some significant differences from instruction in a traditional secondary school, where students work on the same content at the same pace. Consequently, the instructional model that teachers use in a competency-based system must be designed with CBE in mind. In addition to guiding teacher instruction, the instructional model is also the framework that leaders use to give feedback to teachers regarding their status and growth on specific pedagogical skills. A school's instructional model should not be tacit or simply a general set of principles informally referenced within the culture of the school. Rather, a school's instructional model should be a detailed, written document, formally adopted by the school. It creates a common language for educators to reference during self-assessment, professional development, goal setting, observations, and feedback. Many of our suggestions relative to this school-level indicator are explained further in the book *Improving Teacher Development and Evaluation* (Marzano, Rains, & Warrick, 2021).

Programs and Practices	Lagging Indicator Data	Potential Standard for High Reliability Status
CBE reporting system	Documents regarding school-level CBE reporting and grading system	100 percent of teachers understand and accurately employ the CBE reporting system
Measurement topic recovery	Records of measurement topics, courses, and activities	100 percent of students successfully complete measurement topic recovery
Communication with constituents	Data from online communication to parents and community	90 percent of parents receive the information explaining the CBE reporting system
Perceptions of students, teachers, and parents	Surveys of students, teachers, and parents	90 percent of teachers report that the CBE reporting system has been beneficial to them 80 percent of students report that the CBE reporting system has been useful to them 70 percent of parents report that the CBE reporting system has been useful to them

FIGURE 2.20: Potential lagging indicators and criteria for school-level indicator 14.

Evidence	
4 **Sustaining** **(quick data)**	Quick data like the following are systematically collected and reviewed: • Examination of report cards generated by the LMS • Quick conversations with teachers, parents, and students about reporting and grading
3 **Applying** **(lagging)**	Performance goals with clear criteria for success like the following are in place: • 100 percent of teachers understand and accurately employ the CBE reporting system • 90 percent of parents receive the information explaining the CBE reporting system • 90 percent of teachers report that the CBE reporting system has been beneficial to them • 80 percent of students report that the CBE reporting system has been useful to them • 70 percent of parents report that the CBE reporting system has been useful to them
2 **Developing** **(leading)**	• A comprehensive CBE reporting system is in place • Systems are in place to inform parents and students with a clear understanding of the CBE reporting system
1 **Beginning**	• Report cards depict status and growth on a few measurement topics only • The school has a plan for a reporting system that depicts status and growth but does not implement that plan
0 **Not Using**	• The school has no written plan for a reporting system that depicts status and growth • There is no reporting of status and growth on any measurement topics

Source: © 2020 by Marzano Academies, Inc. Adapted with permission.

FIGURE 2.21: Customized high reliability scale for school-level indicator 14.

An Explicit Model of Instruction for CBE

Our preferred model of instruction is based on research and theory that spans decades (Marzano, 1992, 2007, 2017; Marzano et al., 1988, 2021; Marzano, Pickering, & Pollock, 2001). The Marzano Academies model specifically adapts the instructional elements in these previous works for competency-based education. Figure 2.22 depicts the Marzano Academies instructional model.

Overarching Domains	Feedback	Content	Context	Self-Regulation
Design Areas	I. Proficiency Scales	III. Proficiency Scale Instruction	V. Grouping and Regrouping	VIII. Belonging and Esteem
	II. Assessment	IV. General Instruction	VI. Engagement	IX. Efficacy and Agency
			VII. Comfort, Safety, and Order	X. Metacognitive and Life Skills

FIGURE 2.22: Marzano Academies framework for CBE instruction.

The academy instructional model is organized into four overarching categories referred to as *domains*: feedback, content, context, and self-regulation. Within each domain are *design areas*. As their name implies, design areas are important to the process of effective preparation and planning. The domain of feedback refers to the constant flow of information regarding students' current status and their growth on specific measurement topics. It involves proficiency scales (design area I) and assessment (design area II). As discussed earlier in this chapter, proficiency scales are at the heart of the academy model and provide teachers with a unique perspective on curriculum, instruction, and assessment within a CBE system.

The domain of content deals with core instructional strategies—these are the tools teachers use to help students initially learn and then further develop their understanding of the content within each proficiency scale. There are two design areas in this domain. Proficiency scale instruction (design area III) focuses on specific instructional strategies for content within each level of specific proficiency scales. When dealing with this design area, teachers examine the specific learning targets in a proficiency scale and determine which instructional strategies best suit them. General instruction (design area IV) focuses on strategies that help students continually develop and revise their knowledge regarding the content in a specific proficiency scale. These strategies respond to students' needs as teachers help them develop and deepen their understanding and skill in the content to which they have previously been exposed.

The domain of context addresses strategies teachers use to create a classroom environment that maximizes support for student learning. It includes grouping and regrouping (design area V), engagement (design area VI), and comfort, safety, and order (design area VII). These design areas develop the foundations for effective teaching and learning. Grouping and regrouping strategies are the primary tools teachers use to differentiate instruction for students. This is probably the area of expertise that most clearly distinguishes CBE teachers from teachers in traditional classrooms. In a CBE classroom, grouping and regrouping are a part of daily planning deliberations. Engagement strategies in a CBE classroom help students attend to academic activities whether they are working in large groups, small groups, or individually. Strategies for comfort, safety, and order help teachers ensure that students have their basic physical and psychological needs met.

Finally, the domain of self-regulation involves strategies designed to help students become independent learners and take responsibility for their own learning. These skills are uniquely important in a CBE system because such a system requires students to take an active role in their education. It involves three design areas: belonging and esteem (design area VIII), efficacy and agency (design area IX), and metacognitive and life skills (design area X). Belonging and esteem, again, deal with basic psychological needs of students. Strategies for efficacy and agency provide students with opportunities to take control of their own learning. Strategies for metacognitive and life skills focus on powerful higher-order skills that students can use both inside and outside of school.

Each of the ten design areas includes a number of *elements* and each element in the instructional model represents a tacit responsibility for teachers—something they must do in the classroom to provide effective CBE instruction. To illustrate, consider design area II, assessment. It involves four elements.

IIa.   Using obtrusive assessments

IIb.   Using student-centered assessments

IIc.   Using unobtrusive assessments

IId.   Generating current summative scores

Each of these elements is an important practice on its own, but when a teacher successfully enacts all of them, he or she effectively addresses assessment as carried out in a CBE classroom. There are a total of forty-nine elements embedded in the ten design areas. The design areas and their associated elements are shown in figure 2.23 (page 78).

Finally, each element includes a variety of specific instructional strategies. For example, element IIb, student-centered assessment, involves instructional strategies such as personal tracking matrices and student-generated assessments. In all, there are over three hundred specific instructional strategies in the model.

In summary, the academy model of instruction contains four domains. Those four domains have ten embedded design areas. The ten design areas involve forty-nine elements, and the forty-nine elements involve some three hundred specific instructional strategies. Figure 2.24 depicts these layers. The details of each element, associated strategies, and how teachers use the model in secondary classrooms are explained in depth in *Teaching in a Competency-Based Secondary School* (Marzano et al., 2022). Here we focus on how school leaders can use the model to improve teachers' pedagogical skills and, in turn, enhance students' learning.

Teacher Development

In the Marzano Academies model, teacher development is an overt responsibility of the school leader, who should approach it in a systematic fashion. Just as students need clear targets to guide their learning, so too do teachers. To this end, each element in the instructional model must have clear, concrete expectations. Figure 2.25 (page 79) lists evidence for element Ib, tracking student progress. Notice that the chart includes information about both what the teacher should know and do and how students should respond if the teacher enacts the element effectively.

| Four Domains |
| Ten Design Areas |
| Forty-Nine Elements |
| Over Three Hundred Specific Strategies |

Source: Adapted from Marzano, Rains, et al., 2021.

FIGURE 2.24: Complete academy model of instruction.

Feedback	Content	Context	Self-Regulation
I. Proficiency Scales Ia. Providing Proficiency Scales Ib. Tracking Student Progress Ic. Celebrating Success **II. Assessment** IIa. Using Obtrusive Assessments IIb. Using Student-Centered Assessments IIc. Using Unobtrusive Assessments IId. Generating Current Summative Scores	**III. Proficiency Scale Instruction** IIIa. Chunking Content IIIb. Processing Content IIIc. Recording and Representing Content IIId. Using Structured Practice IIIe. Examining Similarities and Differences IIIf. Engaging Students in Cognitively Complex Tasks IIIg. Generating and Defending Claims **IV. General Instruction** IVa. Reviewing Content IVb. Revising Knowledge IVc. Examining and Correcting Errors IVd. Highlighting Critical Information IVe. Previewing Content IVf. Stimulating Elaborative Inferences IVg. Extending Learning Through Homework	**V. Grouping and Regrouping** Va. Supporting Group Interactions Vb. Supporting Group Transitions Vc. Providing Support **VI. Engagement** VIa. Noticing and Reacting When Students Are Not Engaged VIb. Increasing Response Rates VIc. Using Physical Movement VId. Maintaining a Lively Pace VIe. Demonstrating Intensity and Enthusiasm VIf. Presenting Unusual Information VIg. Using Friendly Controversy VIh. Using Academic Games **VII. Comfort, Safety, and Order** VIIa. Organizing the Physical Layout of the Classroom VIIb. Demonstrating Withitness VIIc. Acknowledging Adherence to Rules and Procedures VIId. Acknowledging Lack of Adherence to Rules and Procedures VIIe. Establishing and Adapting Rules and Procedures VIIf. Displaying Objectivity and Control	**VIII. Belonging and Esteem** VIIIa. Using Verbal and Nonverbal Behaviors That Indicate Affection VIIIb. Demonstrating Value and Respect for Reluctant Learners VIIIc. Understanding Students' Backgrounds and Interests VIIId. Providing Opportunities for Students to Talk About Themselves **IX. Efficacy and Agency** IXa. Inspiring Students IXb. Enhancing Student Agency IXc. Asking In-Depth Questions of Reluctant Learners IXd. Probing Incorrect Answers With Reluctant Learners **X. Metacognitive and Life Skills** Xa. Reflecting on Learning Xb. Using Long-Term Projects Xc. Focusing on Specific Metacognitive and Life Skills

Source: © 2020 by Marzano Academies, Inc. Used with permission.

FIGURE 2.23: Elements in the Marzano Academies instructional model.

Teacher Evidence	Student Evidence
Behaviors I systematically track the progress of individual students on the proficiency scales. I systematically track progress of the entire class by showing what percentage of students scored at a proficient (3.0) level or above for a particular assessment. I systematically ask students to set goals relative to the proficiency scales and track their own progress. I systematically design assessments that generate formative scores for proficiency scales. **Understandings** I thoroughly understand the nature of tracking student progress in terms of enhancing students' learning. I thoroughly understand the various ways I can use tracking student progress in the classroom.	**Behaviors** My students commonly update their status on a proficiency scale by tracking their progress. My students commonly examine their progress on specific topics. **Understandings** My students can describe how they have progressed on a particular proficiency scale. My students can describe what they need to do to get to the next level of performance on a proficiency scale in their own words.

Source: © 2021 by Robert J. Marzano. Adapted with permission.

FIGURE 2.25: Evidence chart for element Ib, tracking student progress.

Based on these clear expectations, teachers can score themselves on specific elements of the academy instructional model. As part of the teacher development program, school leaders should ask teachers to rate their level of expertise in each of the forty-nine elements of the model each year. For this purpose, a self-reflection scale like the one in figure 2.26 is useful.

	4 Innovating	3 Applying	2 Developing	1 Beginning	0 Not Using
Tracking Student Progress	I engage in all behaviors at the applying (3) level. In addition, I identify those students who do not exhibit the desired effects and develop strategies and activities to meet their specific needs.	I engage in activities to track student progress without significant errors or omissions and the majority of students exhibit the desired effects.	I engage in activities to track student progress without significant errors or omissions.	I engage in activities to track student progress but do so with errors or omissions (for example, not keeping track of the progress of individual students or not making students aware of their individual progress).	I do not engage in activities to track student progress.

Source: © 2021 by Robert J. Marzano. Adapted with permission.

FIGURE 2.26: Teacher self-reflection scale for element Ib, tracking student progress.

This self-reflection scale deals with element Ib, tracking student progress. The scores on the scale range from not using (0) to innovating (4). At the not using (0) level, teachers should provide activities that help students track their progress but do not do so. At the beginning (1) level, teachers are engaging in such activities but exhibit significant errors or omissions. A level up from there is developing (2). At this level, teachers are using appropriate strategies without significant errors or omissions. In other words, they are using the specific behaviors and exhibiting the specific knowledge listed in the Teacher Evidence column of the evidence chart. While this is certainly noteworthy, in the academy model it is not the desired level of performance. Rather, teachers are expected to reach the applying (3) level on the scale for each element. At the applying (3) level, not only is the teacher implementing strategies without significant errors or omissions, but those strategies are having an observable effect on the majority of students in class. That is, most students display the behaviors and understandings listed in the Student Evidence column of the evidence chart. Finally, at the innovating (4) level, the teacher is making adaptations to strategies to meet the needs of specific students for whom the strategies are not producing the desired effects.

For an in-depth discussion of the underlying theory of teacher development and more detail on how school leaders should approach this important practice, consult *Improving Teacher Development and Evaluation* (Marzano, Rains, et al., 2021).

Teacher Goal Setting

Once teachers have baseline scores on each element of the instructional model, they should set goals to improve. For the purpose of teacher development, Marzano and Kosena (2022) recommended that teachers focus on only three or four elements each year. These selected elements should be in areas where teachers perceive an opportunity for growth. Specifically, selected elements will probably be those for which teachers score themselves as developing (2) or lower on the self-reflection scale. For each selected element, teachers should write professional goals they wish to accomplish in the current school year. Then, using the evidence charts for a teacher's selected growth goals, school leaders and fellow teachers can provide focused feedback and coaching. We suggest that teachers keep professional development notebooks that include their goals, artifacts, and other information related to these goals. For example, teachers can keep the evidence charts, self-reflection scales, and lists of strategies for each growth-goal element in their notebooks for easy reference.

All teachers should write time-bound, measurable goals for the growth they intend to achieve on specific elements within the school year, as well as actions they intend to implement to improve. We also suggest that leaders provide a template, as shown in figure 2.27, where teachers formally record their goals and track their progress. Leaders should encourage teachers to adopt a continuous improvement perspective when setting their professional goals (Marzano & Kosena, 2022). If a teacher reaches applying status on a year-long goal early in the first semester, that teacher should identify a new instructional element and write another appropriate growth goal to work on.

With individual teacher goals in place, the school leader can support teachers' efforts by establishing a coaching schedule to provide feedback on their personal goals. The principal can determine the frequency and timing of coaching sessions; the principal, assistant principal, instructional coach, and department heads should meet regularly with teachers to discuss instructional goals. Ideally, teachers should experience coaching sessions on a monthly basis, though we realize this level of frequency might not be feasible given the existing responsibilities of those who would conduct coaching sessions such as administrators, department heads, and instructional coaches. These meetings should be preplanned and built into a protected coaching calendar. During these meetings,

Name: ____

Instructional strategy: ____

My initial score: __________ My goal is to be at __________ by __________________.

Specific things I am going to do to improve: ____________________________

____

____

____.

Instructional Strategy: ________________________________

Innovating 4										
Applying 3										
Developing 2										
Beginning 1										
Not Using 0										
	a	b	c	d	e	f	g	h	i	S

a. __________ f. __________

b. __________ g. __________

c. __________ h. __________

d. __________ i. __________

e. __________ Summative Score: __________

Source: © 2012 by Marzano Resources. Used with permission.

FIGURE 2.27: Teacher progress chart.

teachers should discuss the challenges they are experiencing with achieving their goals. Coaches would then guide teachers to resources that address their goals and needs. Resources might include books, articles, video recordings, and materials developed internally by the school or district.

Whole-Staff Trends

One of the benefits of having teachers score themselves on each element of the instructional model each year is that school leaders can use the information as a snapshot of the staff's collective strengths and weaknesses across the elements of the model. The leader can compute average scores for each element across the faculty, then identify four or five elements with low average scores and focus professional development on those elements. For example, assume that a school's average self-rated score for element Ib, tracking student progress, is 1.89. This means that, on average, teachers in this school are implementing strategies for this element but can't quite do so without errors yet, clearly representing an area of growth for the school. The principal would then write a measurable schoolwide goal such as, *By February 1 of this academic year, the school's collective self-rated score on element Ib, tracking student progress, will be at least 3.0.*

Examining whole-staff trends and setting schoolwide goals enable school leaders to direct professional development resources toward selected areas of growth. School leaders can complement the individual coaching schedule with a professional development calendar that will allow teachers to receive support and feedback on schoolwide instructional goals in addition to their personal goals.

Instructional Rounds

For both individual and schoolwide goals, instructional rounds are a powerful way to provide teachers with opportunities to observe and analyze effective instructional practices. In essence, instructional rounds involve teachers observing other teachers to learn from their instructional expertise. Here we present two versions.

The first version of instructional rounds focuses on specific elements of the instructional model and specific teachers. To set these up, the leader examines an individual teacher's specific professional growth goals and schedules an instructional round in the classroom of a colleague who is particularly strong in one or more of the targeted areas. For example, if Teacher A's goal is increasing response rates (element VIb in the academy model), and Teacher B is strong in this element, Teacher A will observe Teacher B's classroom at a time when Teacher B will be employing strategies for increasing response rates. Individual rounds require a relatively high degree of coordination, but the benefits outweigh the time and energy required. Teacher A can observe highly effective practices for the exact instructional element she has selected to work on.

The second version of instructional rounds is general rounds. Here, small groups of teachers visit the classrooms of other teachers who have volunteered to be observed. With this approach, the observer teachers are not looking for the use of specific strategies that relate to their personal goals so much as they are looking for examples of exemplary instruction, including new strategies they might use in their own classrooms. A simple protocol teachers can use in general instructional rounds is to ask themselves the following three questions after an observation.

1. What did I see that validates what I do?

2. What did I see that I have questions about?

3. What new ideas do I have based on what I saw?

Relative to the first question, a teacher might note that the observed teacher adheres to rules and procedures the same way he does and feel validated that a trusted colleague uses a strategy the same way he does. Relative to the second question, the observing teacher might wonder why the observed teacher asked questions in a certain way such that only a few students answered. The observing teacher makes a note to ask his colleague about this at some later date. Finally, relative to the third question, the observing teacher makes a mental note to try out a new way to get students to interact in small groups based on the observation.

In addition to benefiting individual teachers, instructional rounds enhance the professional culture of a school, helping to break down the traditional teaching silos that exist in many schools by providing opportunities for teachers to observe their colleagues and discuss instructional practice. Instructional rounds also highlight the strengths of existing faculty and leverage those strengths to improve the overall instructional capacity of the building. Instructional rounds are a win-win for a school and we highly recommend them as part of any professional development model.

Targeted Instructional Practices

Like the priority measurement topics described in our discussion of measurement topics and proficiency scales (SLI 9, page 41), targeted instructional practices identify those instructional strategies and instructional resources the leader believes should be a schoolwide emphasis. Leaders identify priority instructional practices by working with department heads and teachers to determine which instructional practices have the highest probability of enhancing students' competency regarding the priority measurement topics. Department heads and teachers would use their personal experiences and expertise to provide this input. Priority measurement topics and targeted instructional practices work together as depicted in figure 2.28.

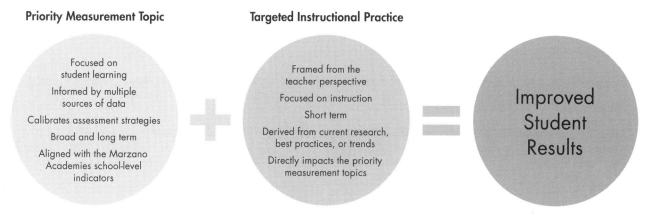

Priority Measurement Topic

Focused on student learning

Informed by multiple sources of data

Calibrates assessment strategies

Broad and long term

Aligned with the Marzano Academies school-level indicators

Targeted Instructional Practice

Framed from the teacher perspective

Focused on instruction

Short term

Derived from current research, best practices, or trends

Directly impacts the priority measurement topics

Improved Student Results

FIGURE 2.28: Priority measurement topics and targeted instructional practices.

Whereas priority measurement topics keep students at the center, the targeted instructional practices are framed from the perspective of the teacher. Figure 2.29 (page 84) provides some examples of priority measurement topics and the targeted instructional practices that teachers will use to address those targets. Note that some of the recommended instructional practices involve specific programs and resources as opposed to specific instructional strategies. This convention provides the school leader with a great deal of latitude in influencing what occurs in classrooms.

High Reliability Leadership for School-Level Indicator 5

Figure 2.30 (page 84) lists some potential lagging indicators for instruction and teacher development. From this list, the leader would then select trim tab indicators to create a customized high reliability scale. Figure 2.31 (page 85) depicts a possible customized scale a school leader might design for school-level indicator 5, instruction and teacher development.

Priority Measurement Topics (What students will learn)	Targeted Instructional Practices (What faculty and staff will do)
Students will be able to develop and revise multi-paragraph texts.	Teachers will use argumentative writing across all classes and content areas. Teachers will use knowledge maps to help students create cohesive essays.
Students will be able to interpret words and phrases in context.	All teachers will use Reading Apprenticeship to model discipline-specific literacy skills and build comprehension strategies. Teachers will use Failure Free Reading for forty-five minutes per day, three days per week to accelerate comprehension and vocabulary development.
Students will be able to create and solve linear equations with two variables.	Mathematics teachers will use Assessment and Learning in Knowledge Spaces (ALEKS) through face-to-face and blended instruction to individualize, differentiate, and personalize instruction. All Integrated Mathematics 1, 2, and 3 teachers will use Khan Academy for forty-five minutes at least one day per week to review linear equations modules. All integrated mathematics teachers will use cumulative reviews to revisit linear equations with one or two variables every three weeks.

FIGURE 2.29: Examples of priority measurement topics and corresponding targeted instructional practices.

Programs and Practices	Lagging Indicator Data	Potential Standard for High Reliability Status
Explicit instructional model	A detailed CBE model of instruction available to teachers along with professional development activities	90 percent of faculty can describe the school's instructional model in depth and the general content of the evidence charts
Teacher growth goals	Protocols and activities for teachers to set growth goals for specific instructional strategies	90 percent of teachers set specific learning goals based on their self-evaluations
Coaching	Coaching protocols and activities that support teachers' pedagogical growth	90 percent of teachers actively engage in the coaching and support that is available to them
Instructional rounds	Protocols and opportunities for instructional rounds	90 percent of teachers engage in instructional rounds
Targeted instructional practices	Processes for identifying generalizations and setting goals for schoolwide instructional practices	100 percent of schoolwide instructional goals are implemented by teachers
Perceptions of students, teachers, and parents	Surveys of students, teachers, and parents	90 percent of teachers report that they are increasing in their competence as a result of the school's policies and practices

FIGURE 2.30: Potential lagging indicators and criteria for school-level indicator 5.

Evidence	
4 **Sustaining** **(quick data)**	Quick data like the following are systematically collected and reviewed: • Examination of teacher improvement plans • Progress charts depicting teacher growth in specific pedagogical skills • Quick conversations with teachers
3 **Applying** **(lagging)**	Performance goals with clear criteria for success like the following are in place: • 90 percent of faculty can describe the school's instructional model in depth and the general content of the evidence charts • 90 percent of teachers set specific learning goals based on their self-evaluations • 90 percent of teachers actively engage in the coaching and support that is available to them • 90 percent of teachers engage in instructional rounds • 90 percent of teachers report that they are increasing in their competence as a result of the school's policies and practices
2 **Developing** **(leading)**	• A written instructional model is in place that is understood by teachers • Self-reflection scales and evidence charts are in place for the instructional model • Systems and routines are in place for teachers to set personal learning goals • Systems and routines are in place to support teachers and enable them to learn from their peers
1 **Beginning**	• The school has written plans to create an instructional model but little progress has been made on a written model • Teachers are aware of a few strategies they use in common but these strategies do not constitute a model of instruction
0 **Not Using**	• The school does not have plans to create a written model of instruction • There is no implementation of common instructional strategies among teachers

Source: © 2020 by Marzano Academies, Inc. Adapted with permission.

FIGURE 2.31: Customized high reliability scale for school-level indicator 5.

Summary

This chapter addressed the second phase of implementing the Marzano Academies model at the secondary school level. The school-level indicators for this phase represent the core changes in instruction, assessment, and grading. The four school-level indicators to implement during this phase are as follows.

1. **Measurement topics and proficiency scales (SLI 9):** The school has well-articulated measurement topics with accompanying proficiency scales for essential academic content.

2. **Classroom assessment (SLI 13):** The school has an assessment system that ensures the use of reliable and valid classroom assessments that measure each student's status and growth on specific measurement topics.

3. **Reporting and grading (SLI 14):** The school has a reporting and grading system that depicts both status and growth for individual students and allows for students to work on multiple levels across different subject areas.

4. **Instruction and teacher development (SLI 5):** The school has an instructional model that provides feedback to teachers regarding their status and growth on specific pedagogical skills.

These indicators deal with the basic infrastructure of secondary education: how the curriculum is organized, how students are assessed, how students' status and growth are recorded and reported, and the pedagogical skills teachers must develop to provide effective CBE instruction.

As before, school leaders should ask the following five questions while they are implementing these indicators.

1. Do the changes in this phase suggest that we should address any school or district policies?

2. Do the changes in this phase suggest that we should address any board of education policies?

3. Do the changes in this phase suggest that we should address any state-level policies?

4. Do the changes in this phase suggest we should address any contractual policies?

5. Do the changes in this phase create or lessen any inequities?

When addressing these questions, the leadership team might determine that the indicator for measurement topics and proficiency scales should lessen inequities in students' learning because the curriculum is so transparent to students. They decide to establish a means of soliciting input from students about whether they feel that the measurement topics make academic goals and expectations clearer. The leadership team might determine that the teachers union should review the classroom assessment system to ensure they have input into the specifics of the system. Finally, the leadership team might realize they need to consult regulations for athletic eligibility to ensure the new grading and reporting system meets the basic state requirements.

CHAPTER 3

Phase 3: Focusing on Learning and Growth

Failure is inevitable but useful when innovating (Portnoy, 2020). Although no one should ever plan to fail, school leaders must accept that failure will always manifest to some degree when they are trying to innovate. By the time a school reaches phase 3, setbacks will have occurred. As long as the leadership team addresses these setbacks, this is a good thing. As we stated in the introduction (page 1), every implementation of the Marzano Academies model is unique. Leaders should view setbacks or what appear to be mistakes as alterations that must be made in the model to meet the unique needs of the school. In light of the symbiotic relationship between innovation and failure, leaders should remind teachers that they are not expected to perfectly employ CBE from the outset. The school leader should create safe space for the educators implementing CBE to fail and then learn from their failures.

Unfortunately, school leaders should also be aware of the possibility that some members of the faculty, staff, community, or even district leadership will seize on inevitable setbacks as opportunities to declare that CBE does not work. In such cases, the school leader should resist the temptation to strike back or ignore the criticism. Indeed, the leader should interact with those who criticize the CBE system, identify the specifics of their criticisms, and use this information to look for areas of improvement.

Phase 3 is a time to solidify the foundation of the work completed during phase 1 and phase 2 without overwhelming the faculty and staff, stakeholders, or students. It is a time to consider revisions of previous decisions, improve on previous solutions, and re-examine plans for the future. Phase 3 and phase 4 address school-level indicators that put the finishing touches on the strong framework provided by phases 1 and 2. Accordingly, school leaders should feel free to swap school-level indicators between phases 3 and 4 to best meet the needs and cultures of their schools. However, we recommend the implementation of the following four indicators during phase 3.

1. Cognitive and metacognitive skills (SLI 10)

2. Vocabulary (SLI 11)

3. Blended instruction (SLI 6)

4. Explicit goals for students' status and growth (SLI 12)

The first three of the phase 3 indicators deal with specific aspects of instruction that help teachers adjust their instructional practices to make them more responsive to the demands of a CBE model. The fourth indicator addresses setting specific goals for student growth.

Cognitive and Metacognitive Skills (SLI 10)

There have been calls for expanding curricula beyond pure academic content for many years. For example, education consultants Copper Stoll and Gene Giddings (2012) argued that America's archaic factory-based model of education does not foster the type of adaptability required of the 21st century. Human development scholar Eric Jensen (2009) examined the impact of poverty on learning and concluded that student achievement will stagnate if learners do not acquire more than rudimentary academic skills to succeed. There are a number of frameworks describing the types of skills students should learn in order to meet these challenges. Researchers at the Partnership for 21st Century Learning (www.battelleforkids.org/networks/p21); education reformers Esther Care, Patrick Griffin, and Mark Wilson (2018) in their book *Assessment and Teaching of 21st Century Skills*; and several others have designed frameworks and critical skills lists identifying essential thinking skills for students.

The Marzano Academies model addresses specific cognitive and metacognitive skills that have a rich history (see Marzano, 2017, 2018; Marzano et al., 2019). We first address the two types of cognitive skills.

Cognitive Skills

Generally speaking, cognitive skills are those involved in thinking, reasoning, and acquiring and using information. Cognitive skills fall into two types: cognitive analysis skills and knowledge application skills.

Cognitive Analysis Skills

Cognitive analysis skills are those that people use to dissect and examine information so that they might understand it at deeper levels. There are eight cognitive analysis skills in the Marzano Academies model, described in table 3.1. Cognitive analysis skills are foundational components of rational thinking and should be directly taught as a formal part of the curriculum with their complexity increasing throughout the grades (Marzano et al., 1988). Cognitive analysis skills are directly related to many of the tasks students encounter in school. Teachers might emphasize this point by demonstrating to students how some of their recent assignments require them to use these skills. For example, a social studies teacher might point out that an assignment examining the official positions of two political parties is a comparing activity. A science teacher might point out that an assignment regarding a meltdown at a nuclear power plant involves analyzing errors.

Knowledge Application Skills

Another type of cognitive skill involves the application of knowledge. These skills are typically employed when using knowledge in unique situations. There are six knowledge application skills in the academy model, described in table 3.2 (page 90). As is the case with the cognitive analysis skills, the knowledge application skills relate directly to many of the classroom tasks students are assigned (Marzano et al., 1988). These tasks are characteristically long term in nature and might take students multiple class periods to complete. Additionally, knowledge application skills apply to a wide variety of situations outside of school. For example, most adults use problem solving and decision making on a daily basis.

Metacognitive Skills

Metacognition is most simply described as thinking about one's thinking. These skills come into play when one is planning, setting goals, making decisions, reflecting, and so on. Metacognition also involves two categories: traditional metacognitive skills and metacognitive life skills.

TABLE 3.1: Cognitive Analysis Skills

Cognitive Analysis Skill	Description
Comparing	Comparing is the process of determining similarities and differences between elements or concepts.
Analogical reasoning	Analogical reasoning is the process of determining how one set of elements or concepts is related to another set of elements or concepts.
Classifying	Classifying is the process of using definable attributes to organize concepts or elements into categories or related subcategories.
Analyzing perspectives	Analyzing perspectives is the process of analyzing one's own perspective and the reasoning supporting it and contrasting that with a different perspective and the reasoning supporting it.
Constructing support	Constructing support is the process of formulating a claim and then developing a well-constructed argument that supports it.
Analyzing errors in reasoning	Analyzing errors is the process of recognizing logical fallacies or errors in information generated by others or oneself.
Analyzing inferences	Analyzing inferences is the process of identifying the inferences one makes automatically and unconsciously as well as the inferences one makes during conscious reasoning.
Generating mental images	Generating mental images is the process of creating images that represent information and procedures.

Source: © 2017 by Marzano Resources. Adapted with permission.

Traditional Metacognitive Skills

Traditional metacognitive skills have been discussed in the literature on education since at least the 1980s. Educators have long been aware that traditional metacognitive skills will help students succeed not only academically but also in a wide variety of endeavors outside of school. The book *Dimensions of Thinking* (Marzano et al., 1988) highlighted metacognitive skills as the ultimate goals of a proposed "thinking skills" curriculum and was one of the first to articulate a framework for how these skills might be directly taught within the K–12 curriculum. The Marzano Academies model builds on these early efforts and specifies a scaffolded approach to teaching metacognitive skills. In the academy model, educators teach and reinforce ten traditional metacognitive skills, which table 3.3 (page 90) describes.

Metacognitive Life Skills

Life skills in the Marzano Academies model are focused on those actions and behaviors that help students become productive members of their school communities and create an environment that supports all learners. The four life skills in the academy model are described in table 3.4 (page 91). The academy model focuses on these particular life skills because of their obvious connection to expectations regarding students' behavior in classrooms and schools. While these skills are clearly

TABLE 3.2: Knowledge Application Skills

Knowledge Application Skill	Description
Decision making	Decision making is the process of generating and applying criteria to select between alternatives that appear equal.
Problem solving	Problem solving is the process of overcoming obstacles or constraints to achieve a goal.
Invention	Invention is the act of creating a new process or product that meets a specific identified need. In a sense, it might be likened to problem solving in that it addresses a specific need. However, problem solving is limited in duration.
Experimental inquiry	Experimental inquiry is the process of generating a hypothesis about a physical or psychological phenomenon and then testing the hypothesis.
Investigation	Investigation is the process of identifying and then resolving differences of opinion or contradictory information about concepts, historical events, or future possible events.
Systems analysis	Systems analysis is the process of describing and analyzing the parts of a system with particular emphasis on the relationships among the parts.

Source: © 2017 by Marzano Resources. Adapted with permission.

TABLE 3.3: Traditional Metacognitive Skills

Metacognitive Skill	Description
Staying focused when answers and solutions are not immediately apparent	This skill helps students overcome obstacles and stay focused when challenges arise. It also helps students to recognize how much effort they are putting into accomplishing a specific task.
Pushing the limits of one's knowledge and skills	This skill helps students set goals and engage in tasks that are personally challenging. When using this skill, students will strive to learn more and accomplish more.
Generating and pursuing one's own standards for performance	This skill enables students to envision and articulate criteria for what a successful project will look like.
Seeking incremental steps	This skill helps students take on complex tasks using small incremental steps so they do not become overwhelmed by the task as a whole.
Seeking accuracy	This skill helps students vet sources of information for reliability and verify information by consulting multiple sources known to be reliable.
Seeking clarity	This skill helps students identify points of confusion when they are learning new information. This allows students to independently seek a deeper understanding.

Resisting impulsivity	When faced with a desire to form a quick conclusion, this skill helps students refrain from doing so until they can gather more relevant information prior to taking action.
Seeking cohesion and coherence	When students are creating something with a number of interacting parts, this skill helps them monitor the relationships between what they are currently doing and the overall intent of the project in which they are engaged.
Setting goals and making plans	This skill helps students set short- and long-term goals, create timelines or blueprints, monitor progress, and make necessary adjustments.
Growth mindset thinking	This skill helps students take on challenging tasks with an attitude that helps them succeed, even when confronted by major obstacles.

Source: © 2017 by Marzano Resources. Adapted with permission.

TABLE 3.4: Life Skills

Life Skill	Description
Participation	Participation involves the set of decisions and actions that helps students add to group discussions and engage actively in questioning and answering questions.
Work completion	Work completion involves the set of decisions and actions that helps students manage their workload and complete tasks efficiently and effectively.
Behavior	Behavior involves the set of decisions and actions that helps students follow classroom rules and norms designed to create an efficient and orderly learning environment for all.
Working in groups	Working in groups involves the set of decisions and actions that helps students function as productive and supportive members of groups designed to enhance the learning of the students within those groups.

Source: © 2017 by Marzano Resources. Adapted with permission.

essential if students are to succeed in the context of secondary schools, teachers should also emphasize their importance in society in general. For example, students will most likely be required to work in groups for their entire lives and behave in a manner that follows the rules of the various situations in which they find themselves. Further, we encourage schools to add more life skills that generalize beyond the classroom to their curriculum.

Proficiency Scales for Cognitive and Metacognitive Skills

Because cognitive and metacognitive skills are as essential a part of the curriculum as academic content, they are also defined by their own proficiency scales. To illustrate, figure 3.1 (page 92) depicts the middle school (grades 6–8) proficiency scale for the cognitive analysis skill of comparing.

As with all proficiency scales, this one illustrates the progression of learning and skill development, with the score 2.0 targets being prerequisites for score 3.0 competency. For example, in figure 3.1,

4.0	The student will: • Describe how the comparison process can be made more rigorous or informative.
3.5	In addition to score 3.0 performance, partial success at score 4.0 content
3.0	The student will: **COM1—Independently execute a comparison process that involves selection of items, characteristics, and self-analysis.**
2.5	No major errors or omissions regarding score 2.0 content, and partial success at score 3.0 content
2.0	**COM1—**The student will perform basic processes such as: • Describe a comparison process that involves selection of items, characteristics, and self-analysis. For example, (1) select the items you wish to compare and the method you will use to record and organize your ideas (such as a Venn diagram, comparison matrix, or double-bubble diagram). (2) Identify the general focus of what you want to learn about the items. (3) Identify characteristics that will provide you with the most information about your focus for learning. (4) Gather and record information about how the items are similar and different for each characteristic. (5) Summarize what you have learned from the comparison task and identify questions about the items that are still unanswered for you.
1.5	Partial success at score 2.0 content, and major errors or omissions regarding score 3.0 content
1.0	With help, partial success at score 2.0 content and score 3.0 content
0.5	With help, partial success at score 2.0 content but not at score 3.0 content
0.0	Even with help, no success

Source: © 2017 by Marzano Resources. Adapted with permission.

FIGURE 3.1: Proficiency scale for comparing, grades 6–8.

the score 2.0 learning target focuses on a concrete set of steps for executing the skill of comparing. The teacher would provide direct instruction, described as follows, on this process to students as a starting point from which they might make alterations to personalize the process.

1. Select the items you wish to compare and the method you will use to record and organize your ideas (such as a Venn diagram, comparison matrix, or double-bubble diagram).

2. Identify the general focus of what you want to learn about the items.

3. Identify characteristics that will provide you with the most information about your focus for learning.

4. Gather and record information about how the items are similar and different for each characteristic.

5. Summarize what you have learned from the comparison task and identify questions about the items that are still unanswered for you.

At the score 3.0 level, students are expected to design their own comparison tasks in which they select the items to be compared and the characteristics on which they will compare them. Additionally, students should be able to analyze their own performance in the comparison task. At the 4.0 level, students must describe how the comparison can be made more rigorous or informative.

It's important to note that within the Marzano Academies model, the various cognitive and meta-cognitive skills become more complex as students move up through the grade levels. The scale in figure 3.1 represents the skill of comparing at the middle school level (grades 6–8). The expectation is that students can independently execute a comparison process using and adapting steps provided by the teacher. If a complete school system is using the academy model, students will be prepared for this expectation because, at the upper elementary level (grades 3–5), the teacher guides students through the steps of comparing. At the high school level (grades 9–12), students generate their own processes for comparison and analyze the different situations in which it can or should be used.

The proficiency scales for cognitive and metacognitive skills should become a formal part of the secondary curriculum. Leaders can do this by assigning the cognitive and metacognitive skills to specific grade levels, subject areas, and courses. For example, at the middle school level, the cognitive analysis skill of analyzing errors in reasoning might be assigned to specific social studies courses. In high school, this cognitive analysis skill might be assigned to specific history courses, literary analysis courses, and science courses. At the middle school level, the knowledge application skill of systems analysis might be assigned to specific computing courses and at the high school level it might be assigned to specific sociology courses and engineering courses. At the middle school level, the traditional metacognitive skill of seeking cohesion and coherence might be assigned to specific writing courses and at the high school level it might be assigned to specific composition courses and art courses. At the middle school and high school levels, the four metacognitive life skills might be assigned to all grade levels and courses simply because they are so central to a well-functioning classroom. It is important to note that just because a metacognitive or cognitive skill is assigned to specific classes does not mean that it cannot be taught and reinforced in other grade levels, subject areas, and courses.

Assessment for Cognitive and Metacognitive Skills

Just as they would with traditional academic content, teachers should assess students on cognitive and metacognitive skills and track their learning. However, cognitive and metacognitive assessments do not employ the same methods that are used with academic content.

To illustrate how such assessment might manifest, consider figure 3.2 (page 94), which contains assessment guidance for the cognitive analysis skill of comparing for grades 6–8. This example illustrates how teachers can approach assessing the cognitive and metacognitive skills without using traditional tests. Rather, teachers will commonly design structured situations where students can demonstrate these skills as they engage in academic tasks.

The assessment guidance does not provide actual assessment items for the content at the score 2.0, 3.0, and 4.0 levels. Rather, it gives teachers an idea of how they might design assessment activities that produce evidence of students' levels of expertise. For example, at the score 2.0 level, simply asking students to describe the comparison process would be an assessment activity. An example of a score 3.0 assessment activity would be providing students with a comparison activity in which they must generate all the parts of the process, including identifying the items to be compared and the characteristics on which they are compared. Additionally, teachers would ask students to analyze their own performance on the task. Finally, at the 4.0 level, students would provide concrete suggestions for how the comparison task they just completed could have been made more rigorous or informative.

Note that figure 3.2 describes the whole-point score values of 2.0, 3.0, and 4.0 only. This is because half-point score values use the whole-point score values as their reference points. In effect, if one defines the assessment practices for the 2.0, 3.0, and 4.0 levels, the remaining values of the scale are also defined.

4.0	After students have completed a complex comparison task, ask them to describe how the task could have been made more rigorous or informative. Student suggestions should include concrete ways to make the characteristics on which items are compared more detailed and nuanced.
3.0	Present students with a comparison task that involves self-analysis and for which they must execute all parts of the process such as identifying the items to be compared, identifying the characteristics on which the items are compared, and summarizing what they have learned through the process. The characteristics on which items are compared should add to a deeper understanding of one or both items. Students should be able to describe new insights they have gained as a result of the process.
2.0	Ask students to describe the comparison process they used. The process should include specific steps such as: (1) select the items you wish to compare and the method you will use to record and organize your ideas (such as a Venn diagram, comparison matrix, or double-bubble diagram); (2) identify the general focus of what you want to learn about the items; (3) identify characteristics that will provide you with the most information about your focus for learning; (4) gather and record information about how the items are similar and different for each characteristic; (5) summarize what you have learned from the comparison task and identify questions about the items that are still unanswered for you. Students should be able to describe what each step entails.

Source: © 2017 by Marzano Resources. Adapted with permission.

FIGURE 3.2: Assessment guidance for comparing, grades 6–8.

Important Decision Points for Cognitive and Metacognitive Skills

Incorporating cognitive and metacognitive skills in the curriculum has implications in some districts for teacher contracts, district curriculum-development practices, and board of education graduation requirements. School leaders must understand their circumstances and deploy innovative strategies that will be effective in their unique school communities. Leaders should shepherd stakeholders to understand the need for these skills by listening to their suggestions and attending to their concerns.

The school leader must also help faculty and staff decide when and where the cognitive and metacognitive skills will be taught and assessed. As described previously, schools should distribute these skills throughout the curriculum based on where they fit best with the subjects. Some content areas are better suited than others to accommodate specific skills, and teachers should be intimately involved in the decision regarding which to include. Ultimately, the leadership team should create a document that assigns each cognitive and metacognitive skill to specific subject areas and grade levels or courses.

Beyond assigning these skills to various courses, the school leader should stress that cognitive and metacognitive skills should be explicitly taught. Teachers' unit plans should articulate how they will instruct and assess the skills, and leaders must review and offer substantive feedback on those plans. Leaders can also maintain high expectations by conducting classroom walkthroughs, arranging peer walkthroughs, facilitating peer reviews of unit plans, adjusting practices based on data, and holding conversations with students, all with a focus on cognitive and metacognitive skills.

If cognitive and metacognitive skills were a systematic part of the curriculum throughout an entire district, a high school might not need to teach the cognitive and metacognitive skills above grade 10 since, by then, the skills would be well formed and students would be able to use them in a variety of ways. However, this scenario reflects an *ideal* situation not found in many actual districts. First, some high schools belong to districts comprised of high schools exclusively, which means they may have little to no direct influence in the K–8 schools. Second, rollouts of CBE do not always occur across entire school districts or in all grade levels or content areas. Third, some districts or high schools may elect to only implement CBE in specific content areas, with small populations of students, or within specified programs (for example, in the alternative school). Those decisions reduce or eliminate the potential for a districtwide focus on cognitive and metacognitive skills. Finally, many high schools face the challenge of significant gaps in academic readiness among incoming ninth graders and transfer students; these students may also have limited if any experience related to cognitive and metacognitive skills. In all of these instances, the foundation is not there. Some students will experience direct instruction in cognitive and metacognitive skills for the first time at the secondary level.

High Reliability Leadership for School-Level Indicator 10

Figure 3.3 lists some potential lagging indicators for cognitive and metacognitive skills. From this list, the leader would then select trim tab indicators to create a customized high reliability scale. Figure 3.4 (page 96) depicts a possible customized scale a school leader might design for school-level indicator 10, cognitive and metacognitive skills.

Programs and Practices	Lagging Indicator Data	Potential Standard for High Reliability Status
Scales for cognitive and metacognitive skills	Proficiency scale documents for cognitive analysis, knowledge application, traditional metacognitive, and metacognitive life skills	90 percent of teachers understand the school's cognitive analysis skills 90 percent of teachers understand the school's knowledge application skills 90 percent of teachers understand the school's traditional metacognitive skills 90 percent of teachers understand the school's metacognitive life skills
Dispersal of cognitive and metacognitive skills throughout content areas and grade levels	An explicit document that depicts the content areas, courses, and grade levels in which various cognitive and metacognitive skills will be directly taught	100 percent of teachers embed the cognitive and metacognitive skills in the curriculum skills as prescribed
Direct instruction of cognitive and metacognitive skills	Data from classroom observations	90 percent of teachers employ the protocols for directly teaching cognitive and metacognitive skills
Assessment of cognitive and metacognitive skills	Data from classroom observations	90 percent of teachers employ the protocols for assessing cognitive and metacognitive skills
Perceptions of students, teachers, and parents	Surveys of students, teachers, and parents	90 percent of teachers report success at teaching cognitive and metacognitive skills 80 percent of students report that they are getting better at the cognitive and metacognitive skills they are taught in school

FIGURE 3.3: Potential lagging indicators and criteria for school-level indicator 10.

Evidence	
4 **Sustaining** **(quick data)**	Quick data like the following are systematically collected and reviewed: • Reviews of teacher lesson plans and unit plans • Quick conversations with teachers and students • Examination of evidence scores in the LMS
3 **Applying** **(lagging)**	Performance goals with clear criteria for success like the following are in place: • 90 percent of teachers understand the school's cognitive analysis skills • 90 percent of teachers understand the school's knowledge application skills • 90 percent of teachers understand the school's traditional metacognitive skills • 90 percent of teachers understand the school's metacognitive life skills • 100 percent of teachers actively engage in the professional development for cognitive and metacognitive skills • 100 percent of teachers embed the cognitive and metacognitive skills in the curriculum skills as prescribed • 90 percent of teachers report success at teaching cognitive and metacognitive skills • 80 percent of students report that they are getting better at the cognitive and metacognitive skills they are taught in school
2 **Developing** **(leading)**	• Cognitive and metacognitive skills with accompanying proficiency scales are in place • Cognitive and metacognitive skills are embedded in the curriculum in a logical and organized fashion
1 **Beginning**	• The school has written plans for the integration of cognitive and metacognitive skills but there is little execution of the plans at the classroom level • Relatively few teachers implement instruction and assessment of cognitive and metacognitive skills
0 **Not Using**	• The school has no written plans for instruction and assessment of cognitive and metacognitive skills • There is no implementation of instruction and assessment of cognitive and metacognitive skills at the classroom level

Source: © 2020 by Marzano Academies, Inc. Adapted with permission.

FIGURE 3.4: Customized high reliability scale for school-level indicator 10.

Vocabulary (SLI 11)

Within the Marzano Academies model, vocabulary development is a revered concept. The academy perspective is that developing students' vocabularies is akin to developing their background knowledge, and well-developed background knowledge provides a sound foundation for academic learning in all subject areas. Education consultant Suzy Pepper Rollins (2014) argued that everything seems more challenging for students who lack adequate vocabulary because vocabulary touches all aspects of students' literacy development, including reading, writing, and conversational proficiencies. ESL teacher and author Judie Haynes (2007) described the use of direct instruction of essential vocabulary combined with visuals to present new words in context as an effective strategy for teaching English learners.

The book *Teaching Basic, Advanced, and Academic Vocabulary* (Marzano, 2020) describes the extensive research on the importance of direct instruction in vocabulary and the need for schools to attend to three tiers of vocabulary. The distinctions between the three tiers provide educators with a concrete framework for direct instruction in vocabulary throughout the K–12 continuum. While tier one and tier two terms are usually the focus of vocabulary development at the elementary level (that is, grades K–5), it is not uncommon for some secondary students to also need this instruction, particularly at the middle school level.

Tier one terms are high-frequency words. This tier includes words like *big, clock, walk,* and *baby.* Such words are so frequent in the English language that elementary students who speak English as a first language might not actually require instruction to learn their meanings. Regarding tier one vocabulary, researchers Isabel L. Beck, Margaret G. McKeown, and Linda Kucan (2002) explained, "Words in this tier rarely require instructional attention to their meaning in school" (p. 8). This is because students frequently encounter these terms outside of school, so much so that by the time they enter school, tier one words are already very familiar to them. However, if students are English learners or come from family backgrounds that offer limited access to literacy experiences, then it is critical that they receive instruction in these terms. Tier two terms are words that may not be encountered frequently enough for teachers to assume that students know them. Words such as *nimble, scrawny,* and *dexterity* exemplify tier two vocabulary. Consequently, tier two terms are often the focus of classroom instruction, specifically in language arts classes.

Academy schools at the elementary level devote a significant amount of time and energy ensuring that by the time their students have completed fifth grade, they have a firm grounding in the tier one and tier two terms. To briefly summarize the instructional approach for tier one and tier two terms at the elementary level (Marzano, 2020), there are 2,845 tier one terms and 5,160 tier two terms. These terms are organized into 420 *semantic clusters*—groups of words with related meanings. To illustrate, consider cluster 102, titled Bodies of Water.

- Tier one terms: *bay, creek, lake, ocean, pond, puddle, river, sea, stream*
- Tier two terms: *bog, brook, cove, current, delta, eddy, estuary, fjord, geyser, gulf, headwaters, inlet, lagoon, marsh, marshland, outlet, rapids, reef, strait, surf, swamp, tide, tributary, waterfall, waterline*

Clusters provide a rich semantic context for students to obtain an initial understanding of unknown words. Students who know the meaning of some or most of the tier one terms will have contextual information with which to understand less common terms like *inlet, eddy,* and *estuary.* Simply stated, teaching vocabulary in semantic clusters aids student learning of those terms (Graves, 2006; Hartati, 2020; Marzano, 2004; Marzano & Marzano, 1988; Sarıoğlu & Yıldırım, 2018). It is useful for secondary leaders to be aware of tier one and tier two terms because they might have students who would benefit from remedial vocabulary instruction. In contrast, instruction in tier three terms is important to all levels, elementary and secondary.

Tier three terms encompass all those terms that are not tier one or tier two terms. A logical question relative to tier three terms is, Which ones should be the subject of direct instruction at the secondary level? The simple answer to this question is that the tier three terms that teachers should teach directly are those that are critical to understanding subject-matter content. For example, words like *meiosis* and *mitosis* in science would fall into this category. While a person will probably not encounter these terms in general interactions with others or in general reading, such terms are critically important to understanding some aspects of biology.

In the academy model, tier three terms that should be the subject of direct instruction are embedded in the proficiency scales for each subject area at each grade level or for each course. To illustrate, consider figure 3.5, which depicts the high school economics proficiency scale for the measurement topic of supply and demand.

4.0	In addition to score 3.0 performance, the student demonstrates in-depth inferences and applications that go beyond what was taught.
3.5	In addition to score 3.0 performance, partial success at score 4.0 content
3.0	The student will: SD—**Explain the causes and effects of changes in supply, demand, and price in a market** (for example, explain the possible results in the gasoline market of an oil shortage, a decrease in the price of electric cars, or a government-enforced price ceiling on gasoline).
2.5	No major errors or omissions regarding score 2.0 content, and partial success at score 3.0 content
2.0	SD—The student will recognize or recall specific vocabulary (for example, *demand curve*, *market-clearing price*, *shortage*, *supply curve*, *surplus*) and perform basic processes such as: • Explain that the demand for a product will normally change (the demand curve will shift) if there is a change in consumers' incomes, tastes, and preferences; a change in the prices of related (complementary or substitute) products; or a change in the number of consumers in a market. • Explain that the supply of a product will normally change (the supply curve will shift) if there is a change in technology, the prices of the productive resources used to make the product, the profit opportunities available to producers from making and selling other products, or the number of sellers in a market. • Explain that changes in supply or demand cause relative prices to change and, in turn, buyers and sellers adjust their purchase and sales decisions. • Explain that shortages of a product usually result in price increases in a market economy, and surpluses usually result in price decreases. • Explain that price controls (government-enforced price ceilings set below the market-clearing price and government-enforced price floors set above the market-clearing price) distort price signals and incentives to producers and consumers and can cause persistent shortages (as a result of price ceilings), persistent surpluses (as a result of price floors), and long-run allocation problems in the economy.
1.5	Partial success at score 2.0 content, and major errors or omissions regarding score 3.0 content
1.0	With help, partial success at score 2.0 content and score 3.0 content
0.5	With help, partial success at score 2.0 content but not at score 3.0 content
0.0	Even with help, no success

Source: © 2019 by Marzano Resources. Adapted with permission.

FIGURE 3.5: Proficiency scale for supply and demand, high school.

The vocabulary terms at the score 2.0 level of this scale (*demand curve, market-clearing price, shortage, supply curve, surplus*) should be the subject of direct instruction. However, it is important to consider the level of depth to which teachers should go when teaching vocabulary terms. To address this, teachers should be aware of the difference between approaching an item as a vocabulary term and approaching it as a concept. The very label *vocabulary term* implies that expectations regarding students' understanding of the term are at a surface level (Marzano & Kendall, 2007). For example, when a science teacher is teaching *ecosystem* as a vocabulary term, the teacher expects students to have a general understanding of an ecosystem as a system of interacting biological organisms and their physical environment. A student who knows *ecosystem* as a vocabulary term might know this definition and at least one example of an ecosystem. In contrast, if *ecosystem* is taught and understood as a concept, then the learner would know multiple generalizations and principles about ecosystems and be able to distinguish among multiple examples. This is an important distinction to keep in mind when secondary teachers are providing direct instruction in tier three terms.

Direct Instruction for Tier Three Terms

Direct instruction can take many forms when teaching vocabulary. The academy model employs a six-step process that has a long history of use (Marzano, 2004, 2010; Marzano & Pickering, 2005; Marzano & Simms, 2013). Those six steps are as follows.

1. Provide a description, explanation, or example of the new term.

2. Ask students to restate the description, explanation, or example in their own words.

3. Ask students to construct a picture, symbol, or graphic representing the term or phrase.

4. Periodically engage students in activities that help them add to their knowledge of the terms to which they have previously been exposed.

5. Periodically ask students to discuss the terms with one another.

6. Periodically involve students in games that allow them to play with terms.

Here, we consider each step briefly. For a detailed description, see *Teaching Basic, Advanced, and Academic Vocabulary* (Marzano, 2020).

Step 1: Provide a Description, Explanation, or Example of the New Term

The first step in the process involves providing students with information that allows them to form a rudimentary but memorable understanding of the new tier three term. This can occur in three ways: a description, explanation, or example of the new term.

Provide a Description

When providing a description, the teacher presents typically nontechnical information that presents students with general but accurate initial understanding of the term. For example, for the chemistry vocabulary term *valence*, the teacher might present the following simple description: *the capacity of an element or radical to combine with another to form a molecule*. While this description is not detailed or complete, it provides students with a general understanding of its meaning.

Provide an Explanation

Although many ways have been proposed to explain new terms to students (Beck, McKeown, & Kucan, 2013), there are four that consider the type of word and students' familiarity (Jenkins & Dixon, 1983):

1. The new term has a simple synonym with which students are familiar or can be explained in very concrete ways. For example, the term *typhoon* has the synonym *hurricane* with which many students are familiar. . . .

2. The new term has a simple synonym, but students are not familiar with the synonym. For example, the term *combustible* is synonymous with the term *flammable* but students might not understand this synonym.

3. The new term does not have a simple synonym, but students have background knowledge they can easily relate to the term. For example, the term *population* has no obvious synonym, but most students would understand the concept of people in a specific group, like the population of a city or school.

4. The new term does not have a simple synonym and students do not have relevant background knowledge from which to draw. For example, the term *cryosphere* refers to areas on Earth where water only occurs in its solid, frozen form. Unless students have seen pictures or video footage of polar regions, they will have no experiential base to understand this concept. (Marzano, 2020, p. 41)

When a new term falls into the first or third category, the teacher provides students with a synonym they recognize or provides a more detailed explanation that is consistent with students' background knowledge. When a new term falls into the second or fourth category, the teacher will have to provide some background information before an explanation or synonym will make sense to students.

Provide Examples

Examples are very concrete ways to introduce new terms and should be used whenever possible. For example, when introducing the term *entropy*, the teacher might present the example of a closet. If you never clean out or organize that closet, it will get more and more chaotic and disheveled over time simply because it takes energy and attention to keep things neat and tidy. Without attention, disorder increases over time. The teacher would then explain how the disorder of the neglected closet corresponds to the definition of entropy.

Step 2: Ask Students to Restate the Description, Explanation, or Example in Their Own Words

In this step, students restate the teacher's description, explanation, or example from step 1. The important part here is that students create their own version of what a new term means; the simple act of restating in their own words forces students to think about the term in depth and helps anchor the term in memory.

Students should have a great deal of freedom to construct their versions of the term's meaning and to connect the term to their own experiences. For example, a student might describe the term *kinetic energy* in the following way: "When I'm running really hard, it takes some time for me to slow down because I have so much kinetic energy." Such personalized descriptions are acceptable at this stage (assuming no significant errors); students will revise their descriptions in later steps of the process.

Students should record the descriptions or explanations that they come up with and other information related to the term. For this purpose, we use the format recommended by Robert J. Marzano and Julia A. Simms (2013). Its components are listed as follows and figure 3.6 shows an example:

- The new term

- The academic subject with which the term is associated, if applicable (for example, science or mathematics)

- The category or measurement topic the term is associated with (for example, Biogeology or Conservation of Matter)

- The student's current level of understanding of the term (for example, 4, 3, 2, or 1)

- The student's description, explanation, and example of the term

- The student's visual depiction of the term (see step 3)

- Words related to the term, such as synonyms or antonyms (Marzano, 2020, p. 43)

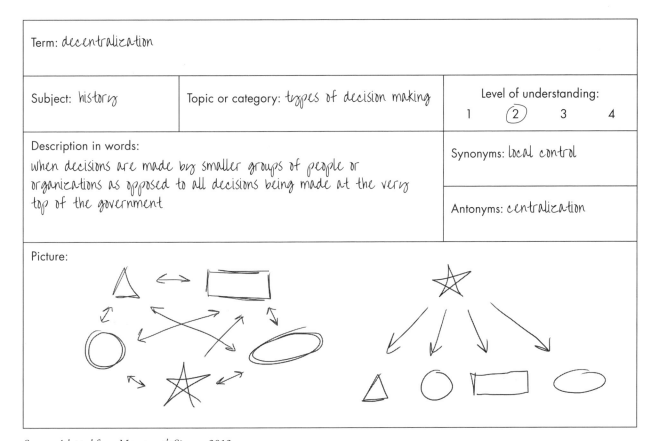

Term: *decentralization*			
Subject: *history*	Topic or category: *types of decision making*		Level of understanding: 1 ② 3 4
Description in words: *when decisions are made by smaller groups of people or organizations as opposed to all decisions being made at the very top of the government*		Synonyms: *local control*	
		Antonyms: *centralization*	
Picture:			

Source: Adapted from Marzano & Simms, 2013.

FIGURE 3.6: Recording page for tier three terms.

Note that the recording sheet has a section where students rate their level of understanding for each term using the following scale.

4.   I understand even more about the term than I was taught.

3.   I understand the term and I'm not confused about any part of what it means.

2. I'm a little uncertain about what the term means, but I have a general idea.

1. I'm very uncertain about the term. I really don't understand what it means.

At this stage, students may rate their understanding as a 1 or a 2 because they have had few exposures to the word. As the six-step process continues and students have more opportunities to examine the word in various contexts, their understanding and ratings will increase.

Step 3: Ask Students to Construct a Picture, Symbol, or Graphic Representing the Term or Phrase

Step 3 continues students' recording their initial understanding of the term, but now they do so with a nonlinguistic representation. In other words, students draw a picture, symbol, or graphic to represent the term. For example, students might draw an abstract picture that reminds them of the meaning of the term, stick figure representations, a realistic picture of the term, symbols that represent the meaning of the term, and so on.

Teachers should be aware that some students may resist this step if they are self-conscious of their drawing abilities or believe that their written descriptions are sufficient. In contrast, other students might display perfectionist tendencies with their drawings and spend too much time on them (Marzano, Rogers, & Simms, 2015). We suggest that demonstrating the variety of different ways that students can create nonlinguistic representations will help alleviate these concerns. Teachers might also incorporate multimedia graphics, videos, animations, or previous students' pictures into their examples of appropriate visual depictions.

Step 4: Periodically Engage Students in Activities That Help Them Add to Their Knowledge of the Terms

Whereas steps 1, 2, and 3 serve to introduce each new term and must occur in order, steps 4, 5, and 6 are intended to provide students with additional and varying exposures to the terms. As Marzano (2020) stated, "Each new exposure to previously introduced terms provides an opportunity for students to deepen their knowledge of the terms" (p. 45). Steps 4, 5, and 6 do not need to occur in a specific order or for every single word. Also, each instance of these steps will involve multiple words. Students should engage in an activity from step 4, 5, or 6 at least once a week.

Step 4 includes the widest range of activities. Activities that help students add to their knowledge of the term can include comparing and contrasting, classifying, creating metaphors, creating analogies, and examining roots and affixes (Marzano, 2020). Here we consider a comparing and contrasting activity as an example; for details on the other categories of activities, see *Teaching Basic, Advanced, and Academic Vocabulary* (Marzano, 2020).

Comparing and contrasting activities involve students examining the similarities and differences between the concepts represented by two or more vocabulary terms. These activities could be as simple as completing sentence stems like the following.

- _____ and _____ are similar because they both:
  - _____
  - _____
- _____ and _____ are different because:
  - _____ is _____, while _____ is _____.
  - _____ is _____, while _____ is _____.

Note that it is sometimes necessary to use verbs other than *is* and *are* in the stems. To illustrate this sentence stems activity, consider the following comparison of the terms *entrepreneur* and *innovator*.

- Entrepreneurs and innovators are similar because they both:
  - Think creatively
  - Set their own standards
- Entrepreneurs and innovators are different because:
  - Entrepreneurs focus on making money, while innovators focus on creating new things
  - Entrepreneurs focus on selling, while innovators focus on designing and producing

Step 5: Periodically Ask Students to Discuss the Terms With One Another

Step 5 uses the context of peer-to-peer interactions to extend students' comprehension of vocabulary terms. These activities can be relatively informal; the teacher might pair or group students and ask them to explain certain vocabulary terms to each other. To deepen the conversation, students can identify points of agreement and disagreement in their understandings and use the internet, ask the teacher, or have other students weigh in to resolve disagreements.

For a more structured activity, students can identify the semantic relationships between terms (Hiebert & Cervetti, 2012). A semantic relationship between words is anything that connects the words in terms of their meaning. Figure 3.7 lists common semantic relationships, examples, and questions that teachers can use to prompt students.

Semantic Relationship	Example	Prompt
Semantic classes	*Novels* are in the category of *books*.	What category does this word belong to?
Words that commonly occur together	*Loaf* is often paired with *bread*.	What other words are commonly associated with this word?
Superordination	*Deciduous* refers to a type of *trees*.	Does this word represent a type of something? If so, what?
Synonym	*Pertinent* and *relevant* have roughly the same meaning.	What is a synonym for this word?
Part-whole	A *crankshaft* is part of an *engine*.	Does this word represent part of something? If so, what?
Instrumentality	A *sponge* is used to scrub *dishes*.	Does this word represent something that causes something else? If so, what is caused?
Theme	*Hard drive* and *random-access memory (RAM)* are both computer-related terms.	Is this word part of some larger theme? If so, what is the theme and what are some other words that belong with that theme?

Source: Adapted from Marzano, 2020.

FIGURE 3.7: Semantic relationships.

Step 6: Periodically Involve Students in Games That Allow Them to Play With Terms

Word games can be brief activities or last multiple class periods. We include a sampling of games for secondary classrooms here. Marzano and colleagues (2015) and Marzano (2020) described additional vocabulary games that are effective for step 6.

- **Alphabet Antonyms:** The teacher selects a particular letter of the alphabet. Students write down several vocabulary words, all beginning with that same letter. Then, they come up with an antonym for each one. Each student reads the antonyms to the class and the class tries to guess the original words. Consider the following example of vocabulary words beginning with *b* and antonyms. The student would read *autobiography, ending,* and so on and the class would try to guess *biography, beginning,* and the rest.

  - biography—autobiography

  - beginning—ending

  - book—chapter

  - back matter—front matter

- **Classroom Feud:** Similar to the game show *Family Feud,* teams of students answer questions about vocabulary terms. If they answer correctly, they earn points.

- **Draw Me:** One student draws a picture of a vocabulary term while others try to guess the word as quickly as possible. This game is similar to the board game *Pictionary.*

- **Name That Category:** The teacher divides students into two teams. A clue-giver on each team has a list of categories provided by the teacher. The clue-giver names vocabulary terms that fit in each category to help the team guess the category. Once teammates guess the category, the clue-giver moves on to the next one on the list and starts listing terms for that category. Whichever team gets through the list first wins.

- **Talk a Mile a Minute:** This game is similar to the board games *Taboo* and *Catch Phrase.* In advance, the teacher creates cards that each list a category and several associated vocabulary terms. During the game, one student on each team receives a card and must lead the rest of the team to say each of the vocabulary terms without using any of the words on the card in the clues. Each round is timed.

- **Vocabulary Charades:** One team silently acts out a vocabulary term while teammates try to guess it.

High Reliability Leadership for School-Level Indicator 11

Figure 3.8 lists some potential lagging indicators for vocabulary. From this list, the leader would then select trim tab indicators to create a customized high reliability scale. Figure 3.9 depicts a possible customized scale a school leader might design for school-level indicator 11, vocabulary.

Programs and Practices	Lagging Indicator Data	Potential Standard for High Reliability Status
Three tiers of terms	Virtual and in-person professional development regarding tier one, tier two, and tier three vocabulary	100 percent of teachers are adequately familiar with the nature and intent of the tier one, two, and three terms
Six-step process for vocabulary instruction	Data from classroom observations	90 percent of teachers employ the six-step process with tier three terms
Perceptions of students, teachers, and parents	Surveys of students, teachers, and parents	80 percent of students report that their knowledge of tier one, two, and three terms is increasing

FIGURE 3.8: Potential lagging indicators and criteria for school-level indicator 11.

Evidence	
4 **Sustaining** **(quick data)**	Quick data like the following are systematically collected and reviewed: • Examination of records indicating students' status on tier one, two, and three vocabulary • Quick conversations with students about their status on tier one, two, and three vocabulary
3 **Applying** **(lagging)**	Performance goals with clear criteria for success like the following are in place: • 90 percent of teachers employ the six-step process with tier three terms • 100 percent of teachers are adequately familiar with the nature and intent of the tier one, two, and three terms • 90 percent of teachers explicitly follow the plans for instruction, assessment, and record keeping regarding tier one, two, and three terms • 80 percent of students report that their knowledge of tier one, two, and three terms is increasing
2 **Developing** **(leading)**	• The six-step process for teaching tier three terms is in place • Tier one, two, and three terms have been identified and have explicit protocols for their use • Critical tier three terms are embedded in proficiency scales
1 **Beginning**	• The school has written plans regarding instruction in tier one, two, and three vocabulary but there is no implementation of the plans • Instruction in tier one, two, and three vocabulary is available but relatively few students have access to it
0 **Not Using**	• The school has no written plans for instruction in tier one, two, and three vocabulary • There is no direct instruction in tier one, two, and three vocabulary at the classroom level

Source: © 2020 by Marzano Academies, Inc. Adapted with permission.

FIGURE 3.9: Customized high reliability scale for school-level indicator 11.

Blended Instruction (SLI 6)

Blended instruction—a system that integrates online learning resources with direct teacher instruction—is essential to CBE implementation. Since students will be working at different paces on the measurement topics within the curriculum, they must have access to virtual instruction that does not require meeting with a teacher in real time. There are a growing number of systems and platforms that provide online learning opportunities for students. Some of these offer free resources (for example, Khan Academy), and others offer fee-based services (for example, Discovery Education). School leaders should make efforts to become familiar with these resources and match them to the measurement topics that constitute their curriculum. Regardless of the platform and system used, there are some general considerations secondary school leaders should keep in mind.

From the beginning of implementation, the school leader should emphasize the fact that blended instruction is an essential component of CBE, not an optional one. Blended instruction provides an optimal platform for meeting the diverse learning needs of individuals and groups of learners. Secondary teachers can have well over a hundred students on their rosters, and blended instruction is vital to honoring their different levels of background knowledge and the varying paces at which they will learn.

One way to approach blended instruction is to align delivery methods with three primary functions.

1. **Supplement and support:** Use flex scheduling to deliver instruction to students who need to recover measurement topics. *Flex scheduling* is a term that means a school provides students with multiple opportunities to work on content. Although typically used in alternative school settings for at-risk students, flex models can support students who need the flexibility to work on previously taught measurement topics, but outside of the traditional classroom. Potential instructional environments and users include before- and after-school tutoring, measurement topic recovery programs, and Saturday school facilitators.

2. **Enrich and enhance:** Utilize a self-blended model with highly motivated students who can work on their traditional courses and an additional course or two independently. Self-blended means that students can determine whether they learn specific types of content virtually. Students interested in advanced classes, classes not offered by the school, and shorter enrichment modules will benefit from a self-blended approach. Another potential circumstance may involve students pursuing early graduation. Similar to a flex model, the self-blended delivery applies to circumstances and environments outside of the traditional classroom.

3. **Individualize, differentiate, and personalize:** Employ a face-to-face delivery model to customize instruction for individual students (individualization), design and provide instruction for homogeneous groups of learners (differentiation), or give students a voice in designing their learning (personalization). The face-to-face model is the delivery method teachers use in classrooms to address various levels of ability and competency.

Although CBE schools should approach blended instruction as a schoolwide strategy, various state regulations, local district policies, and course requirements may impede or restrict the full use of blended instruction in those cases. For example, driver's education requires physical, behind-the-wheel instruction and is therefore not amenable to a fully blended approach. That said, within the classroom, some students will receive face-to-face delivery from the teacher while others who have demonstrated competency participate in online instruction to increase their pace. Still others, including English learners and those who need individualized support, may need remediation to advance their learning and can use blended instruction to access previous measurement topics or individualized education goals.

Giving students access to content, lessons, activities, and resources through blended instruction is an essential supplement to teacher instruction in a CBE system. In the following sections, we discuss the importance of playlists, the added benefit of real-time data on student status, and the need to prepare teachers for blended instruction.

Playlists

In general terms, a *playlist* is a progression of virtual learning activities students can utilize at any time. The LMS selected by a secondary school should have some type of playlist feature that allows teachers to create specific, differentiated lessons for particular measurement topics. These virtual learning progressions provide a sequenced set of tasks, activities, resources, and assessments for students to follow. Figure 3.10 displays an example from the Empower LMS.

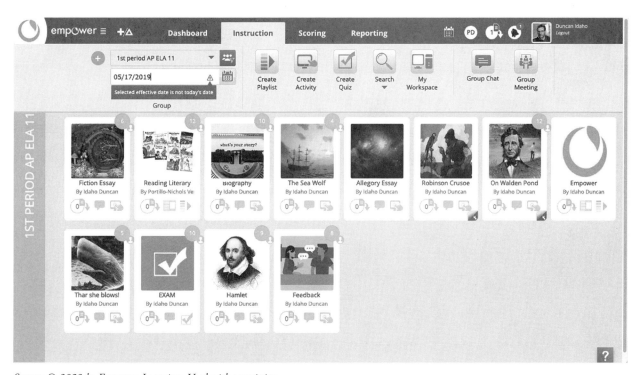

Source: © 2023 by Empower Learning. Used with permission.

FIGURE 3.10: ELA playlist.

This playlist is for a measurement topic in eleventh-grade ELA. Each tile links to a separate lesson or activity. Some lessons present new content to students, such as information about literary works. Such information may be presented in short video segments, written materials, or both. Some tiles lead to quizzes. In short, teachers can create tiles with any type of virtual activity and sequence them to produce a coherent virtual instructional experience for students. The teacher would also specify which tiles relate to score 2.0, 3.0, and 4.0 content on a specific proficiency scale. Typically, the tiles in the beginning of a playlist deal with score 2.0, followed by tiles that relate to score 3.0 content, and so on. This noted, teachers have a great deal of flexibility in terms of how they construct and organize the tiles in a playlist.

Figure 3.11 depicts a playlist created for a STEM class. Notice that the left side of the screen provides a legend so students can identify which tiles contain big idea information, which tiles contain activities, which tiles contain quizzes, and so on. This provides students with a *mental set* or advance organizer regarding what they can expect in the learning sequence.

Source: © 2023 by Empower Learning. Used with permission.

FIGURE 3.11: STEM class playlist.

Playlists are a unique way to leverage the power of a blended classroom to differentiate instruction and personalize the learning experience. The teacher can create learning activities and assign them to different groups of students. This tool enables students to move through the content at their own pace, anywhere and anytime they have internet access.

Real-Time Data on Student Status

One less obvious benefit of blended instruction is that it increases the availability of real-time data about each student's status on each measurement topic in the curriculum. This helps the teacher identify students who are starting to lag behind in pace and guide them to individual support through blended learning activities. Without such access to data, blended learning resources might sit unused by the very students who need them most. In the academy model, the school's chosen LMS must have the capability to report students' status in an ongoing manner. As mentioned previously, Marzano Academies use the Empower Learning platform, but there is a growing number of systems that can display reports like that in figure 3.12.

Source: © 2023 by Empower Learning. Used with permission.

FIGURE 3.12: View of students' current status.

This screen depicts a report for an eleventh-grade Advanced Placement (AP) English course on classical literature. Each row represents a specific student and each column represents a specific measurement topic. At the top of each column, a code denotes each of the measurement topics seen here (for example, LA.RI.11.4). These school-specific codes refer to the local system for organizing standards and measurement topics in the curriculum and linking various learning resources to their parent topics.

Each cell within a row contains the student's current summative score for that particular measurement topic. In figure 3.12, each student has a current summative score on each of the measurement topics (or a blank if there are not enough evidence scores to make a determination). Analyzing this report, the teacher might note that there are four students who have not yet demonstrated competence (that is, achieved score 3.0) in the first measurement topic and two students who have not demonstrated competence in the sixth measurement topic. The teacher might organize these students into small groups to work through the playlists on those topics together. The teacher would periodically check in with the group members to see how they are doing and provide support when necessary. As this example illustrates, the report on students' current status helps teachers determine which individual students or groups of students need additional support from the teacher or from the online resources of the playlist.

Preparation for Teachers

A secondary school leader should recognize that not all faculty are equally adept with technology. Consequently, to effectively implement this school-level indicator, the principal should provide a wide array of training opportunities for teachers. Certainly, face-to-face, all-staff professional development is a must, especially regarding the general functionality of the LMS. All faculty members should receive the same initial training regardless of their level of expertise. In addition, the principal should provide supplemental training opportunities, both in person and virtual, for teachers to access on an on-demand basis. After the school has adopted an LMS, the leader's attention should turn to selecting the online platforms (both subscription-based and free) that offer resources teachers can build into playlists. Be sure to provide teachers with appropriate professional development on accessing the chosen platforms and building playlists within the LMS.

In addition to providing professional development on the tools that enable blended instruction, school leaders must emphasize the importance of blended instruction. Establish an expectation that teachers' lesson plans explicitly state which online resources will be used, at what point in the instructional process, and for what learning targets. Review lesson plans and provide feedback to ensure teachers habitually include blended instruction as an integral part of lessons. Finally, the school leader should conduct both physical and virtual walkthroughs of classrooms to support the blended instruction requirements and identify next steps for professional development.

High Reliability Leadership for School-Level Indicator 6

Figure 3.13 lists some potential lagging indicators for blended instruction. From this list, the leader would then select trim tab indicators to create a customized high reliability scale. Figure 3.14 depicts a possible customized scale a school leader might design for school-level indicator 6, blended instruction.

Explicit Goals for Students' Status and Growth (SLI 12)

This school-level indicator deals with keeping track of student achievement and growth both at the individual level and at the school level. To begin, we emphasize that the indicator is stated in terms of students' growth *and* status as opposed to status alone. The logic here is that if a school sets a focus on learning (that is, growth) for all students, then, over time, students and the school will reach high status. When schools focus only on students' status, it is easy for educators to fall victim to the *ecological fallacy*, a misinterpretation of data where one attributes the characteristics of the group to all the individuals within the group. For example, it is common for schools to measure student achievement by average scores across an entire grade or school. When a school sets a goal based on the average achievement of all students, it is easy for leaders to be satisfied with the mean achievement score of students and ignore the fact that half of students have scores below the mean—some well below it. One might even argue that the ecological fallacy leads to some schools' failure to identify learning gaps between subgroups of students, let alone do anything to alleviate those gaps. While secondary schools will probably always have to report average status, this school-level indicator can help reorient leaders' metrics toward growth. To operationalize this indicator, we discuss setting explicit goals using proficiency scales, setting goals using external tests, and going beyond the scores.

Setting Explicit Goals Using Proficiency Scales

Within the academy model, one of the best places to start when working on explicit goals for students' status and growth is student growth as measured by proficiency scales. Growth is easy to compute with proficiency scales since it is simply the difference between a student's first score on a given measurement topic and his or her current score on that topic. To illustrate, consider figure 3.15 (page 112), which depicts a student's initial status (the darker portion of the bars) and current status (the lighter portion of the bars) on each measurement topic for science. For example, the first row concerns the measurement topic of matter and its interactions. The dark part of the bar stops

Programs and Practices	Lagging Indicator Data	Potential Standard for High Reliability Status
Playlists	LMS data regarding the frequency of playlist use	100 percent of teachers use the playlist feature in the LMS
Real-time data on student status	Assessment data stored in the LMS	100 percent of teachers keep data on students' current status and growth
Professional development on blended instruction	Records of professional development regarding blended instruction	100 percent of teachers engage in the professional development activities for blended instruction
Perceptions of students, teachers, and parents	Surveys of students, teachers, and parents	90 percent of teachers report that they feel confident about using the school's blended instruction process

FIGURE 3.13: Potential lagging indicators and criteria for school-level indicator 6.

Evidence	
4 **Sustaining** **(quick data)**	Quick data like the following are systematically collected and reviewed: • Examination of the online resources in the LMS • Reviews of teacher lesson plans and unit plans • Walkthrough observational data • Quick conversations with teachers and students
3 **Applying** **(lagging)**	Performance goals with clear criteria for success like the following are in place: • 100 percent of teachers use the playlist feature in the LMS • 100 percent of teachers engage in the professional development activities for blended instruction • 90 percent of teachers report that they feel confident about using the school's blended instruction process
2 **Developing** **(leading)**	• An LMS that adequately supports CBE is identified • Adequate professional development for blended instruction is in place
1 **Beginning**	• The school has written plans for the design and use of online resources for score 2.0, 3.0, and 4.0 content but there is no implementation at the school level • Only a few teachers use online resources for content in proficiency scales
0 **Not Using**	• The school has no written plans for the design and use of online resources • There is no use of online resources for proficiency scales at the classroom level

Source: © 2020 by Marzano Academies, Inc. Adapted with permission.

FIGURE 3.14: Customized high reliability scale for school-level indicator 6.

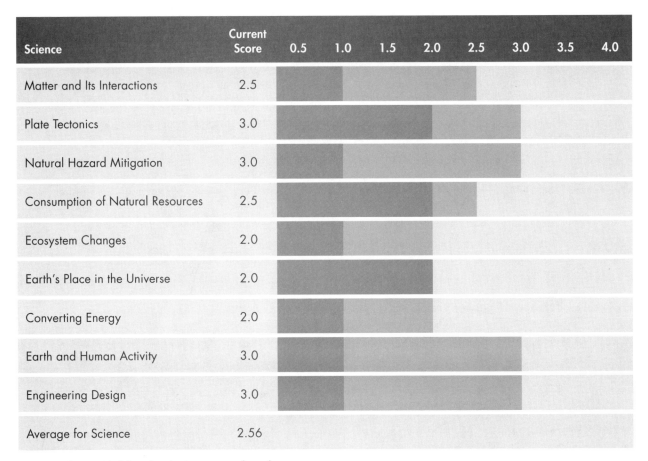

Science	Current Score	0.5	1.0	1.5	2.0	2.5	3.0	3.5	4.0
Matter and Its Interactions	2.5								
Plate Tectonics	3.0								
Natural Hazard Mitigation	3.0								
Consumption of Natural Resources	2.5								
Ecosystem Changes	2.0								
Earth's Place in the Universe	2.0								
Converting Energy	2.0								
Earth and Human Activity	3.0								
Engineering Design	3.0								
Average for Science	2.56								

FIGURE 3.15: Middle school science growth and status report.

at 1.0, which means that the student's first score was 1.0. The light part of the bar extends up to the score of 2.5, which is the student's current score. Therefore, the student's growth score for this topic is 1.5 levels (that is, 2.5 – 1.0 = 1.5).

A reporting system like this makes it easy to set goals and understand progress. Teachers can set goals for growth on the proficiency scale for individual students and their classes as a whole. For example, a teacher might set goals regarding the average increase in proficiency scale scores for each student. Likewise, a teacher might set an overall goal for the average increase in proficiency scale scores for the class as a whole. Departments can also set growth goals for a course. For example, with a healthy awareness of the ecological fallacy, the mathematics department might establish a goal that average student growth will be at least 2.0 levels in a specific course over the school year.

Students can also set personal growth goals for measurement topics in each of their courses. Students would set their goals immediately after receiving their first scores on specific measurement topics. To illustrate, consider figure 3.16. The first column lists the specific measurement topics for which the student is setting goals (in this example, several topics for 20th-century U.S. history). The second column, titled My Initial Score, is where students record the first score they receive. Then, there are two ways that students might go about setting goals for status and growth. One is to first establish their final status goal. When they receive their first score, they set their goal for the final status they want to achieve. Their growth, then, is a simple function of the difference between their initial status and their final status goal. The other method is to first establish their growth goal. In turn, the final status goals will then be easy to compute.

Measurement Topic	My Initial Score	My Growth Goal	My Final Status Goal
Post-War Society and Economy	1.5	2 scale levels	3.5
U.S. Foreign Policy in the Forties and Fifties	2.0	2 scale levels	4.0
U.S. Domestic and Foreign Policy in the Sixties	2.0	1.5 scale levels	3.5
Vietnam War	1.5	1.5 scale levels	3.0
Civil Rights Movements	1.0	2 scale levels	3.0

Source for measurement topics: Dodson, 2019.

FIGURE 3.16: Individual student goals.

Setting Goals Using External Assessments

While growth goals using proficiency scales provide very useful information, secondary school leaders will no doubt want to set goals for external tests. Common fare in K–12 education, external tests are those designed and scored by an organization outside the school or district. It is probably safe to say that there is a cultural expectation that schools set and meet goals for scores on external tests simply because of the importance they have accreted. In *Ethical Test Preparation in the Classroom*, Robert J. Marzano, Christopher W. Dodson, Julia A. Simms, and Jacob P. Wipf (2022) explained that external and standardized tests have a long history in education, dating back to the mid-1800s. To this day, such tests play a major role in decisions about individual students, schools, and districts. That external assessments will be a major part of K–12 education for the foreseeable future seems a reasonable prediction. It is important to note, though, that many educators believe that measuring students' current status and growth is too complex an issue to rely solely on external assessments, especially infrequent standardized exams.

It was at the turn of the millennium that education scholar W. James Popham (2001) wrote about the uses and misuses of standardized achievement tests and argued that test makers designed such tests to set up sensitive norm-referenced comparisons by detecting differences among test takers. He maintained that educators should use standardized achievement test results to inform parents and students about students' relative achievements, identify students for enrichment and remediation programs, and allocate resources, but not to evaluate schools (Popham, 2001). Similarly, educator and author Michael J. Higgins (2009) stated that although achievement tests have value, the emphasis on a single test score, coupled with their use as high-stakes measurements, has been like extinguishing fire with gasoline. According to educational consultant and author Anthony Muhammad (2015), school accountability ratings or letter grades and the focus on standardized test scores have resulted in public humiliation and forced schools into survival mode. Interestingly, over a thousand colleges and universities have deemphasized standardized testing in the admissions process due to lingering concerns about the discriminatory history of test development, the racial gaps in average scores, and testing bias against disadvantaged and low-income students (Buckley, 2020). This notwithstanding, general perceptions of a school's success are still commonly based on external tests, and secondary leaders should be well aware of this.

If school leaders wish to set growth goals using external tests, they should focus on interim assessments. As their name implies, interim assessments occur multiple times during the year, typically at the beginning of the year, middle of the year, and end of the year. Their frequency of administration makes them good tools with which to compute growth at the individual student level. Secondary schools commonly employ interim assessments for mathematics and ELA, at least. Schools typically use the data from these assessments to determine individual student needs and prescribe interventions as appropriate. Once beginning-of-year scores have been recorded, individual goals can be set for each student in the same fashion as goals are set for proficiency scale growth. As is the case with setting individual goals using proficiency scales, students should be intimately involved in setting their goals for external assessments. The main difference is the metric employed by external interim assessments; where proficiency scales for subject areas have a common scale that ranges from 0.0 to 4.0, external interim assessments have their own unique scales. Therefore, the scale for a mathematics interim assessment might differ from the scale for a reading interim assessment. Fortunately, interim assessment makers provide detailed guidance as to reasonable expectations for student growth using their specific metrics. Knowing these characteristics of their interim assessments, leaders can design specific growth goals for the school as a whole as well as for individual students. Indeed, some secondary schools make it a point to explain the scale score interpretations to students so that they can set such goals themselves.

Finally, end-of-year tests are also used for goal setting. Note that the end-of-year administration of an interim assessment is different from the end-of-year test typically administered by the state. Here we consider this latter type of end-of-year test. As their name implies, such tests occur at the end of the year and are commonly administered by state departments of education. Leaders who wish to set goals relative to state test results should do so at the schoolwide level (as opposed to individual student or class goals). It is also important to note that high schools often identify one particular assessment as a marker for the overall success of the school. For example, a high school might identify one of the forms of the SAT as its primary indicator of student achievement.

In some states, students must receive specific scores on specific tests to qualify for graduation (see table 3.5). If students' graduation is in some way determined by their scores on end-of-year assessments, then it is the secondary leader's responsibility not only to set schoolwide goals for these assessments, but also to adequately prepare each student for these tests. We address how this can be done in our discussion of school-level indicator 7, cumulative review (chapter 4, page 126).

Setting Goals in Terms of Percentage Gain

One straightforward way to establish schoolwide goals that are easy to understand and communicate is to state them in terms of percentage gain. To illustrate, consider figure 3.17 (page 116). This figure is a representation of how school leaders might set and communicate schoolwide percentage gain goals. The first two columns refer to external interim assessments. In this example, the goal is to see a 5 percent increase in scores from the baseline (that is, the beginning-of-year interim assessment) on the middle-of-year interim assessments for each subject area. Percentage gain for proficiency scale scores is easily computed by comparing the first scores assigned to students on measurement topics to their final summative scores. Percentage gain goals on state assessments are a different perspective because the scores being compared represent different students. For example, to compute gain for ninth-grade mathematics on the state assessment, leaders would compare the state assessment scores for the current class of ninth graders to the state assessment scores of the previous year's ninth graders.

TABLE 3.5: States With Tests as a Graduation Requirement

State	Exit Exam	Notes
Florida	Florida Standards Assessments (FSA)	Students must pass exit exams or achieve specified scores on the ACT or SAT.
Louisiana	Louisiana Educational Assessment Program (LEAP 2025)	Students must pass one subject in each of three subject pairs.
Maryland	Maryland Comprehensive Assessment Program (MCAP)	Students can substitute Advanced Placement or International Baccalaureate test scores. A Bridge Plan project-based alternative is available after failing an MCAP exam twice.
Massachusetts	Massachusetts Comprehensive Assessment System (MCAS)	Students who do not pass the requisite MCAS exams can fulfill the requirement through completion of a portfolio and an Educational Proficiency Plan. There is also an MCAS performance-appeals process.
New Jersey	New Jersey Student Learning Assessments (NJSLA)	Students must pass NJSLA or pass alternative assessments, including the ACT or SAT. There is a portfolio-based appeals process for those who fail the requisite exams.
New York	Regents Examinations	Students must pass five exams.
Ohio	Ohio's State Tests	Students must pass end-of-course exams, or achieve specified scores on other tests, such as the ACT or SAT. Ohio also has a graduation pathway requiring an industry credential and minimum score on the WorkKeys career-readiness assessment.
Texas	State of Texas Assessments of Academic Readiness (STAAR)	Students must pass five end-of-course exams.
Virginia	Standards of Learning (SOL)	Students must pass SOL exams or achieve specified scores on other tests, including ACT, SAT, Advanced Placement, or International Baccalaureate.

Source: Adapted from Gewertz, 2019; Marzano et al., 2022.

High Reliability Leadership for School-Level Indicator 12

Figure 3.18 (page 116) lists some potential lagging indicators for explicit goals for students' status and growth. From this list, the leader would then select trim tab indicators to create a customized high reliability scale. Figure 3.19 (page 117) depicts a possible customized scale a school leader might design for school-level indicator 12, explicit goals for students' status and growth.

	Middle-of-year interim assessment	End-of-year interim assessment	Proficiency scale scores	End-of-year state assessment	SAT
Mathematics	5 percent	10 percent	30 percent	5 percent	5 percent
English Language Arts	5 percent	10 percent	30 percent	5 percent	5 percent
Science	5 percent	10 percent	30 percent	5 percent	N/A

FIGURE 3.17: Percentage gain goals.

Programs and Practices	Lagging Indicator Data	Potential Standard for High Reliability Status
Proficiency scale goals	Data regarding each student's status and growth on measurement topics	90 percent of class goals are met 90 percent of individual student goals are met
External test goals	Data regarding each student's status and growth on external tests	90 percent of schoolwide goals are met
Percentage gain goals	Percentage gain scores on various internal and external assessments	90 percent of schoolwide goals are met
Perceptions of students, teachers, and parents	Surveys of students, teachers, and parents	90 percent of teachers report that setting goals for students has been beneficial to student learning 90 percent of students report that setting goals has helped them learn

FIGURE 3.18: Potential lagging indicators and criteria for school-level indicator 12.

Summary

This chapter addressed the third phase of implementing the Marzano Academies model at the secondary level. The school-level indicators for this phase represent important elements of the model that might seem like isolated initiatives with their own specific purposes, but in fact fill in important pieces of the whole. Metaphorically, without these indicators, the model would have the basic skeletal structure of a CBE system but there would be little meat on the bones. The same can be said of the indicators in phase 4.

The four school-level indicators to implement during phase 3 are as follows.

1. **Cognitive and metacognitive skills (SLI 10):** The school has well-articulated measurement topics and proficiency scales for cognitive and metacognitive skills that are systematically taught and assessed throughout the curriculum.

2. **Vocabulary (SLI 11):** The school has programs and practices in place to ensure that all students have a working knowledge of tier one, tier two, and tier three vocabulary.

Evidence	
4 **Sustaining** **(quick data)**	Quick data like the following are systematically collected and reviewed: • Examination of growth scores and summative scores in the LMS • Examination of benchmark assessment scores • Examination of end-of-year assessment scores
3 **Applying** **(lagging)**	Performance goals with clear criteria for success like the following are in place: • 90 percent of schoolwide goals are met • 90 percent of class goals are met • 90 percent of individual student goals are met
2 **Developing** **(leading)**	• Schoolwide goals using external assessments are in place and monitored • Teacher-level goals are in place and monitored • Individual student goals are in place and systematically monitored
1 **Beginning**	• The school has written goals but those goals are not translated into quantifiable student outcomes • The school has written goals but they do not address both status and growth
0 **Not Using**	• The school has no written goals for students' status and growth • Data regarding student status and growth are not analyzed

Source: © 2020 by Marzano Academies, Inc. Adapted with permission.

FIGURE 3.19: Customized high reliability scale for school-level indicator 12.

3. **Blended instruction (SLI 6):** The school procures online resources and engages teachers in activities that help them develop online activities for score 2.0, 3.0, and 4.0 content on all proficiency scales.

4. **Explicit goals for students' status and growth (SLI 12):** The school has explicit goals for students' status and growth at the individual student level and at the school level.

As before, school leaders should ask the following five questions while they are implementing these indicators.

1. Do the changes in this phase suggest that we should address any school or district policies?

2. Do the changes in this phase suggest that we should address any board of education policies?

3. Do the changes in this phase suggest that we should address any state-level policies?

4. Do the changes in this phase suggest we should address any contractual policies?

5. Do the changes in this phase create or lessen any inequities?

When addressing these questions, the leadership team might determine that the indicator for cognitive and metacognitive skills should be brought to the teachers union for approval as it represents a change in the overall curriculum. They might also decide that the indicator for blended instruction should be presented to the school board since it has significant implications for the school budget. Finally, they decide that the indicator for vocabulary has the potential to address inequities in students' background knowledge and decide to gather data on its implementation to verify its effects.

CHAPTER 4

Phase 4: Finishing Strong

Journalist B. C. Forbes is commonly credited as the author of the well-known statement, "How you start is important, but it is how you finish that counts" (QuoteFancy, n.d.). This certainly applies to CBE implementation. The final phase of implementation should involve powerful and meaningful programs and practices that put the finishing touches on the school's CBE model. The four school-level indicators in this phase, although very different in their focus, all send a message that the academy has a common way of engaging in the teaching and learning process and even a common way of talking about the teaching and learning process. The four school-level indicators addressed in phase 4 are as follows.

1. Personal projects (SLI 4)

2. Cumulative review (SLI 7)

3. Knowledge maps (SLI 8)

4. Collective responsibility (SLI 15)

The following sections detail each one.

Personal Projects (SLI 4)

While some academic content holds deep interest for students, it is also true that secondary students are interested in a wide variety of topics and issues, many of which are nowhere to be found in the academic curriculum. Therefore, it is prudent for secondary educators to offer opportunities to explore areas that are connected to students' lives and related to their interests (Brough, Bergmann, & Holt, 2006). The school-level indicator of personal projects accomplishes this. Here we discuss capstone projects, personal projects, and the integral link to metacognitive skills.

Capstone Projects

A *capstone* is the final decorative stone placed on a building or a monument. In education, particularly at the high school and college levels, capstone projects are the final projects students complete to demonstrate their ability to organize information focused on a particular topic or issue into a unified whole. Capstone projects are powerful. In the academy model, they should exhibit specific characteristics.

The student must have control over the topic of the capstone project. More specifically, students should be able to select the academic domain or domains on which the project will focus (for example, mathematics, art, music, science, health, physical education, athletics, and so on). Within the selected domain or domains, students should be able to select specific issues they might address. For example, if a student selects the domain of mathematics, they should be able to identify a specific issue within mathematics on which to focus, such as an investigation of the historical origins of calculus.

Capstone projects should employ a concrete process with discernable steps and milestones. To this end, it is very useful for teachers to use the six knowledge application processes described in school-level indicator 10 (chapter 3, page 88), which are designed to guide students through the execution of complex tasks (Marzano, 2019). For each of the six knowledge application skills (decision making, problem solving, invention, experimental inquiry, investigation, and systems analysis), there is a concrete set of steps that students can follow to execute that skill (see Marzano et al., 2022). For example, the following steps comprise the process for investigation.

1. Identify the type of investigation you are going to do (definitional, historical, or projective) and the specific question you will be answering—What event or idea do I want to explain?

2. Gather the necessary information to be able to describe what is already known about your topic—What do people already know?

3. Summarize what is already known—What is the best way to relate what people already know?

4. Based on what is already known, describe one or more confusions or contradictions—What confusions do people have or what contradictions are present for this idea or event?

5. Select at least one confusion or contradiction and develop a plausible resolution, collecting more information to support your resolution if necessary—What suggestions do I have for clearing up these confusions or contradictions? How can I defend my suggestions?

6. Evaluate how well you have done in your investigation and summarize what you have learned—How do I feel about the investigation? What have I learned?

As is the case with other skills and procedures, teachers should model each step and provide guidance as students learn the knowledge application processes. The following sections cover how each knowledge application skill might form the basis of a capstone project.

Decision Making

Decision making is the process of generating and applying criteria to select between alternatives that appear equal. Relative to a capstone project, a student might choose to study important decisions that have been made historically. For example, a student who is interested in the domain of history might examine the decision President Truman made to drop the atomic bombs on Japan in August of 1945. During the project, the student would collect primary-source information on that decision and come up with reasonable estimates of the different alternatives that were being considered, criteria that were used to select among the alternatives, and the importance Truman and his team likely applied to the various criteria.

Another student interested in science might design a decision-making capstone project around the alternative actions being proposed to arrest the negative effects of climate change. The student would articulate the criteria that she will use when selecting among alternatives and the relative importance of the various alternatives. Based on these parameters, the student would then select an alternative and explain the logic underlying her decision.

Problem Solving

At its core, problem solving can be described as the process of addressing and overcoming constraints and limiting conditions that are impeding the accomplishment of a goal. As a capstone project, one student interested in health might study the problem-solving process related to the COVID-19 vaccination effort. This initiative certainly involved obstacles and limiting conditions. In the student's study of how this problem was addressed, they would report on:

- The original goal
- The obstacles or limiting conditions
- The solutions that were considered
- Why the final solution was selected
- Whether an alternative goal had been considered

Alternatively, students might undertake problem-solving capstone projects to define and attempt to solve problems in their own lives. For example, music students who are working on a specific classical piece for the piano might realize that the fingering provided for a specific piece doesn't work for the size and shape of their hands. They might alter the protocol to account for the physical constraints they must operate with. They would develop the new fingering protocol and describe the changes they made and why they made them. Finally, they would perform the piece using the new fingering protocol.

Invention

Invention is the process of creating a new process or product that meets a specific identified need. In a sense, it might be likened to problem solving in that it addresses a specific need. However, problem solving is limited in duration. Once the initial obstacle or limiting condition has been overcome, the problem-solving process ends. Invention commonly starts by trying to overcome a problem but it continues over time as the new process or product keeps getting refined.

Capstone projects might explore historical inventions or endeavor to invent something new. A science student interested in the early uses of electricity might examine the process Thomas Edison followed to come up with a durable filament for his light bulb. The student would report on early versions of the filament, changes that Edison made in the various versions of the filament, and the standards Edison set for the new invention. A student interested in mechanical engineering might attempt to design a conversion kit that can be used to transform a normal bicycle into one with a motor that the rider can charge by pedaling and then use to propel the bicycle without the need to pedal anymore.

Experimental Inquiry

Experimental inquiry is the process of generating a hypothesis about a physical or psychological phenomenon and then testing the hypothesis. As an experimental inquiry capstone project, a physics student might examine the Manhattan Project, which resulted in the first atomic bomb. The student might focus on describing the observations that were made, the hypotheses that were generated, how the hypotheses were tested, and how theories were changed.

A student interested in nutrition and health might keep a log of her exercise and nutrition routine over a two-week period of time. The student would note the time of day, how long before and after a meal she exercised, the type of meal, and how effective the exercise seemed to be. At the end of the two weeks, the student would examine her data and generate a hypothesis about the best ways for her to exercise. She would then design her individual routine, try it out for a month, and then analyze the results in terms of the effectiveness of the new exercise routine.

Investigation

Investigation is the process of identifying and then resolving differences of opinion or contradictory information about concepts, historical events, or future possible events. As this definition implies, there are three types of investigation tasks (Marzano, 2021b).

1. **Definitional investigation:** Designing and defending a precise definition for a concept for which there is no generally agreed-on definition and differing opinions

2. **Historical investigation:** Articulating and defending an explanation for a past event for which there is no generally agreed-on account and differing opinions as to what occurred

3. **Projective investigation:** Articulating and defending a prediction for a possible future event for which there is no generally agreed-on account and differing opinions as to what might occur

The investigation process offers students a great many options for capstone projects. For example, a student interested in coral reefs might investigate a 1972 project off the coast of Florida during which two million old tires were dropped into the ocean about a mile offshore in an effort to create an artificial reef. While the project was conceived with good intentions, it did not turn out well. In fact, the artificial reef turned out to be a huge environmental problem. For the project, the student would investigate what happened and how the issue was addressed.

A student interested in journalism might study the famous investigations conducted by Bob Woodward and Carl Bernstein around the Watergate scandal in the early 1970s. The student would undertake the following actions as part of the investigation process for the project.

- Describe the general findings articulated by Woodward and Bernstein.

- Describe how they collected their information.

- Describe controversies associated with Woodward and Bernstein's conclusions.

- State a position regarding one or more of the controversies and defend that position.

Systems Analysis

Systems analysis is the process of describing and analyzing the parts of a system with particular emphasis on the relationships among the parts. As a capstone project, a science student who has become interested in open systems might analyze how students engage in schools. The science student would articulate the way students come to school in the morning, take classes during the day, and then return home as an open system. The student would identify the boundaries of the system, the component parts and subparts of the system, and how those parts and subparts interact.

A student interested in history might examine the conceptual development of how humanity has understood the solar system, from the origins of astronomy to the current understanding of the parts of the solar system and how they interact. The student would address the following questions as part of the systems analysis.

- How have notions of the parts of the solar system changed?

- How have notions of the boundaries of the solar system changed?

- How have notions of the relationships between the planets and the sun changed?

In summary, capstone projects are an option schools might use for this school-level indicator since they provide students with creative latitude relative to domains, topics, and execution.

The Personal Project

The other option within this indicator is simply known as *the personal project*. Personal projects allow students to work on short-term or long-term goals of their own design regardless of whether those goals have any connection to academic content. They provide students with the most flexibility for voice and choice. The academy model for personal projects involves seven phases.

Phase I: Identifying a personal goal to pursue

Phase II: Eliciting support

Phase III: Gathering information about the goal

Phase IV: Discerning discrepancies between current and future self

Phase V: Creating a plan

Phase VI: Moving into action

Phase VII: Evaluating the effectiveness of your actions

The specifics of these phases are described in detail in the book *Motivating and Inspiring Students* (Marzano, Scott, et al., 2017). Briefly, though, the working dynamic of a personal project is that each year, each student selects a project to work on and progresses through these seven phases. A student might select a different topic each year. For example, a seventh-grade student might select the goal of learning how to play the guitar. The next year that same student as an eighth grader might set the goal of learning how to play the drums. Alternatively, students might select long-term goals that represent dreams they have about themselves in the future. For example, a student might select the long-term goal of visiting specific countries by the time she is twenty-one. Another student might set the long-term goal of a military career, and so on.

Each of the seven phases is designed to teach students something about their goal and about themselves. Phase I (identifying a personal goal) teaches students about the specifics of goal setting and how to articulate goals. To illustrate, consider the example of a ninth grader named Maria. One of the activities in the first phase of the personal project process is to respond to the prompt, What would you do if you knew you wouldn't fail? Maria's response is to declare that she would like to be a fighter pilot in the Navy. Her teacher or advisor provides her with guidance as to how to set an effective long-term goal, such as having a concrete outcome, specific timelines, and concrete components.

Phase II (eliciting support) helps students understand the nature and importance of support from others while working toward a goal; it further helps students create a system of support for their personal goals. Maria realizes that she will need support to accomplish such a lofty goal and it can come from a variety of sources. As part of this phase, Maria identifies people she will ask to support her. She selects her aunt who was in the Marines to help her learn about the military lifestyle. She selects her mother as her coach regarding how to live a disciplined yet balanced life.

Phase III (gathering information about the goal) guides students to begin finding out what they need to know and be able to do to realize their goals. Maria researches key steps along the path to being a Navy pilot, including going to college and getting a technical degree, knowing how and when to enlist in the Navy, keeping herself in good physical shape, and so on.

Phase IV (discerning discrepancies between current and future self) requires students to examine their current actions and habits and identify changes they might have to make in themselves to accomplish their goals. Maria compares skills and knowledge she has now with those she will need to fully realize her goal. During this phase, Maria sees that there are some habits she will have to acquire and some current habits she will have to get rid of.

Phase V (creating a plan) requires students to actually create written plans, mapping out the steps they will have to take to accomplish their goals. Maria writes a fairly detailed plan that lays out specific events and timelines.

Phase VI (moving into action) requires students to identify and engage in actions that they can take immediately relative to their goals. Maria identifies those things she can do right now that might be small steps to her ultimate goal. As a small step, she initiates a specific exercise routine. She reads about the type of technical skills that fighter pilots should have, such as a good sense of orientation in space.

Finally, during phase VII (evaluating the effectiveness of your actions), students reflect on what they have done. Maria continually assesses how well she is doing, identifying and celebrating those things that are going well and those things she can improve on.

School leaders should ensure they provide a clear explanation to faculty as to why personal projects are important for every student, as well as create clear, easy-to-follow instructional protocols for when and how personal projects will be deployed.

Metacognitive Skills and Personal Projects

The seven phases of the personal projects are excellent vehicles to teach and reinforce virtually any of the metacognitive skills (SLI 10, chapter 3, page 88). Recall that the metacognitive skills in the academy model are as follows.

1. Staying focused when answers and solutions are not immediately apparent

2. Pushing the limits of one's knowledge and skills

3. Generating and pursuing one's own standards for performance

4. Seeking incremental steps

5. Seeking accuracy

6. Seeking clarity

7. Resisting impulsivity

8. Seeking cohesion and coherence

9. Setting goals and making plans

10. Growth mindset

When executed well, personal projects implicitly help students utilize many of these skills. For example, students are asked to push the limits of their knowledge and skills and set their own standards for excellence as they develop their plans. They must seek accuracy and clarity as they research the requirements of their goals. In addition to relying on the implicit reinforcement of the metacognitive skills, teachers can use personal projects to directly teach and reinforce selected skills. A specific teacher might select one or two metacognitive skills for students to demonstrate as they engage in their personal projects.

High Reliability Leadership for School-Level Indicator 4

Figure 4.1 lists some potential lagging indicators for personal projects. From this list, the leader would then select trim tab indicators to create a customized high reliability scale. Figure 4.2 depicts a possible customized scale a school leader might design for school-level indicator 4, personal projects.

Programs and Practices	Lagging Indicator Data	Potential Standard for High Reliability Status
Capstone projects	Protocols for completion of capstone projects	90 percent of students complete capstone projects 90 percent of teachers follow the written protocols for capstone projects
Personal projects	Protocols for personal projects	90 percent of students complete personal projects 90 percent of teachers follow the written protocols for personal projects
Metacognitive skills and personal projects	Specific metacognitive skills embedded in personal projects	90 percent of teachers embed specific metacognitive skills in personal projects or capstone projects
Perceptions of students, teachers, and parents	Surveys of students, teachers, and parents	90 percent of students say they enjoy and value their personal projects or capstone projects

FIGURE 4.1: Potential lagging indicators and criteria for school-level indicator 4.

Evidence	
4 **Sustaining** **(quick data)**	Quick data like the following are systematically collected and reviewed: • Quick conversations with students, teachers, and parents • Artifacts from personal projects or capstone projects, which are archived
3 **Applying** **(lagging)**	Performance goals with clear criteria for success like the following are in place: • 90 percent of students complete personal projects or capstone projects • 90 percent of teachers embed specific metacognitive skills in personal projects or capstone projects • 90 percent of teachers follow the written protocols for personal projects or capstone projects • 90 percent of students say they enjoy and value their personal projects or capstone projects
2 **Developing** **(leading)**	• Personal projects or capstone projects are in place that provide students opportunities to work on projects of their own design that demonstrate multiple types of skills • Personal projects or capstone projects have well-defined phases • Metacognitive skills are identified for use in personal projects or capstone projects
1 **Beginning**	• The school has written plans for the use of personal projects or capstone projects but there is no implementation at the school level • Some teachers implement their own versions of personal projects or capstone projects but there is no schoolwide approach
0 **Not Using**	• The school has no written plans for the use of personal projects or capstone projects • There is no implementation of personal projects or capstone projects at the classroom level

Source: © 2020 by Marzano Academies, Inc. Adapted with permission.

FIGURE 4.2: Customized high reliability scale for school-level indicator 4.

Cumulative Review (SLI 7)

The school-level indicator of cumulative review is designed to ensure Marzano Academies students have multiple opportunities to review and revise content they are learning. The cumulative review process makes extensive use of recall. Unfortunately, the cognitive process of recall has been much maligned in K–12 education. When educators think of recall, they think of a lower-order operation. This negative interpretation can be traced to what is popularly referred to as Bloom's taxonomy (Bloom, 1956) and its later revision (Anderson & Krathwohl, 2001). In the 1956 version, the lowest order of cognition was *recall of knowledge*; in the 2001 version, the lowest order of cognition was referred to as *remembering*. Since then, the field of neuroscience has established the fact that when employed properly, the act of recall or remembering can be one of the most powerful learning tools available to students. As learning researchers Barbara Oakley, Beth Rogowsky, and Terry Sejnowski (2021) described in their book *Uncommon Sense Teaching*, when students use recall as a learning tool, they don't just download stored information in a verbatim fashion. Instead, recall involves reassembling information from permanent memory into working memory. Each time students do this, it provides an opportunity for them to reshape and improve their understanding of the content recalled. This is the essence of cumulative review as employed in the academy model.

The Process of Cumulative Review

The cumulative review process is designed to be used systematically throughout the year in every class. Of course, the idea of review is not new in K–12 education, but the connected nature of the cumulative review sessions in the academy model is new. In general, cumulative review sessions are designed to help students not only recall and reprocess what they have recently learned but also make connections with content that goes back to the beginning of the year. Ideally, cumulative review is done once per week or, at least, once every other week.

To illustrate, assume that a ninth-grade health class addressed twenty measurement topics over the course of the year. Each topic represents a specific measurement topic and each measurement topic has an associated proficiency scale. Assume the first topic was addressed in a unit that spanned the first two weeks of school. The first cumulative review session would focus on the content from that topic. During the second two weeks, topic 2 would be addressed. Now the cumulative review session embedded in this unit would address the content from topic 2 and would make any logical connections to the content in topic 1. By the time the last unit of the year was presented with a focus on topic 20, students and teachers would be making connections with this new content and the content in previous topics where appropriate. This is not to say that during the final unit, the cumulative review process would be designed to review all nineteen previous topics. Rather, the connections would be only those that make intuitive sense and help deepen students' understanding of the original content and any relationships that have been disclosed through the process.

The cumulative review process has three distinct phases: (1) recording, (2) reviewing, and (3) revising. Each phase is intentional and requires students to do something different with the content.

Recording

In the first phase of cumulative review, students record what they have learned about a topic that the teacher has introduced to them. Typically, this is recently taught content. For example, if the cumulative review session were conducted on the Friday of the first week of a unit, students would record what they think they know about the content that had been presented that week. In their recordings, students represent what they understand about the content using their own words or representations. Students might do this by recording brief summaries of the content or creating graphic organizers depicting their understanding. This phase requires students to recall information from memory and represent it in words, symbols, pictures, or a combination of all these formats. By the end of the recording phase, students should have a concise representation of what they believe to be true about the topic that is the subject of cumulative review.

Reviewing

The reviewing phase of the cumulative review process requires students to examine or test their understandings of the content they have just recorded. The teacher might simply ask students to explain why they believe their representations are accurate or why they believe a certain piece of content to be true. Students might first respond in writing and then share their responses with the whole class or in small groups.

Another activity teachers can use in the review phase is practice test items that relate directly to the content. To this end, the book *Ethical Test Preparation in the Classroom* (Marzano, Dodson, et al., 2022) provides teachers with clear guidance regarding prevalent topics and common types of items that appear on standardized tests in ELA, mathematics, and science. Knowing this, teachers can use the cumulative review process to ensure that students not only know the important content but also become familiar with the types of questions they will encounter on high-stakes tests. For example, a mathematics teacher might present the practice test question in figure 4.3 during the reviewing phase of the cumulative review process.

Prudence bought a book that had a 30 percent discount off its original price. The total amount she paid was d dollars, including an 11 percent sales tax on the discounted price. Which of the following represents the original price of the book in terms of d?

A. $0.81d$ B. $\dfrac{d}{0.81}$ C. $(0.7)(1.11)d$ D. $\dfrac{d}{(0.7)(1.11)}$

Source: Marzano, Dodson, et al., 2022, p. 311.

FIGURE 4.3: Sample practice test item for mathematical expressions.

Within the cumulative review process, teachers can create specific types of items for specific content and engage students in detailed discussions about the nuances of the content they are reviewing as well as the nuances of the types of items that are used to assess the content. These discussions provide students with insights into themselves as learners and as test takers. Teachers can even have students create their own examples of specific types of items and analyze how their items can be made easier or harder to answer simply based on the construction of the item.

Revising

Revising is the third phase of the cumulative review process. It is the step where learners formally add to and make changes in what they thought they knew to be true. It is also the step where students can forge linkages to previous content. To this end, teachers typically stimulate student revisions by asking questions like the following.

- What gaps have you discovered in your understanding?

- What new information have you added to what you previously knew?

- What errors in your previous thinking have you corrected?
- What relationship have you found between this content and what we have previously addressed in class?

Students can use the corrections and connections they identify in response to these prompts to update their understanding and representations (notes and so on) of the content.

Support for Cumulative Review

The school leader should be cognizant of and plan for necessary support for teachers to implement cumulative review. Probably the best place to start is the reason behind this process. Veteran teachers might bring up questions about the emphasis on recall. This is an important issue to address overtly. Leaders will find that when faculty and staff actually delve into the nature of recall and the research on its importance, they quickly become advocates for the cumulative review process. As mentioned previously, one of the biggest misconceptions a leader will likely have to address is that recall is a lower-order cognitive process involving verbatim repetition of previously learned information. Engaging in book studies with resources like *Uncommon Sense Teaching* (Oakley et al., 2021) can be of great benefit in changing teachers' views.

The school leader should make frequent visits to classrooms using cumulative review and collect success stories and examples of best practices. One of the more powerful things leaders can do in this regard is interview students about their experiences and relate the results of these interviews to faculty. Leaders might record some of their interviews with students and share them with faculty. Doing so can lead to open discussions with teachers about ways to make cumulative review as powerful as possible.

High Reliability Leadership for School-Level Indicator 7

Figure 4.4 lists some potential lagging indicators for cumulative review. From this list, the leader would then select trim tab indicators to create a customized high reliability scale. Figure 4.5 depicts a possible customized scale a school leader might design for school-level indicator 7, cumulative review.

Programs and Practices	Lagging Indicator Data	Potential Standard for High Reliability Status
Cumulative review process	Data from classroom observations	90 percent of teachers systematically use the cumulative review process
Practice test items	Data from classroom observations	100 percent of teachers use sample test items in the cumulative review process and can explain why they are important to that process
Regular, frequent reviews	Data from classroom observations	100 percent of teachers use the cumulative process at least once every two weeks
Perceptions of students, teachers, and parents	Surveys of students, teachers, and parents	90 percent of teachers and 80 percent of students perceive cumulative review to be useful to their learning

FIGURE 4.4: Potential lagging indicators and criteria for school-level indicator 7.

Evidence	
4 **Sustaining** **(quick data)**	Quick data like the following are systematically collected and reviewed: • Reviews of teacher lesson plans and unit plans • Walkthrough observational data • Quick conversations with teachers and students
3 **Applying** **(lagging)**	• 100 percent of teachers use sample test items in the cumulative review process and can explain why they are important to that process • Observational data are in place indicating that 90 percent of teachers systematically use the cumulative review process • 90 percent of teachers and 80 percent of students perceive cumulative review to be useful to their learning
2 **Developing** **(leading)**	• Teachers follow specific protocols for systematically reviewing critical content • Cumulative review is executed on a systematic basis according to schedule
1 **Beginning**	• The school has written plans for the use of cumulative review but there is no implementation at the school level • Only a few teachers utilize cumulative review
0 **Not Using**	• The school has no written plans for the use of cumulative review • There is no implementation of cumulative review at the classroom level

Source: © 2020 by Marzano Academies, Inc. Adapted with permission.

FIGURE 4.5: Customized high reliability scale for school-level indicator 7.

Knowledge Maps (SLI 8)

Knowledge maps as used in the Marzano Academies model are a comprehensive system of what educators commonly refer to as *graphic organizers*. We use the term *knowledge maps* for two reasons. The first is that the typical use of graphic organizers is strongly engrained within K–12 education, hindering teachers' adoption of the approach we recommend. For the most part, educators use graphic organizers to help students visually organize information they have just learned (hence the term *graphic organizer*). Typically, once students have used a graphic organizer with certain content and perhaps discussed why they represented it a certain way, they move on to other activities and do not return to that graphic organizer. There is nothing inherently wrong with this use of graphic organizers. However, there are much more powerful and systematic ways to use graphic organizers, which lead to the second reason we prefer the term *knowledge maps*.

The term *knowledge maps* is intended to convey that learning involves creating a mental model or mental map of content. In effect, this occurs when students create a graphic representation of content. It is not the graphic representation itself that helps students understand the content; it is the corresponding representation in the students' minds that enhances their learning. The academy model's use of knowledge maps goes beyond students' drawing a knowledge map (and thus creating a mental model) for content, however. A central feature of employing knowledge maps is that teachers ask students to identify which knowledge maps are appropriate for representing certain content, rather than provide a single graphic organizer. Students should find multiple types of maps to represent information. For example, when students read an expository passage about climate change, the teacher might ask them to identify at least two knowledge maps that they could use to organize the information in the passage. One student might make the case that the causation knowledge map and the problem-solution knowledge map both fit the content equally well. The general awareness such activities provide to learners is that comprehending information is a constructive process and there is typically more than one way to construct an overall understanding of information as presented.

To accommodate the wide range of content in the curriculum, there are various types of knowledge maps, which we discuss next.

Types of Knowledge Maps

Each type of knowledge map represents a unique type of content. Additionally, the Marzano Academies maps progress from simple to complex to accommodate the increasing level of complexity of academic content as students progress through the grades. In all, there are fourteen different types of knowledge maps. Figure 4.6 depicts the continuum of knowledge maps from preK to grade 12 for each of the fourteen types. Ideally, a secondary school would coordinate the use of knowledge maps with its feeder schools so that the teachers throughout a student's education are using consistent terminology and graphic representations.

To illustrate the spiral nature of knowledge maps in terms of their complexity and how teachers at various levels might use them, consider the category of collections. At their core, collection maps are lists. There are four different collection knowledge maps, one for each of the four grade-level bands.

- Simple list (K–2)
- Combined list (3–5)
- Intersecting list (6–8)
- Nested list (9–12)

A simple list is an articulation of items that fit in a category. Figure 4.7 shows the generic form of a simple list knowledge map. For example, a music teacher might engage K–2 students in a unit of instruction that introduces them to different types of musical instruments. As a knowledge representation activity, the teacher simply asks students to list the various instruments mentioned in the unit.

category
item
item
item
item
item

Source: © 2017 by Marzano Resources. Used with permission.

FIGURE 4.7: Simple list knowledge map.

- Trombone
- Trumpet
- French horn
- Cello
- Violin
- Flute
- Clarinet
- Oboe
- Bassoon
- Harp

Structure	PreK	K–2	3–5	6–8	9–12
1. Basic Relationships	x	x	x	x	x
2. Description	x	x	x	x	x
3. Sequence	simple	x	complex	x	x
4. Causation		simple	complex	x	x
5. Problem-Solution		simple	complex	advanced	x
6. Comparison		x	x	x	x
7. Collection		simple lists	combined lists	intersecting lists	nested lists
8. Classification		simple	complex	x	x
9. Argumentation		simple	complex	x	x
10. Reasoning				inductive	x
				deductive	x
11. Systems		process	x	x	x
		cycle	x	x	x
		flowchart	x	x	x
			system	x	x
12. Episode			x	x	x
13. Metaphor			x	x	x
14. Analogy			x	x	x
TOTALS	3	12	16	18	18

Source: © 2020 by Marzano Academies, Inc. Used with permission.

FIGURE 4.6: Vertical alignment of knowledge maps.

item category	data category	data category
item	data	data
item	data	data
item	data	data
item	data	data
item	data	data

Source: © 2017 by Marzano Resources. Used with permission.

FIGURE 4.8: Combined list knowledge map.

Musical Instrument	Type of Instrument	Typical Pitch Range
Trombone	Brass	Medium
Trumpet	Brass	High
French horn	Brass	High
Cello	String	Low
Violin	String	High
Flute	Woodwind	High
Clarinet	Reed	Medium
Oboe	Reed	High
Bassoon	Reed	Low
Harp	String	Low, Medium, and High

FIGURE 4.9: Combined list of instruments, categories, and pitches.

data category A / data category B	data	data
data		item
data	item item	
data	item	item
data		item item
data	item	

Source: © 2017 by Marzano Resources. Used with permission.

FIGURE 4.10: Intersecting list knowledge map.

At the level of grades 3–5, teachers would give students a more complex task using the combined list knowledge map. A combined list pairs a collection of items with data for each item. Figure 4.8 shows the generic form of the combined list knowledge map. For example, the music teacher might ask upper elementary students to create a combined list that incorporates the following categories of instruments.

- Strings
- Reeds
- Brasses
- Woodwinds

In effect, when students use a combined list knowledge map, they are representing the target content as belonging to multiple categories. Students could also pair the instruments with data about their typical pitch range: high, medium, or low. A combined list map depicting the instruments, their categories, and their ranges might look like figure 4.9.

In grades 6–8, students employ the intersecting list knowledge map, which eliminates the redundancy of the combined list. Figure 4.10 shows the generic form of the intersecting list knowledge map. Using the same information about the instruments depicted previously, an intersecting list knowledge map might use instrument categories on one axis and the pitch range of instruments on the other axis. This is depicted in figure 4.11.

The nested list is introduced at the high school level (9–12). It allows for the creation of an intersecting list that contains more than three sets of information. Figure 4.12 shows the generic form of the nested list knowledge map. Students using this map might decide to add data pertaining to how the various instruments are played (bowing, plucking, blowing, striking), and also indicate in which type of group (symphony orchestra, marching band) the instruments are typically played (see figure 4.13).

Support for Knowledge Maps

As with other new instructional practices, school leaders must support teachers as they learn about and implement knowledge maps. Leaders can begin by addressing why the Marzano

Academies system of knowledge maps is important. Virtually all teachers in a secondary school will be familiar with and already using graphic organizers in their own idiosyncratic ways. Therefore, the discussion should address reasons why teachers need to use the same maps and the same terminology. The simple answer to this question is that a common language provides students with consistency across content areas. When a science teacher asks students to organize content using the combined list knowledge map, she means the same thing as when the music teacher asks students to use the combined list map. Using the knowledge maps schoolwide facilitates and improves student learning.

Once teachers begin using knowledge maps in the classroom, the school leader should monitor their use, gathering information from walkthroughs and from discussions with teachers. While some teachers might use knowledge maps a great deal and others more sparingly, they should all refer to the maps by their proper names and allow students to choose which maps are most appropriate for specific content and within specific tasks.

	Low	Medium	High
String	Cello Harp	Harp	Violin Harp
Reed	Bassoon	Clarinet	Oboe
Brass		Trombone	Trumpet French horn
Woodwind			Flute

FIGURE 4.11: Intersecting list of instruments, categories, and pitches.

		data A1			data A2		
		data B1	data B2	data B3	data B1	data B2	data B3
data C1	data D1	item	item	item	item	item	item
	data D2	item	item	item	item	item	item
data C2	data D3	item	item	item	item	item	item
	data D4	item	item	item	item	item	item
data C3	data D5	item	item	item	item	item	item

Source: © 2017 by Marzano Resources. Used with permission.

FIGURE 4.12: Nested list knowledge map.

		Symphony			Marching Band		
	Category	High	Medium	Low	High	Medium	Low
Bowed or plucked	**Strings**	Violin	Viola Harp	Cello or Bass			
Blown through mouthpiece	**Reeds**	Oboe	Clarinet Saxophone	Bassoon		Clarinet Saxophone	Bassoon
	Brasses	Trumpet French horn	Trombone	Tuba	Trumpet Mellophone	Trombone	Tuba
	Woodwinds	Piccolo Flute			Piccolo Flute		
Striking a surface	**Percussion**	Triangle	Piano	Bass drum	Triangle		Bass drum

FIGURE 4.13: Nested list of instruments.

High Reliability Leadership for School-Level Indicator 8

Figure 4.14 lists some potential lagging indicators for knowledge maps. From this list, the leader would then select trim tab indicators to create a customized high reliability scale. Figure 4.15 depicts a possible customized scale a school leader might design for school-level indicator 8, knowledge maps.

Programs and Practices	Lagging Indicator Data	Potential Standard for High Reliability Status
Vertical alignment of knowledge maps	Documents describing the alignment of knowledge maps in various courses, subject areas, and grade levels	100 percent of teachers are aware of the alignment of knowledge maps in courses, subject areas, and grade levels
Professional development for knowledge maps	Virtual and in-person professional development regarding the use of knowledge maps	100 percent of teachers actively participate in the professional development activities
Systematic use of knowledge maps	Data from classroom observations	100 percent of teachers demonstrate systematic use of knowledge maps in their classrooms
Perceptions of students, teachers, and parents	Surveys of students, teachers, and parents	90 percent of students report that they understand knowledge maps and that the maps help their learning 100 percent of teachers respond that they understand how to use knowledge maps and employ them on a systematic basis

FIGURE 4.14: Potential lagging indicators and criteria for school-level indicator 8.

Collective Responsibility (SLI 15)

The school-level indicator of collective responsibility is directly related to the concept of collective efficacy, which was popularized by education scholars Jenni Donohoo, John Hattie, and Rachel Eells (2018) in an article titled "The Power of Collective Efficacy." The authors traced the concept of collective efficacy to the work of psychologist Albert Bandura in the 1970s. They noted that in 1977 Bandura observed that a group member's confidence in their teammates affects the team's overall performance for the better (Donohoo et al., 2018). When a team of individuals share the belief that they can overcome challenges through their unified efforts, that team is more effective than it would be if the competent individuals simply worked independently. In 1997, Bandura referred to this phenomenon as *collective efficacy*, which he defined as "a group's shared belief in its conjoint capability to organize and execute the courses of action required to produce given levels of attainment" (Bandura, 1997, p. 477).

Since then, there have been a number of studies conducted on the topic (see Eells, 2011), along with the development of instruments to measure the collective efficacy of educators in a school (see Eells, 2011; Goddard, 2002; Goddard, Hoy, & Woolfolk-Hoy, 2004). The event that solidified the prominence of collective efficacy in the minds of K–12 educators was its high ranking in Hattie's list of variables that are related to student achievement. Specifically, in 2015, Hattie ranked collective efficacy second among 195 variables in terms of its relationship with student achievement. This is

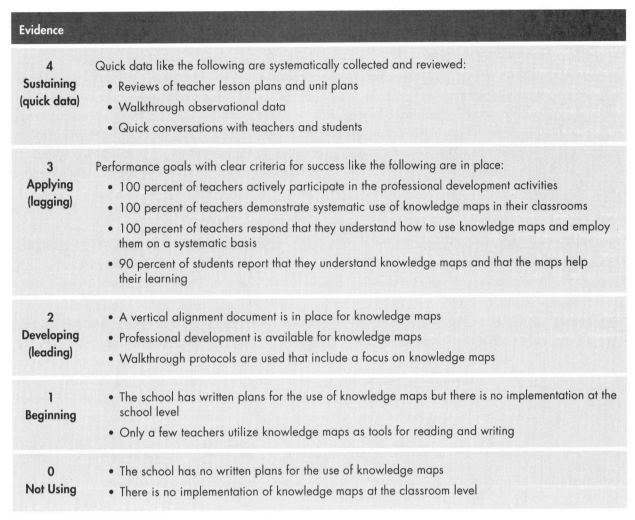

Evidence	
4 **Sustaining** **(quick data)**	Quick data like the following are systematically collected and reviewed: • Reviews of teacher lesson plans and unit plans • Walkthrough observational data • Quick conversations with teachers and students
3 **Applying** **(lagging)**	Performance goals with clear criteria for success like the following are in place: • 100 percent of teachers actively participate in the professional development activities • 100 percent of teachers demonstrate systematic use of knowledge maps in their classrooms • 100 percent of teachers respond that they understand how to use knowledge maps and employ them on a systematic basis • 90 percent of students report that they understand knowledge maps and that the maps help their learning
2 **Developing** **(leading)**	• A vertical alignment document is in place for knowledge maps • Professional development is available for knowledge maps • Walkthrough protocols are used that include a focus on knowledge maps
1 **Beginning**	• The school has written plans for the use of knowledge maps but there is no implementation at the school level • Only a few teachers utilize knowledge maps as tools for reading and writing
0 **Not Using**	• The school has no written plans for the use of knowledge maps • There is no implementation of knowledge maps at the classroom level

Source: © 2020 by Marzano Academies, Inc. Adapted with permission.

FIGURE 4.15: Customized high reliability scale for school-level indicator 8.

noteworthy not only for its high ranking but also for the fact that collective efficacy was not even mentioned in the previous lists of variables reported by Hattie (2009, 2012) as important correlates of student achievement.

Most of the discussion about collective efficacy has focused on what educators believe—do teachers believe, as a group, that they can advance student learning? In the academy model, belief is considered an important first step, but those beliefs must turn into concrete actions. The leader of a secondary school using the academy model can operationalize the underlying belief of collective efficacy by ensuring teachers share key responsibilities—hence the term *collective responsibility*. The following sections cover four ways teachers might engage in collective responsibility: recording evidence scores and summative scores, support for individual students, common planning, and transitions from level to level.

Recording Evidence Scores and Summative Scores

One powerful way to manifest collective responsibility in a secondary school is to have multiple teachers submit evidence scores for students on specific proficiency scales. Recall from the discussion of school-level indicator 13, classroom assessment (chapter 2, page 49), that teachers using the academy model collect multiple evidence scores for each student on each measurement topic. When implementing collective responsibility, multiple teachers submit evidence scores for a given student on a given topic.

To accomplish this, designate specific teachers as responsible for specific measurement topics; these teachers can enter evidence scores into the LMS for any students working on those topics. For example, consider the science measurement topics in a specific high school chemistry course. Certainly, the teacher of record for that course would enter multiple evidence scores for these measurement topics for each student in the class. In addition, though, other teachers who teach chemistry or have been vetted for their knowledge of chemistry could enter scores for these topics if they observe a student demonstrating knowledge or skill at a particular level of the proficiency scale. This would typically occur during the times when students are free to work with teachers other than those who are officially teaching a given course—FIT blocks or other flexible scheduling structures (SLI 16, chapter 1, page 36). A student who goes to the science bullpen during a FIT block for help with a chemistry measurement topic might receive instruction from a different teacher, but that teacher could still enter evidence scores into the LMS based on those interactions with the student.

A school might also expand collective responsibility for entering scores to assigning current summative scores. Specifically, groups of teachers who share responsibilities for teaching and assessing students on common measurement topics can periodically meet to examine evidence scores for students they have in common. Based on the evidence scores in the LMS, these teachers would come to agreements on a current summative score for each student. This can be especially useful when a student has a very uneven pattern of evidence scores for a particular measurement topic. High scores followed by low scores followed by more high scores, for example, can make it difficult to assign a summative score. Two or more teachers who have interacted with the student about the content might meet, examine the uneven pattern, and jointly arrive at the most reasonable summative score.

Support for Individual Students

Collective responsibility can also manifest in the school's systems of support for individual students. To illustrate, consider the response to intervention model. Within RTI, Tier 1 instruction (not to be confused with tier one vocabulary) refers to general classroom instruction, or core instruction, that all students will experience. Tiers 2 and 3 represent interventions that do not apply to all students. Tier 2 interventions are supplemental to what all students receive during regular instruction and typically occur in small-group settings. Working in collaborative teams, teachers identify groups of students with common needs and ensure those groups receive adequate and targeted instruction in those common areas of need. Such instruction might occur during a FIT block. Finally, Tier 3 interventions are for students whose specific needs are more significant and require one-to-one interaction. In many cases, such interventions require the attention of teachers who do not have whole-class responsibilities.

In the context of collective responsibility, teachers who interact with the same students would periodically meet to determine which students need Tier 2 or Tier 3 interventions and how best to structure those interventions in as effective and efficient a manner as possible.

Common Planning

Another way that secondary teachers can employ collective responsibility is through common planning. Instead of individual teachers creating their own idiosyncratic unit plans, teams of teachers operating collectively engage in this activity. For example, teachers responsible for content at the same grade level or in the same course might meet and design units. The collective unit design process should be guided by questions like the following.

1. What proficiency scales will this unit address? (Measurement topics and proficiency scales, SLI 9, page 41)

2. What specific instructional activities will teachers employ for various learning targets within the proficiency scales? (Instruction and teacher development, SLI 5, page 74)

3. What tier one, tier two, or tier three vocabulary will be part of the unit? (Vocabulary, SLI 11, page 96)

4. What knowledge maps will students use to represent the content? (Knowledge maps, SLI 8, page 129)

5. Which cognitive and metacognitive skills will the unit address? (Cognitive and metacognitive skills, SLI 10, page 88)

6. What topics will be addressed during cumulative review? (Cumulative review, SLI 7, page 126)

7. What types of classroom assessments will teachers use in this unit? (Classroom assessment, SLI 13, page 49)

As these questions indicate, collective unit planning brings together a number of school-level indicators. Question 1 requires collaborating teachers to determine the proficiency scales that will be the focus of a unit of instruction. Question 2 involves collaborating teachers determining which strategies from the forty-nine elements of the academy instructional model they will use throughout the unit. Question 3 requires teachers to make decisions about the tier three vocabulary terms (not to be confused with Tier 3 interventions) that will be directly taught to students during the unit and which, if any, tier one and tier two terms should be taught to specific students. Question 4 requires collaborating teachers to identify the specific knowledge maps that their classes will use with specific content within the unit. Question 5 has teachers identify the specific cognitive and metacognitive skills that they will introduce or reinforce within the unit. Question 6 involves the specific topics and activities that they will employ during cumulative review. Finally, question 7 deals with the types and timing of specific common assessments that teachers will use.

Collective planning requires participating teachers to articulate their ideas and values and then reconcile differences when they occur. For example, a team of teachers might initially disagree on which content to prioritize during cumulative review or which types of assessments to use. Coming to joint decisions about such issues distributes the responsibility for students' learning across the faculty.

Transitions From Level to Level

One of the most important types of decisions teachers in an academy must make is when students are ready to move up to the next level of content for a specific subject area. In middle school, such decisions might involve determining if particular students are ready to move from sixth-grade mathematics to seventh-grade mathematics. At the high school level, such decisions might involve moving from an introductory composition course to an advanced composition course. In a CBE system, teachers can make decisions regarding these transitions quarterly or even every six weeks.

Teachers who have been involved in entering evidence scores or determining current summative scores should meet periodically to determine if specific students should be moved up to a higher level of content. For example, after discussing a specific student they have in common, two teachers might strongly agree that the student would be best served by moving up a level so that she can engage in content that is more challenging to her and thus alleviate the boredom she seems to exhibit. For some students, teachers might deliberate on whether they should be moved down a level in the rare situations where a student does not seem to have mastered the content at the next lower level.

High Reliability Leadership for School-Level Indicator 15

Figure 4.16 lists some potential lagging indicators for collective responsibility. From this list, the leader would then select trim tab indicators to create a customized high reliability scale. Figure 4.17 depicts a possible customized scale a school leader might design for school-level indicator 15, collective responsibility.

Programs and Practices	Lagging Indicator Data	Potential Standard for High Reliability Status
Recording evidence scores and summative scores	Protocols for collectively assigning evidence scores and summative scores	100 percent of teachers engage in collective assignment of evidence scores and summative scores
Support for individual students	Protocols for collective decisions about student support	100 percent of teachers engage in collective decisions about addressing individual student needs
Common planning	Protocols for common planning	100 percent of teachers engage in collective unit planning
Transitions from level to level	Protocols for collective decisions regarding students' transitioning to different levels	100 percent of teachers engage in collective decisions about student transitions
Perceptions of students, teachers, and parents	Surveys of students, teachers, and parents	90 percent of teachers report that they participate in collective responsibility activities and that students benefit from these efforts

FIGURE 4.16: Potential lagging indicators and criteria for school-level indicator 15.

Summary

This chapter addressed the fourth phase of implementing the Marzano Academies model at the secondary school level. As with the phase 3 indicators, those in this phase help fill out the model such that it represents a comprehensive, integrated approach to competency-based education. The four school-level indicators to implement during this phase are as follows.

1. **Personal projects:** The school has programs and practices in place that allow students to engage in projects of their own design.

2. **Cumulative review:** The school has programs and practices in place that ensure students continually review and revise critical content and practice various forms of assessment relative to that content.

Evidence	
4 **Sustaining** **(quick data)**	Quick data like the following are systematically collected and reviewed: • Records from Empower indicating multiple teachers are providing evidence scores for measurement topics • Quick conversations with teachers and students about the extent to which multiple teachers are engaged in decisions about individual students
3 **Applying** **(lagging)**	Performance goals with clear criteria for success like the following are in place: • 100 percent of teachers engage in collective assignment of evidence scores and summative scores • 100 percent of teachers engage in collective decisions about student transitions • 100 percent of teachers engage in collective decisions about addressing individual student needs • 100 percent of teachers engage in collective unit planning
2 **Developing** **(leading)**	• Protocols are in place for teachers to collectively assign evidence scores and summative scores • Protocols are in place for teachers to collectively make decisions about student transitions • Protocols are in place for teachers to collectively make decisions about addressing individual students' needs • Protocols are in place for teachers to collectively develop unit plans
1 **Beginning**	• The school has written plans to facilitate collective responsibility but they are not specific enough to be actionable • Some teachers attempt to work with other teachers to implement their own versions of collective responsibility
0 **Not Using**	• The school has no written plans to facilitate collective responsibility • No teachers try to implement aspects of collective responsibility on their own

Source: © 2020 by Marzano Academies, Inc. Adapted with permission.

FIGURE 4.17: Customized high reliability scale for school-level indicator 15.

3. **Knowledge maps:** The school ensures that students use knowledge maps to comprehend and write various types of texts.

4. **Collective responsibility:** The school has programs and practices in place that ensure teachers collectively provide instruction, support, and assessments on measurement topics regardless of whose class students are officially assigned to.

As before, school leaders should ask the following five questions while they are implementing these indicators.

1. Do the changes in this phase suggest that we should address any school or district policies?

2. Do the changes in this phase suggest that we should address any board of education policies?

3. Do the changes in this phase suggest that we should address any state-level policies?

4. Do the changes in this phase suggest we should address any contractual policies?

5. Do the changes in this phase create or lessen any inequities?

When addressing these questions, the leadership team might determine that the indicators for cumulative review and collective responsibility should be brought to the teachers union for approval as they represent required aspects of the teaching and learning process. They might also decide that the indicator for personal projects should be presented to the school board since it has significant implications for the school budget. This might be the case when personal projects require students to seek experiences and resources outside of the school, like visiting a nearby training facility for a specific profession they aspire to.

Having outlined the four phases for implementing the Marzano Academies model, we next turn our attention to transformational leadership.

CHAPTER 5

The Four Roles of a
Transformational Leader

In his book *Futuring: The Exploration of the Future*, Edward Cornish (2004) said:

> We are all time travelers on a journey into the future. However, we are not tourists accompanied by a guide who can tell us just what lies ahead and will keep us safe and comfortable. Instead, we are explorers in an unknown and dangerous region that no one has ever seen before us. (p. 1)

One might legitimately make the claim that leading a secondary school trying to implement a CBE system is a bit of a journey into the future without precise instructions. Even though the previous four chapters provide guidance and benchmarks in terms of the school-level indicators, each secondary school embarks on a unique journey. Heeding Cornish's message, leaders of CBE middle schools and high schools should understand their roles as pioneers traveling into a new region of education.

Striking out into uncharted territory requires leaving behind old practices and mindsets that will steer you in the wrong direction. Leaders trying to effect the significant changes inherent in a move to CBE are sometimes the unwitting victims of misguided beliefs about leadership, making substantive change extremely difficult if not impossible. Specifically, limiting beliefs that hamper large-scale changes include the following.

1. School leaders must have buy-in before initiating an innovation.

2. Traditional secondary schools, particularly high schools, are too complex to transform.

3. A new innovation must perfectly mirror the latest trends, or some previously created intervention.

4. School leaders can effect significant change by evaluating teachers.

We maintain that to overcome these limiting beliefs, secondary leaders must think differently and behave differently. At an operational level, this involves cultivating their skills in four different roles, each of which mitigates the effects of a specific limiting belief. These roles are lead coalitionist, lead cultivator, lead creator, and lead coach. Table 5.1 (page 142) lists which leadership role counteracts each limiting belief.

In this chapter, we consider each role and the limiting belief it addresses. Through a detailed examination of each of these four leadership roles, we present practical strategies for implementing change and moving forward in your school.

TABLE 5.1: Leadership Roles and Limiting Beliefs

Limiting Belief	Leadership Role
School leaders must have buy-in before initiating an innovation.	Lead coalitionist
Traditional secondary schools, particularly high schools, are too complex to transform.	Lead cultivator
New innovations must perfectly mirror the latest trends, or some previously created intervention.	Lead creator
School leaders can effect significant change by evaluating teachers.	Lead coach

Lead Coalitionist

Educational leaders have traditionally tried to cultivate buy-in from teachers and other staff members before launching educational innovations. On the surface this makes some sense—if leaders are going to implement significant change, shouldn't they wait until those affected by the change agree that it is a good thing to do? While this idea has intuitive appeal, widespread buy-in rarely occurs in advance of second-order change.

Second-order change refers to changes to the existing paradigm, marking "a large break from the past" (Marzano et al., 2018, p. 145), as opposed to *first-order change*, which describes more basic changes within the current system. This is an important distinction for leaders of any type of organization, educational or otherwise. However, whether a change is second order or not is a matter of perception. In a secondary school, particularly a large one, there will most likely be some who perceive CBE as a necessary first-order change, and others who perceive it as a near-impossible or unnecessary second-order change. In the books *School Leadership That Works* (Marzano, Waters, & McNulty, 2005) and *District Leadership That Works* (Marzano & Waters, 2009), Marzano and colleagues applied the research and theory on first- and second-order change to K–12 schooling. Using different terminology, others have addressed these same two types of change (Argyris & Schön, 1974, 1978; Heifetz, 1994). Table 5.2 depicts some of the important characteristics of first-order and second-order change.

Even a cursory analysis of these characteristics demonstrates that leaders promoting initiatives that are second order in nature will have a much more difficult task than promoting initiatives that involve first-order changes. To determine the order of change regarding any type of initiative under consideration, a leader should ask the following questions.

- Are the changes a logical and incremental extension of what we have done in the past?

- Do the changes fit within our existing paradigms and beliefs?

- Are the changes consistent with prevailing values and norms?

- Can we implement the changes with the knowledge and skills we already possess?

- Can we implement the changes with the resources and conditions that are available to us?

- Is there general agreement that these changes are necessary?

TABLE 5.2: Characteristics of First-Order Change Versus Second-Order Change

First-Order Change	Second-Order Change
Is perceived as an extension of the past	Is perceived as a break with the past
Fits within existing paradigms	Lies outside existing paradigms
Is consistent with prevailing values and norms	Conflicts with prevailing values and norms
Can be implemented with existing knowledge and skills	Requires the acquisition of new knowledge and skills
Requires resources and conditions currently available to those responsible for implementing the innovations	Requires resources and conditions not currently available to those responsible for implementing the innovations
Is easily accepted because of common agreement that the innovation is necessary	Is easily resisted because only those who have a broad perspective of the school see the innovation as necessary

Source: Adapted from Marzano & Waters, 2009; Marzano et al., 2005.

Leaders can pose these questions to faculty and staff and collect and analyze their answers. By carefully examining the pattern of responses, leaders can determine if their stakeholders consider the proposed changes to be second-order change. If responses indicate that a majority or even a significant minority of constituents perceive the coming changes as second order, then the leader should not expect immediate or unquestioning buy-in. In addition to the fact that some people will perceive moving to a CBE system as second-order change, various other reasons can severely hamper buy-in, such as regressive bargaining unit stances, educational politics, and outdated state policies.

All of these obstacles notwithstanding, it is legitimate for a secondary leader to attempt to foster buy-in if for no other reason than such efforts will demonstrate a concern for the opinions and beliefs of all members of the school community. Stated differently, it is legitimate for school leaders to make efforts at buy-in even knowing that they will not accomplish universal agreement. Interestingly, the term *buy-in* does not necessarily mean the same thing to all secondary leaders. Education consultant Daniel Venables (2018) described buy-in as a necessary but intangible, amorphous commodity characterized by a commitment to embrace or try a new way of doing things or a novel idea. Education advisors Michael Fullan and Lyle Kirtman (2019) suggested that buy-in is less a function of beliefs than it is a byproduct of peoples' early involvement and input into an initiative that results in their ownership of a plan. We contend that educators commonly miss Fullan and Kirtman's point that buy-in is a *byproduct* of something else; to obtain buy-in, something else must have already happened. This flies in the face of current "common-sense" wisdom, which posits that before educational leaders attempt substantive change, they must have widespread buy-in or any one of a number of derivative responses such as enthusiasm, agreement, or support. Given the nature of buy-in and the inherent resistance to second-order change, we recommend that secondary leaders reduce their focus on obtaining buy-in and increase their efforts to build a coalition of the willing.

We define a *coalition of the willing* as a professional community comprised of previously separate individuals or smaller groups with diverse perspectives who are motivated to achieve various objectives of a broader shared vision. Unlike buy-in, a coalition of the willing does not seek universal agreement. It does not attempt to measure attitudes or emotions by asking if people *feel* included, whether they *enthusiastically* embrace the initiative or *support* a decision. A coalition of the willing does not ask all parties to accept the plan. Instead of focusing on feelings, enthusiasm, and expressions of support, a coalition of the willing gets people involved and creates a unified effort through authentic collaboration rather than chasing a sense of agreement. Table 5.3 compares characteristics between buy-in and a coalition of the willing.

TABLE 5.3: Comparison of Buy-In and a Coalition of the Willing

Buy-In	Coalition of the Willing
• Based on agreement • Asks team members to plan, usually in the form of SMART (strategic and specific, measurable, attainable, results oriented, time bound) goals • Pursues acceptance of the larger plan as valid from most individuals and groups • Relies on integrating all voices to gain support for the overall goal • Measures majority support through surveys • Ceases coalition-building efforts once an arbitrary level of agreement is reached (for example, once 75 percent of staff agree) • Ignores disagreement as long as the majority agrees • Must have agreement from superiors • Seeks to empower all team members • Must be obtained before launching the plan	• Based on collaboration • Unifies around a bold vision supported by SMART goals, targets, and tasks • Asks stakeholders to collaborate in pursuit of the goal • Joins people in pursuit of diverse objectives of the larger goal • Seeks input continually • Can be temporary or permanent based on need or purpose • Welcomes productive disagreement • Incorporates various smaller tasks that access people's specific interests • Relies on research and expertise to inform implementation • Seeks feedback from students, parents, and community members about the plan's implementation

Of course, to establish and maintain a coalition of the willing, secondary school leaders must shift their roles from salesperson to lead coalitionist. *Lead coalitionists* guide the coalition of the willing by laying out audacious visions that define the initiative's realistic long-term destination. Virtually all secondary leaders are aware of the importance of setting relatively short-term SMART goals. While this is certainly a good practice, the lead coalitionist understands the importance of keeping the shared vision alive. Big ideas are essential to innovation because they communicate the vision, expand mindsets, set direction, realign focus, and constrain tendencies to stray. After defining the school's audacious CBE vision, lead coalitionists deliberately parse that shared vision into SMART goals, supported by discrete targets and tasks that integrate the voices of the school's faculty, staff, students, parents, and community. The school's vision remains intact over time, always reminding the school community of the intended destination. At the same time, lead coalitionists use the vision as a filter to gather input from stakeholders regarding short-term objectives that reflect the various perspectives of the group. For example, one part of the school vision might be that all students have access to advanced courses. In turn, the school leader might ask for specific proposals as to how this might manifest. Only practices that align with the vision are allowed to move forward.

Instead of seeking agreement, lead coalitionists invite stakeholders to consider how their distinct interests align with the school's vision. Thus, individuals and smaller disparate groups may join the coalition of the willing for different reasons, but all understand the intended destination. The intent of such efforts is authentic collaboration, not agreement. For example, assume that a particular teacher is not a full supporter of the school's audacious vision of becoming the region's showcase school for personalized competency-based education (that is, the destination). However, the principal, functioning as a lead coalitionist, knows this teacher is sincerely interested in creating hope and celebrating students. So, the principal asks her to assist the vanguard team as they implement a new schoolwide program that acknowledges acts of kindness and recognizes academic achievement. After learning how important the program is and its direct connection to the school-level indicator of inspiration (SLI 3, chapter 1, page 29), the reluctant teacher agrees. She joins the coalition of the willing because the lead coalitionist connected her to a target that reflects her interests rather than trying to convince her to buy in. Over time, the reluctant teacher partners with others within the coalition whose interests align with her own. Together, they pursue the long-term vision of becoming a showcase school for CBE because they see their work as significant to the broader plan. The principal never asks the reluctant teacher to agree, accept, submit, or support.

With a compelling vision and strategically designed objectives, lead coalitionists can build their coalitions of the willing person by person and group by group. Out of necessity and with a sense of urgency, secondary school leaders must abandon the strategy of chasing an arbitrary level of the ambiguous notion of buy-in (such as establishing the rule that an initiative will not move ahead unless 75 percent of teachers indicate agreement on the survey). We believe such a perspective actually hinders the successful completion of new initiatives. As education leadership expert Douglas Reeves (2006) noted, "If you wait for people to have buy-in, be happy, or change belief systems, then change will never happen" (p. 97). Investing one's leadership energy into establishing a coalition of the willing is much more powerful and attainable. To establish a coalition of the willing, lead coalitionists can employ three key strategies: (1) building relational trust, (2) welcoming productive conflict, and (3) working with community influencers.

First, a lead coalitionist must establish relational trust with the stakeholders who will join the coalition and maintain it with existing members. Business management author Patrick Lencioni (2002) suggested that functioning cohesive teams rely on trust, and it is impossible to have teamwork without it. He defined trust as "the confidence among team members that their peers' intentions are good, and that there is no reason to be protective or careful around the group" (Lencioni, 2002, p. 195). Lead coalitionists foster a sense of openness, vulnerability, and honesty in relationships with and between coalition members. They also ensure members have confidence in each other when the team agrees and resist mistrust when disagreement occurs. Lead coalitionists understand that without trust, the team can quickly become dysfunctional. Educational leader Alan M. Blankstein (2004) maintained that trust and relationships hold a community together and that effective leaders create relational trust by demonstrating respect, personal regard, and integrity. Certainly, establishing relational trust is not a new concept. However, it is a crucial element of the role of lead coalitionist, whose responsibility is to hold together and expand a community of previously separate individuals and small groups with divergent opinions.

Second, while lead coalitionists work to maintain relational trust, they must also allow for conflict and diversity of thought. It's tempting for secondary school leaders to avoid conflict and stake their hopes on obtaining buy-in characterized by a sense of agreement. Many school leaders fall into the trap of excluding those whose views are different from their own. Unfortunately, in some schools and districts, professionals who ask informed, challenging questions, have divergent opinions, or disagree with decisions find themselves on the outside of an initiative, regarded as oppositional, negative, and resistant to change. Lead coalitionists build on relational trust by welcoming productive conflict, constructive criticism, purposeful disagreement, and divergent but informed opinions. Educators and authors Shelley Burgess and Beth Houf (2017) stated that leaders should create environments that welcome people with unique voices, value diversity of thought, and challenge one another's ideas without attacking. Lead coalitionists do not avoid conflict and ideological challenges; they embrace them as essential to solidifying the coalition. Lencioni (2002) argued that relationships that focus on quickly resolving issues and producing the best outcomes require productive conflict. While it's a natural tendency to view any dispute as destructive, lead coalitionists seek to strengthen innovative ideas by welcoming conflicting opinions, respecting those who challenge, and allowing open, and sometimes heated, debate. They understand that if they evade meaningful conflict and disagreement, the coalition of the willing cannot thrive or expand and is unlikely to produce the desired results.

Third, lead coalitionists know they cannot build a strong coalition by themselves; they cannot go it alone! Throughout the process of establishing and maintaining a coalition of the willing, lead coalitionists should surround themselves with people who have influence and information. Some of the key roles to consider are assistant principals, department chairs, instructional coaches, and other teacher-leaders. All these *second-chair leaders* have the potential to make or break the coalition. Education consultants Mike Bonem and Roger Patterson (2005) stressed the idea that the second-chair leaders' most valuable tool is their influence throughout the organization. In most high schools, second-chair leaders have executive authority over specific areas (for example, assistant principal for curriculum, science department chair, athletic director). Equally important are those who do not have formal titles, such as teachers known for their pedagogical skills and those who oversee coaching or helping other teachers. In all cases, the individual's influence—that is, people's readiness to follow them (Bonem & Patterson, 2005)—serves a vital function in building and maintaining a coalition of the willing. Stated plainly, principals influence faculty and staff by leveraging their broad perspective, but second chairs do so through their profound influence. Comprehensive middle schools and high schools tend to be too large for principals to have deep schoolwide influence. Therefore, principals should view the influence of their second chairs not as a threat but as an asset.

In addition to valuing influential team members, lead coalitionists also appreciate and incorporate individuals who have information. Social science author Malcolm Gladwell (2002) described information carriers as *mavens*—people who accumulate knowledge and then share and trade the information they have. Lead coalitionists would do well to identify and incorporate individuals in their schools who have this quality. Sometimes, they are easy to find. School leaders can simply look for those people who regularly "hold court" with members of the faculty and staff—those whom others seem to listen to and respect. To build a strong community, lead coalitionists must utilize the energy and determination of information carriers in the coalition of the willing. The dynamic combination of influencers and information carriers will be of great value to lead coalitionists as they unify the school community in pursuit of the vision.

In summary, one of the limiting beliefs school leaders must confront is the idea of obtaining buy-in before an initiative begins or throughout its implementation. School leaders should build coalitions instead of selling the initiative. Lead coalitionists focus on collaboration by building relational trust, valuing conflict and disagreement, and utilizing the influencers and information carriers within the organization. In response to the over-applied concept of buy-in, the shift to lead coalitionist is one of the most subtle but essential components of transformational leadership.

Lead Cultivator

The second limiting belief that hinders second-order change is that comprehensive middle schools and high schools are too large and too complex to transform. Leaders who are influenced by this belief will attempt innovations but limit their scope. For example, they might implement an SAT prep program but carefully select the students who have access to the program, join networks that give them opportunities to hang banners for school recognition, or partner with a new community-based program to offer more after-school and lunchtime tutoring but only for students whose scores are very close to demonstrating competence on the state test, thus prioritizing the appearance of improvement over learning for all students. In effect, the limiting belief that secondary schools are too large and complex to transform can make leaders focus on small regular gains in lieu of tackling systemic issues. To be sure, small gains and recognition are good things, but when they distract leaders from major issues within the system, they are harmful. Leaders who succumb to this limiting belief unwittingly become part of the inertia keeping traditional secondary education in place.

It is certainly true that secondary schools are complex organizations and high schools are the most complex of the lot. However, school leaders should resist the impulse to minimize the complexity and instead pivot to the role of lead cultivator. *Lead cultivators* communicate values, norms, learning, language, and everyday practices that continuously develop mindsets for systemic change. In agriculture, preparing for cultivation involves breaking up or loosening the soil to promote growth. The process destroys weeds around existing plants and increases water filtration and aeration. Lead cultivators confront the central problem of limiting mindsets around complexity by breaking it up or loosening it. They employ strategies that destroy unwanted beliefs, values, language, and practices that can choke desirable structures or practices. Lead cultivators recognize that a supportive culture is essential to the choice between taking risks for systemic change and tinkering with low-yield programmatic change.

To act as lead cultivators, secondary leaders must have the courage to change themselves. Too often, leaders who want to transform their schools do not recognize that they also must do things differently. Fullan and Kirtman (2019) concluded that the environment of leadership is changing; therefore, leadership must also change. Many aspects of a school's ecosystem are continually evolving, including policy, technology, instructional strategies, family structures, and the community. Leadership must change in response to alterations in the environments. To implement any innovation, lead cultivators must foster an innovative culture.

Lead cultivators seek out co-leaders who are within the school, district, or local area or who have extensive experience in the community. Some of the most effective school transformations have occurred when efforts include a mix of local and external experts (Tait & Faulkner, 2019). The combination of fresh perspectives tempered by hometown wisdom and oft-needed reality checks increases support for and sustainability of initiatives. Lead cultivators assemble teams that utilize local champions' knowledge and experience in combination with the creative thinking outside leadership can bring to the table.

Lead cultivators also listen to the interests of students, staff, and community members to identify their passions and beliefs, and use this information to assess the teams' overall commitment to the initiative (Tait & Faulkner, 2019). By taking intentional steps to listen and account for the teams' passions, lead cultivators add to the culture of collaboration. According to education scholars Steve Gruenert and Todd Whitaker (2017), the collaborative school culture is the optimal setting to which schools should aspire. Collaborative cultures are vital because they attract people and then support them (Fullan & Kirtman, 2019). By maintaining a culture that values its constituents' interests and believes in collaboration, lead cultivators construct teams of cultivators who work diligently to break up and loosen closed mindsets, readying them for systemic change. For example, a lead cultivator would identify specific formal and informal groups within the school and hold focus group interviews with them. This simple activity recognizes and values the opinions of these groups.

Lead cultivators must also make the decision not to waste time and energy on directly confronting people who will not get on board. Business leadership author Jon Gordon (2007) made this clear when he stated, "Some people are going to get on your bus and some people won't. Do not worry about the people who refuse to board your bus. Don't waste your energy on them" (p. 70). Recall that one of the unintended consequences of the limiting belief that school leaders must have buy-in before they can initiate an innovation is that substantive change never gets off the ground. Similarly, it's useful to remember that the task of lead cultivators is to break up and loosen all parts of the culture that do not reflect the values, norms, learning, language, and everyday practices of the coalition of the willing. Lead cultivators gently create cracks in the culture that allow for the members of the coalition to grow, for them to coalesce as a team, and for others to join (Gruenert & Whitaker, 2017).

In summary, the perceived organizational complexity of secondary schools has become a major obstacle to systemic innovation. Lead cultivators overcome this obstacle by nurturing and communicating values, norms, learning, language, and everyday practices that continuously prepare mindsets for systemic change. Lead cultivators convert the complexity into a unified commitment to innovation. They focus on establishing a collaborative culture in which the coalition of the willing can thrive. Lead cultivators listen to their stakeholders to understand and identify their passions and interests. They also intentionally incorporate local expertise into their leadership structures. Equally important, lead cultivators exhibit courage by choosing not to perseverate on resisters. The results of the shift from being the manager of school complexity to lead cultivator mean the complexity or size of a secondary school is not a challenge to change but a vehicle for it.

Lead Creator

The third limiting belief to transformational change is that a new innovation must perfectly mirror the latest trends or some previously created intervention. This limiting idea also includes the assumption that every new practice must be validated by the same quantitative metric. While it is certainly true leaders should use innovations supported by documented research, they must also broaden their perspectives and understand studies in context.

The most popular metric used to interpret education research is effect size, and the most well-known reporting of effect sizes associated with educational interventions is the body of work by Hattie (2009, 2012, 2015). In his 2009 book *Visible Learning*, Hattie took the position that an effect size of 0.40 is a general "hinge point," or "cut point," that educators should be cognizant of. If an intervention has an average effect size of 0.40 or above across a number of studies, then it should be considered viable. If the average effect size is below 0.40, then it should not. There are a number of problems with this perspective that require an understanding of the nature of effect sizes to discern.

Although *effect size* is technically a generic term for any measure of the relationship between two variables, two metrics are commonly used as the effect size: standardized mean difference and correlation coefficient. When educators use the term *effect size*, they are typically referring to the standardized mean difference. In general terms, the *standardized mean difference* (denoted by the variable d) is the difference in the mean scores between a group that received a specific intervention (that is, the experimental group) and a group that did not receive the intervention (that is, the control group). For example, the standardized mean difference could be used to compute the differences in average achievement scores between competency-based classrooms (the experimental group) and classrooms that did not use a CBE approach (the control group).

A correlation coefficient (denoted by the variable r) is also a type of effect size because it, too, quantifies the relationship between two variables. However, a correlation does not involve distinct experimental and control groups. Rather, a correlation coefficient is computed when a study involves a number of subjects, all of which use a specific intervention at varying levels of fidelity. For example, a correlation coefficient could quantify the relationship between how well a classroom employs a CBE approach and the average achievement of the students in the class. If a study involved twenty classes that used CBE at differing levels of fidelity, for instance, a correlation coefficient would be computed between the twenty levels of CBE fidelity represented in the classes and the twenty average achievement scores from the classes.

A correlation coefficient has a direct mathematical relationship with a standardized mean difference. Specifically, the following formula transforms a standardized mean difference (d) to a correlation coefficient (r).

$$r = \frac{d}{(d^2 + 4)^{1/2}}$$

Conversely, the following formula transforms a correlation coefficient (r) to a standardized mean difference (d).

$$d = \frac{2r}{(1 - r^2)^{1/2}}$$

Many researchers have provided guidance as to what can be considered small, medium, and large correlations and standardized mean differences (see Ellis, 2010; Rosenthal, 1996). Drawing on the work of psychologist and statistician Jacob Cohen (1988), psychology researchers Andrey Lovakov and Elena R. Agadullina (2021) noted that the most common thresholds for interpreting effect sizes are those listed in table 5.4. An analysis of the relative sizes of the two types of effect sizes indicates that, in general, the standardized mean difference is about twice the size of the correlation coefficient.

Relative to the discussion here, it is important to note that other researchers have argued against classifying any type of effect size by its magnitude. For example, researchers Gene V. Glass, Barry McGaw, and Mary Lee Smith (1981) explained:

TABLE 5.4: Thresholds for Interpreting Effect Sizes

Metric	Small	Medium	Large	Very Large
Standardized mean difference (d)	0.20	0.50	0.80	1.30
Correlation (r)	0.10	0.30	0.50	0.70

Source: Adapted from Lovakov & Agadullina, 2021.

> There is no wisdom whatsoever in attempting to associate regions of the effect size metric with descriptive adjectives such as "small," "moderate," "large," and the like. Dissociated from a context of decision and comparative value, there is little inherent value to an effect size of 3.5 or .2. Depending on what benefits can be achieved at what cost, an effect size of 2.0 might be "poor" and one of .1 might be "good." (p. 104)

In addressing this issue, psychology scholar Mark Lipsey and his colleagues (2012) explained that those interpreting effect sizes must think in terms of practical significance, which involves a comparison with typical expectations. They noted:

> Practical significance is not an inherent characteristic of the numbers and statistics that result from intervention research—it is something that must be judged in some

context of application. To interpret the practical significance of an intervention effect, therefore, it is necessary to invoke an appropriate frame of reference external to its statistical representation. (p. 26)

They further explained that appropriate frames of reference for educational interventions include expectations for normal growth, other similar interventions, and the cost and resources associated with the intervention under study.

In effect, the notion that programs and practices can be judged on the basis of a simple metric like an effect size makes little sense. Leaders seeking to move to a CBE system should certainly consult all the available research. But they should keep in mind that all research is highly situational in that the results for one study most probably will not precisely transfer to another situation. As Reeves (2006) noted, "The reality is that perfect research does not exist" (p. 97). Consequently, the leader seeking change by implementing an off-the-shelf program is looking for an easy fix. These do not exist when it comes to transforming secondary schools, especially when the change is second order in nature, hence the need for the lead creator.

Lead creators consult the extant research and use it to guide their deliberation. But they are also not afraid to challenge the status quo and break traditions when an innovation is not working. As this definition implies, leaders cannot create if they are simply using programs developed by others. This is not to say that they are averse to using previously developed programs as critical parts of a bigger plan. Ultimately, lead creators study and learn from others but rely on their unique talents and plans (Cousins, 2008). One cannot innovate by following someone else's blueprint (Gallagher & Thordarson, 2018).

Leadership literature has provided insight on the characteristics of a lead creator. According to Fullan and Kirtman (2019), one of the competencies of highly effective leaders is their willingness to challenge the status quo and take risks. Fullan (2014) argued that leaders maximize impact by challenging practices that may not improve student achievement, and by taking risks to achieve results. According to education scholars Alyssa Gallagher and Kami Thordarson (2018), breaking long-held traditions and rules can be daunting but that "intentional rule-breaking can help us step into the universe of possibility" (p. 113).

In summary, lead creators do not simply implement programs created by others. They learn from education research and the efforts of others, but ultimately create innovations that are specific to their unique situations. One might liken the actions of a lead creator to a sculptor with a raw piece of granite. The sculptor has a picture of the heretofore uncreated work in mind and continually chisels off small chips of granite that are not part of that vision. So, too, the lead creator begins with a strong vision and then gradually changes or discards those aspects of the system that are not part of that vision. Finally, the lead creator inspires others in the school and community to collaborate in the creative process (Boyatzis & McKee, 2005).

Lead Coach

The limiting belief that spawns the need for the role of lead coach is that school leaders can stimulate school improvement and substantive change through the teacher evaluation process. On the surface, this might seem like a reasonable idea: if teachers are evaluated on behaviors specific to an innovation, they will learn to exhibit these behaviors, which in turn will produce the desired effects of the innovation. Indeed, this thinking was central to the massive Race to the Top (RTT) legislation under the administration of President Barack Obama (see Marzano et al., 2021). While that legislation had many components, a central theme was that the evaluation process could increase teachers' pedagogical skills and focus their efforts on improving student learning. Although the reform seemed reasonable conceptually, once data started coming in regarding its effects, it became clear that the evaluation process is simply not useful as a tool for teacher development. In effect, then, the whole enterprise of teacher evaluation as envisioned by the RTT legislation failed to make any substantive changes in the teaching and learning in K–12 classrooms. While some metrics show improvement, the system still does not sufficiently differentiate between excellent and ineffective teachers or help weak teachers improve (Kraft & Gilmour, 2017; Lash, Tran, & Huang, 2016). In terms of moving a secondary school to a CBE system, the leader who tries to use the evaluation process as the lever to produce transformational change is doomed to failure.

Instead of using evaluation as the lever for change, school leaders should focus on developing their skills as lead coach. A *lead coach* establishes a culture of coaching characterized by ongoing, collaborative, and job-embedded learning, accompanied by personalized goals and specific feedback. Lead coaches are dedicated to unlocking the potential of their teachers. As a result of effective coaching, teachers should become more confident about their abilities (Whitaker, 2012). This is accomplished by focusing on teacher growth as opposed to rating competence.

Unfortunately, the evaluation process is sometimes the antithesis of the coaching process. Characteristically, evaluators hurriedly complete each teacher's obligatory preconference, perform the required number of classroom observations, write up feedback on the predetermined documents, conduct post-conferences, and do all of it within a predetermined timeline. Additionally, many evaluation systems trivialize the complexity of effective teaching by employing lengthy checklists. As we described in the discussion of instruction and teacher development (SLI 5, chapter 2, page 74), effective teaching involves using instructional strategies in a manner that ensures those strategies are having a visible effect on student learning. Checklists imply that the mere use of a strategy demonstrates expertise. Finally, the high-stakes nature of teacher evaluation tends to dominate the attention of teachers and leaders. Education leadership scholar David B. Reid (2017) pointed out that principals are less likely to rate teachers critically due to the possible consequences to teacher employment, further confusing the issue. Thus, teacher evaluation scores probably do not even provide teachers accurate feedback about their pedagogical skills.

This is not to say that the evaluation process is inherently deleterious to teacher development. Indeed, in the hands of an effective lead coach, the evaluation process can produce positive effects and even be an agent of change. Education consultant Todd Whitaker (2012) alluded to this when he stated that effective leaders focus on improving people because they understand it is people who will improve the quality of a school, not programs. By stressing the importance of developing people, lead coaches can engage teachers in professional learning that enables them to lean into vulnerability, try new strategies, and make mistakes without fear.

Within the Marzano Academies model, the scale teachers use to examine their pedagogical skills is specifically designed for teacher development. The five levels of this scale, which we introduced in the discussion of school-level indicator 5 (see figure 2.26, page 79), include not using (0), beginning (1), developing (2), applying (3), and innovating (4). This scale provides teachers with a schema for developing their use of specific strategies. Even if a teacher is not currently using a pedagogical strategy, they have clear guidance as to the next level up—beginning (1)—which means that they use the particular strategy, albeit with some errors or omissions. This descriptor sends a message to teachers that making errors or omissions is simply part of the process when developing a skill. As teachers move to the developing (2) level, they focus on executing the strategy without significant errors or omissions, before turning their attention to students and the strategy's discernable effect on them at the applying (3) level. Finally, the innovating (4) level encourages teachers to grow their skills to a point where they can adapt the strategy to ensure it produces the desired effect with all students.

As mentioned previously, academy teachers rate themselves on the forty-nine elements and then set goals for improvement on specific instructional elements each year. In effect, in the Marzano Academies model, teacher development begins with self-reflection. This is an essential component of coaching, "which continuously flows from goal setting to action to reflection" (Bloom, Castagna, Moir, & Warren, 2005, p. 49). In their study of teacher reflection, education scholars Tushar Gupta, Abha Shree, and Lokanath Mishra (2019) maintained that reflection prompts people to decipher what they learned, why they learned it, and how that specific increment of learning occurred. Similarly, management studies researchers Payal Sharma and Jagwinder Singh Pandher (2018) found that teachers should undergo regular self-assessment and self-reflection as it is the most critical teacher professional development activity. Teachers can meet with instructional coaches or other school leaders, and students can meet with assigned mentors or teachers to monitor progress, reflect, design action steps, and set new incremental growth goals. For the lead coach, then, the teacher evaluation process focuses on teacher development. Outside of the evaluation process, there are a number of activities in which lead coaches engage.

Lead coaches encourage collaboration among teachers. Blankstein (2004) asserted that in high-achieving schools, teachers work interdependently, become active learners, and work collaboratively to improve teaching strategies. Since collaboration is not necessarily the norm at the secondary level, the lead coach should encourage and facilitate teamwork, partnership, relationship, and cooperation. With teacher development in mind, lead coaches may ask teachers to engage in lesson study. Lesson study was introduced to American educators through the book *The Teaching Gap* by education scholars James Stigler and James Hiebert (1999). Stigler and Hiebert (1999) described a collaborative approach to lesson design used in Japan called *kounaikenshuu*:

> One of the most common components of *kounaikenshuu* is lesson study (*jugyou kenkyuu*). In lesson study, groups of teachers meet regularly over long periods of time (ranging from several months to a year) to work on the design, implementation, testing, and improvement of one or several "research designs" (*kenkyuu jugyou*). By all indicators, lesson study is extremely popular and highly valued by Japanese teachers, especially at the elementary level. It is the linchpin of the improvement process. (pp. 110–111)

Education consultants and authors Richard DuFour and Robert J. Marzano (2011) explained that, since the introduction of the concept of lesson study to U.S. educators, those educators have developed several adaptations (see, for example, Jalongo, Rieg, & Helterbran, 2007). DuFour and Marzano (2011) noted that collaborative teams within professional learning communities are perfect vehicles for developing and vetting effective units, as described in our discussion of school-level indicator 5 (page 74). Within the Marzano Academies model, the concept of *lesson design* has expanded to *unit design*. This expansion introduces many benefits. First, the development of a common unit helps ensure that students receive well-crafted and vetted instruction that is similar from teacher to teacher. Second, focusing on unit design as opposed to lesson design provides individual teachers with day-to-day flexibility to meet the specific needs of their students while still operating within a well-defined structure.

Lead coaches do not emphasize end-of-course scores, interim assessment results, end-of-year data, state assessments, or other macrodata. Instead, they utilize more frequent microdata grounded in student evidence from classroom assessments like quizzes, exit tickets, student questions during lessons, journals, quick checks for understanding, responses to guided practice, and so on (Venables, 2014). Microdata such as these keep the focus on student learning at a granular level as teachers make data-informed decisions about their instruction (Sweeney, 2013; Venables, 2014). By concentrating on current micro-level student data, lead coaches remain centered on evidence of where students are in their learning and what teachers can do to improve their learning (Sweeney, 2011), rather than on the students' general achievement as measured by omnibus external assessments.

Finally, lead coaches work to identify a team of coaches who will support teachers throughout the execution of an initiative like CBE. The leadership team should reframe the roles of principal, assistant principal, deans, department chairs, and any other titles that supervise teachers. These roles should no longer be supervisory with the responsibility to judge competence. Instead, lead coaches apply a coaching stance to these roles to support individuals and groups of teachers focusing on professional practice. Lead coaches adjust their budgets to hire as many instructional coaches as possible. They also invest in and establish teacher-leaders who can serve as instructional coaches. The end goal is to form a group of instructors who function as coaches and support teachers as they learn and apply new knowledge.

In summary, lead coaches must work diligently to establish and maintain a general culture of coaching. Such a culture improves the quality of community and learning by fostering professional collaboration, extending leadership beyond the principal, and involving teachers in crafting learning experiences over which they take ownership (Johnson, Leibowitz, & Perret, 2017). Establishing a culture of coaching can transform the school by improving teacher practices and confronting systemic issues (Aguilar, 2013). Within a culture of coaching, members of the coalition of the willing seek opportunities to collaborate and teachers take more responsibility for their learning, with an eye toward improving the talent and skills of teachers and leaders alike.

Summary

In this chapter, we have described four different roles that leaders of secondary schools seeking to adopt CBE should pursue: lead coalitionist, lead cultivator, lead creator, and lead coach. Each of these roles mitigates the negative effects of common limiting beliefs in K–12 education. The role of lead coalitionist focuses the leader's attention on creating a coalition of the willing and counters the limiting belief that leaders must have buy-in before undertaking a complex change. The role of lead cultivator addresses the limiting belief that secondary schools are too complex to sustain large-scale change by focusing attention on generating and supporting big ideas in the service of CBE. The role of lead creator alleviates the limiting belief that any changes in secondary education must mirror someone else's strategy for innovation. This role focuses on inspiring those involved in designing and implementing CBE to trust their interpretations of how they should apply research and best practices to their situations. The role of lead coach works against the limiting belief that significant change in secondary schools should be powered by the teacher evaluation process and focuses attention on coaching as the primary vehicle for developing expertise in CBE. Leaders who adopt these four roles will find more success in transitioning their organizations to a competency-based system.

In this book, we have provided a comprehensive overview of a specific approach to competency-based education at the secondary level: the Marzano Academies model. Throughout the preceding chapters, we have attempted to provide a detailed and comprehensive discussion that enables secondary leaders to apply the sixteen school-level indicators to their current situations to transform their schools into CBE systems or make significant next steps in this endeavor. As we mentioned in the introduction (page 1), this book is intended for two audiences. One audience is those schools seeking official status as academies. Those schools should contact Marzano Academies (MarzanoAcademies.org) to begin this journey. The other audience is those schools who wish to implement some but not all of the components of the academy model. Those schools should select the indicators of interest and make any adaptations or alterations to those indicators they see fit. We wish these schools great success and satisfaction in their efforts.

Regardless of whether a school embraces the full Marzano Academies model or adapts the indicators in the model to meet their specific needs, we hope this book provides a stimulus for school leaders to evolve their systems into the next generation of secondary schools. We believe that this model operationalizes the foundational pillars of that next-generation school, and hope that our comments not only inspire secondary school leaders in this endeavor but also offer a concrete roadmap.

REFERENCES AND RESOURCES

Aguilar, E. (2013). *The art of coaching: Effective strategies for school transformation.* San Francisco: Jossey-Bass.

Anderson, L. W., & Krathwohl, D. R. (Eds.). (2001). *A taxonomy for learning, teaching, and assessing: A revision of Bloom's taxonomy of educational objectives.* New York: Longman.

Argyris, C., & Schön, D. (1974). *Theory in practice: Increasing professional effectiveness.* San Francisco: Jossey-Bass.

Argyris, C., & Schön, D. (1978). *Organizing learning: A theory of action perspective.* Reading, MA: Addison-Wesley.

Bandura, A. (1977). Self-efficacy: Toward a unifying theory of behavioral change. *Psychological Review, 84*(2), 191–215.

Bandura, A. (1993). Perceived self-efficacy in cognitive development and functioning. *Educational Psychologist, 28*(2), 117–148.

Bandura, A. (1997). *Self-efficacy: The exercise of control.* New York: Worth Publishers.

Beck, I. L., McKeown, M. G., & Kucan, L. (2002). *Bringing words to life: Robust vocabulary instruction.* New York: Guilford Press.

Beck, I. L., McKeown, M. G., & Kucan, L. (2013). *Bringing words to life: Robust vocabulary instruction* (2nd ed.). New York: Guilford Press.

Benard, B. (2004). *Resiliency: What we have learned.* San Francisco: WestEd.

Blankstein, A. M. (2004). *Failure is not an option: Six principles that guide student achievement in high-performing schools.* Thousand Oaks, CA: Corwin.

Bloom, B. S. (Ed.). (1956). *Taxonomy of educational objectives: The classification of educational goals. Handbook I: Cognitive domain.* New York: David McKay.

Bloom, G., Castagna, C., Moir, E., & Warren, B. (2005). *Blended coaching: Skills and strategies to support principal development.* Thousand Oaks, CA: Corwin.

Blum, R., & Libbey, H. P. (2004). School connectedness: Strengthening health and education outcomes for teenagers. *Journal of School Health, 74*(4), 229–299.

Bonem, M., & Patterson, R. (2005). *Leading from the second chair: Serving your church, fulfilling your role, and realizing your dreams.* San Francisco: Jossey-Bass.

Boyatzis, R., & McKee, A. (2005). *Resonant leadership: Renewing yourself and connecting with others through mindfulness, hope, and compassion.* Boston: Harvard Business School Press.

Brewer, H. (2019). *Relentless: Changing lives by disrupting the educational norm.* San Diego, CA: Dave Burgess Consulting, Inc.

Brough, J. A., Bergmann, S., & Holt, L. C. (2006). *Teach me, I dare you!* New York: Routledge.

Buckley, J. (2020). *Standardized tests can serve as a neutral yardstick.* Accessed at https://www.proquest.com/scholarly-journals /standardized-tests-can-serve-as-neutral-yardstick/docview/2417866713/se-2 on April 23, 2022.

Burgess, S., & Houf, B. (2017). *Lead like a PIRATE: Make school amazing for your students and staff.* San Diego, CA: Dave Burgess Consulting, Inc.

Care, E., Griffin, P., & Wilson, M. (Eds.). (2018). *Assessment and teaching of 21st century skills: Research and applications.* New York: Springer.

Chen, Y. (2021). Beyond the ordinary: Designing a mobile-assisted funds-of-knowledge-featured instructional framework for English learners. *International Journal of Designs for Learning, 12*(2), 49–58.

Cohen, J. (1988). *Statistical power analysis for the behavioral sciences* (2nd ed.). Hillsdale, NJ: Lawrence Erlbaum.

Collins, J. (2001). *Good to great: Why some companies make the leap . . . and others don't.* New York: HarperBusiness.

Convertino, C. (2016). Beyond ethnic tidbits: Toward a critical and dialogical model in multicultural social justice teacher preparation. *International Journal of Multicultural Education, 18*(2), 125–142.

Cornish, E. (2004). *Futuring: The exploration of the future.* Bethesda, MD: World Future Society.

Cousins, D. (2008). *Experiencing leadershift: Letting go of leadership heresies.* Colorado Springs, CO: David C. Cook.

Cox, J. W., Rich, S., Chiu, A., Muyskens, J., & Ulmanu, M. (2022, May 25). More than 311,000 students have experienced gun violence at school since Columbine. *Washington Post.* Accessed at www.washingtonpost.com/graphics /2018/local/school-shootings-database/ on May 26, 2022.

Croninger, R. G., & Lee, V. E. (2001). Social capital and dropping out of high school: Benefits to at-risk students of teachers' support and guidance. *Teachers College Record, 103*(4), 548–581.

Deas, K. (2018). Evaluating Common Core: Are uniform standards a silver bullet for education reform? *The Journal of Educational Foundations, 31*(3), 47–62. Accessed at https://search.proquest.com/docview/2204807034?accountid =36783 on April 23, 2022.

de Brey, C., Musu, L., McFarland, J., Wilkinson-Flicker, S., Diliberti, M., Zhang, A., et al. (2019). *Status and trends in the education of racial and ethnic groups 2018* (NCES 2019-038). Washington, DC: National Center for Education Statistics. Accessed at https://nces.ed.gov/pubs2019/2019038.pdf on April 30, 2022.

Diem, S., & Carpenter, B. W. (2012). Social justice and leadership preparation: Developing a transformative curriculum. *Planning and Changing, 43*(1/2), 96–112.

DiMartino, J., & Wolk, D. L. (Eds.). (2010). *The personalized high school: Making learning count for adolescents.* San Francisco: Jossey-Bass.

Dodson, C. (2019). *The critical concepts in social studies.* Accessed at www.marzanoresources.com/critical-concepts-social -studies.html on March 1, 2021.

Donohoo, J., Hattie, J., & Eells, R. (2018). The power of collective efficacy. *Educational Leadership, 75*(6), 40–44.

DuFour, R., & Marzano, R. J. (2011). *Leaders of learning: How district, school, and classroom leaders improve student achievement.* Bloomington, IN: Solution Tree Press.

Dweck, C. S. (2006). *Mindset: The new psychology of success.* New York: Ballantine Books.

Eells, R. (2011). *Meta-analysis of the relationship between collective efficacy and student achievement* [Doctoral dissertation, Loyola University of Chicago]. Loyola eCommons. Accessed at https://ecommons.luc.edu/cgi/viewcontent.cgi?article= 1132&context=luc_diss on June 14, 2022.

Ellis, P. D. (2010). *The essential guide to effect sizes: Statistical power, meta-analysis, and the interpretation of research results.* Cambridge, UK: Cambridge University Press.

Esposito, J., & Swain, A. N. (2009). Pathways to social justice: Urban teachers' uses of culturally relevant pedagogy as a conduit for teaching for social justice. *Perspectives on Urban Education, 6*(1), 38–48.

Esquith, R. (2003). *There are no shortcuts.* New York: Pantheon.

Finn, D., III, & Finn, M. (2021). *Scheduling for personalized competency-based education.* Bloomington, IN: Marzano Resources.

Frey, N., Fisher, D., & Smith, D. (2019). *All learning is social and emotional: Helping students develop essential skills for the classroom and beyond.* Alexandria, VA: Association for Supervision and Curriculum Development.

Fullan, M. (2014). *The principal: Three keys to maximizing impact.* San Francisco: Jossey-Bass.

Fullan, M., & Kirtman, L. (2019). *Coherent school leadership: Forging clarity from complexity.* Alexandria, VA: Association for Supervision and Curriculum Development.

Furman, G. (2012). Social justice leadership as praxis: Developing capacities through preparation programs. *Educational Administration Quarterly, 48*(2), 191–229.

Gallagher, A., & Thordarson, K. (2018). *Design thinking for school leaders: Five roles and mindsets that ignite positive change.* Alexandria, VA: Association for Supervision and Curriculum Development.

Garmezy, N. (1974). The study of competence in children at risk for severe psychopathology. In E. J. Anthony & C. Koupernik (Eds.), *The child in his family: Children at psychiatric risk* (Vol. 3, pp. 77–97). New York: Wiley.

Gewertz, C. (2019, April 9). Which states require an exam to graduate? An interactive breakdown of states' 2016–17 testing plans. *Education Week.* Accessed at www.edweek.org/ew/section/multimedia/states-require-exam-to-graduate.html on February 9, 2021.

Gladwell, M. (2002). *The tipping point: How little things can make a big difference.* New York: Little, Brown and Company.

Glass, G. V., McGaw, B., & Smith, M. L. (1981). *Meta-analysis in social research.* Beverly Hills, CA: SAGE.

Goddard, R. D. (2002). A theoretical and empirical analysis of the measurement of collective efficacy: The development of a short form. *Educational and Psychological Measurement, 62*(1), 97–110.

Goddard, R. D., Hoy, W. K., & Woolfolk-Hoy, A. (2004). Collective efficacy beliefs: Theoretical developments, empirical evidence, and future directions. *Educational Researcher, 33*(3), 3–13.

Goens, G. A. (2021). *Getting the message: The wisdom of listening and thinking.* Lanham, MD: Rowman & Littlefield.

Gomez-Velez, N. (2013). Urban public education reform: Governance, accountability, outsourcing. *The Urban Lawyer, 45*(1), 51–104.

Gordon, J. (2007). *The energy bus: 10 rules to fuel your life, work, and team with positive energy.* Hoboken, NJ: Wiley.

Graves, M. F. (2006). *The vocabulary book: Learning and instruction.* New York: Teachers College Press.

GreatSchools Staff. (2021, May 3). *The most important class in high school isn't what you think.* Accessed at www.greatschools .org/gk/articles/advisory-the-most-important-class-in-high-school-isnt-what-you-think on May 25, 2022.

Gruenert, S., & Whitaker, T. (2017). *School culture recharged: Strategies to energize your staff and culture.* Alexandria, VA: Association for Supervision and Curriculum Development.

Gupta, T., Shree, A., & Mishra, L. (2019). Reflective teaching as a strategy for effective instruction. *Educational Quest, 10*(1), 37–43.

Harrison, L., Jr., & Clark, L. (2016). Contemporary issues of social justice: A focus on race and physical education in the United States. *Research Quarterly for Exercise and Sport, 87*(3), 230–241. Accessed at http://dx.doi.org/10.1080 /02701367.2016.1199166 on June 14, 2022.

Hartati, V. (2020). *The influence of word cluster strategy toward students' vocabulary mastery at the second semester of the eighth grade of SMPN 19 Bandar Lampung in academic year 2019/2020* [S1 degree thesis, Tarbiyah and Teacher Training Facility, State Islamic University of Raden Intan]. Accessed at http://repository.radenintan.ac.id/11745/1 /PUSAT1-2.pdf on May 20, 2022.

Hattie, J. A. C. (2009). *Visible learning: A synthesis of over 800 meta-analyses relating to achievement.* New York: Routledge.

Hattie, J. A. C. (2012). *Visible learning for teachers: Maximizing impact on learning.* New York: Routledge.

Hattie, J. A. C. (2015). The applicability of visible learning to higher education. *Scholarship of Teaching and Learning in Psychology, 1*(1), 79–91.

Haynes, J. (2007). *Getting started with English language learners: How educators can meet the challenge.* Alexandria, VA: Association for Supervision and Curriculum Development.

Heifetz, R. A. (1994). *Leadership without easy answers.* Cambridge, MA: Belknap Press of Harvard University Press.

Heifetz, R. A., & Linsky, M. (2002). *Leadership on the line: Staying alive through the dangers of leading.* Boston: Harvard Business Review Press.

Hiebert, E. H., & Cervetti, G. N. (2012). What differences in narrative and informational texts mean for the learning and instruction of vocabulary. In E. J. Kame'enui & J. F. Baumann (Eds.), *Vocabulary instruction: Research to practice* (2nd ed., pp. 322–344). New York: Guilford Press.

Higgins, M. J. (2009). Standardized tests: Wristwatch or dipstick? *Research in Education, 81*(1), 1–11.

Hodges, A. (2010). Venture to a new frontier: The need for partnerships between postsecondary academic advisors and secondary schools. *Academic Advising Today, 33*(4). Accessed at https://nacada.ksu.edu/Resources/Academic-Advising-Today /View-Articles/Venture-to-a-New-Frontier-The-Need-for-Partnerships-between-Postsecondary-Academic-Advisors-and -Secondary-Schools.aspx on May 23, 2022.

Hoegh, J. K. (2020). *A handbook for developing and using proficiency scales in the classroom.* Bloomington, IN: Marzano Resources.

Hoerr, T. R. (2017). *The formative five: Fostering grit, empathy, and other successful skills every student needs.* Alexandria, VA: Association for Supervision and Curriculum Development.

Jalongo, M. R., Rieg, S. A., & Helterbran, V. R. (2007). *Planning for learning: Collaborative approaches to lesson design and review.* New York: Teachers College Press.

Jenkins, J. R., & Dixon, R. (1983). Vocabulary learning. *Contemporary Educational Psychology, 8*(3), 237–260.

Jensen, E. (2009). *Teaching with poverty in mind: What being poor does to kids' brains and what schools can do about it.* Alexandria, VA: Association for Supervision and Curriculum Development.

Johnson, J., Leibowitz, S., & Perret, K. (2017). *The coach approach to school leadership: Leading teachers to higher levels of effectiveness.* Alexandria, VA: Association for Supervision and Curriculum Development.

Kallick, B., & Zmuda, A. (2017). *Students at the center: Personalized learning with habits of mind.* Alexandria, VA: Association for Supervision and Curriculum Development.

Kane, T. J., & Staiger, D. O. (2012). *Gathering feedback for teaching: Combining high-quality observations with student surveys and achievement gains.* Seattle, WA: Bill & Melinda Gates Foundation.

Koltko-Rivera, M. E. (2006). Rediscovering the later version of Maslow's hierarchy of needs: Self-transcendence and opportunities for theory, research, and unification. *Review of General Psychology, 10*(4), 302–317.

Kondor, C., Owusu-Ansah, A., & Keyne-Michaels, L. (2019). Intercultural fortuitous learning: Preparing prospective teachers to teach culturally diverse populations. *Multicultural Education, 26*(3–4), 17–26.

Kraft, M. A., & Gilmour, A. F. (2017). Revisiting the Widget Effect: Teacher evaluation reforms and the distribution of teacher effectiveness. *Educational Researcher, 46*(5), 234–249.

Kulaas, A., Ryerse, M., & Vander Ark, T. (2017, August 24). *The role of advisory in personalizing the secondary experience.* Accessed at www.gettingsmart.com/2017/08/24/the-role-of-advisory-in-personalizing-the-secondary-experience-2 on May 19, 2022.

Lash, A., Tran, L., & Huang, M. (2016, May). *Examining the validity of ratings from a classroom observation instrument for use in a district's teacher evaluation system.* Accessed at http://ies.ed.gov/ncee/edlabs/regions/west/pdf/REL_2016135.pdf on February 17, 2022.

Lencioni, P. (2002). *The five dysfunctions of a team: A leadership fable.* San Francisco: Jossey-Bass.

Lipsey, M. W., Puzio, K., Yun, C., Hebert, M. A., Steinka-Fry, K., Cole, M. W., et al. (2012, November). *Translating the statistical representation of the effects of education interventions into more readily interpretable forms.* Washington, DC: Institute of Education Sciences, U.S. Department of Education.

Lovakov, A., & Agadullina, E. R. (2021, February). Empirically derived guidelines for effect size interpretation in social psychology. *European Journal of Social Psychology.* Accessed at www.researchgate.net/publication/349082997 _Empirically_Derived_Guidelines_for_Effect_Size_Interpretation_in_Social_Psychology on May 25, 2022.

Lund, D. E. (2011). Examining shades of grey with students: Social justice education in action. *Journal of Praxis in Multicultural Education, 6*(1), 79–91.

Malone, H. J. (2009). Build a bridge from high school to college: Transition programs are essential for many disadvantaged students. *Phi Kappa Phi Forum, 89*(3), 23.

Marion, S., Worthen, M., & Evans, C. (2020). *How systems of assessments aligned with competency-based education can support equity.* Accessed at https://aurora-institute.org/resource/how-systems-of-assessments-aligned-with -competency-based-education-can-support-equity/ on March 18, 2022.

Marzano, R. J. (1992). *A different kind of classroom: Teaching with Dimensions of Learning.* Alexandria, VA: Association for Supervision and Curriculum Development.

Marzano, R. J. (2003). *What works in schools: Translating research into action.* Alexandria, VA: Association for Supervision and Curriculum Development.

Marzano, R. J. (2004). *Building background knowledge for academic achievement: Research on what works for schools.* Alexandria, VA: Association for Supervision and Curriculum Development.

Marzano, R. J. (2006). *Classroom assessment and grading that work.* Alexandria, VA: Association for Supervision and Curriculum Development.

Marzano, R. J. (2007). *The art and science of teaching: A comprehensive framework for effective instruction.* Alexandria, VA: Association for Supervision and Curriculum Development.

Marzano, R. J. (2010). *Teaching basic and advanced vocabulary: A framework for direct instruction.* Boston: Cengage.

Marzano, R. J. (2011). *Formative assessment and standards-based grading.* Bloomington, IN: Marzano Resources.

Marzano, R. J. (2017). *The new art and science of teaching.* Bloomington, IN: Solution Tree Press.

Marzano, R. J. (2018). *Making classroom assessments reliable and valid.* Bloomington, IN: Solution Tree Press.

Marzano, R. J. (2019). *Understanding rigor in the classroom.* West Palm Beach, FL: Learning Sciences International.

Marzano, R. J. (2020). *Teaching basic, advanced, and academic vocabulary: A comprehensive framework for elementary instruction.* Bloomington, IN: Marzano Resources.

Marzano, R. J. (2021a). *Element IId: Generating current summative scores.* Accessed at https://marzanoacademies.org /wp-content/uploads/2021/03/Marzano-Academies-Element-IId-Generating-Current-Summative-Scores-in-a-CBE -Classroom.pdf on January 19, 2022.

Marzano, R. J. (2021b). *Element IIIf: Engaging students in cognitively complex tasks in a CBE classroom.* Accessed at https://marzanoacademies.org/wp-content/uploads/2021/04/Element-IIIf-12-Engaging-Students-in-Cognitively-Complex-Tasks-in-a-CBE-Classroom.pdf on January 19, 2022.

Marzano, R. J., & Abbott, S. D. (2022). *Teaching in a competency-based elementary school: The Marzano Academies model.* Bloomington, IN: Marzano Resources.

Marzano, R. J., Aschoff, A. S., & Avila, A. (2022). *Teaching in a competency-based secondary school: The Marzano Academies model.* Bloomington, IN: Marzano Resources.

Marzano, R. J., Brandt, R. S., Hughes, C. S., Jones, B. F., Presseisen, B. Z., Rankin, S. C., et al. (1988). *Dimensions of thinking: A framework for curriculum and instruction.* Alexandria, VA: Association for Supervision and Curriculum Development.

Marzano, R. J., Dodson, C. W., Simms, J. A., & Wipf, J. P. (2022). *Ethical test preparation in the classroom.* Bloomington, IN: Marzano Resources.

Marzano, R. J., Heflebower, T., Hoegh, J. K., Warrick, P., & Grift, G. (2016). *Collaborative teams that transform schools: The next step in PLCs.* Bloomington, IN: Marzano Resources.

Marzano, R. J., & Kendall, J. S. (2007). *The new taxonomy of educational objectives* (2nd ed.). Thousand Oaks, CA: Corwin.

Marzano, R. J., & Kosena, B. J. (2022). *Leading a competency-based elementary school.* Bloomington, IN: Marzano Resources.

Marzano, R. J., & Marzano, J. S. (1988). *A cluster approach to elementary vocabulary instruction.* Newark, DE: International Reading Association.

Marzano, R. J., & Marzano, J. S. (2015). *Managing the inner world of teaching: Emotions, interpretations, and actions.* Bloomington, IN: Marzano Resources.

Marzano, R. J., Norford, J. S., Finn, M., & Finn, D., III (with Mestaz, R., & Selleck, R.). (2017). *A handbook for personalized competency-based education.* Bloomington, IN: Marzano Resources.

Marzano, R. J., Norford, J. S., & Ruyle, M. (2019). *The new art and science of classroom assessment.* Bloomington, IN: Solution Tree Press.

Marzano, R. J., & Pickering, D. J. (2005). *Building academic vocabulary: Teacher's manual.* Alexandria, VA: Association for Supervision and Curriculum Development.

Marzano, R. J., Pickering, D. J., & Pollock, J. E. (2001). *Classroom instruction that works: Research-based strategies for increasing student achievement.* Alexandria, VA: Association for Supervision and Curriculum Development.

Marzano, R. J., Rains, C. L., & Warrick, P. B. (2021). *Improving teacher development and evaluation: A guide for leaders, coaches, and teachers.* Bloomington, IN: Marzano Resources.

Marzano, R. J., Rogers, K., & Simms, J. A. (2015). *Vocabulary for the new science standards.* Bloomington, IN: Marzano Resources.

Marzano, R. J., Scott, D., Boogren, T. H., & Newcomb, M. L. (2017). *Motivating and inspiring students: Strategies to awaken the learner.* Bloomington, IN: Marzano Resources.

Marzano, R. J., & Simms, J. A. (2013). *Vocabulary for the Common Core.* Bloomington, IN: Marzano Resources.

Marzano, R. J., & Toth, M. D. (2013). *Teacher evaluation that makes a difference: A new model for teacher growth and student achievement.* Alexandria, VA: Association for Supervision and Curriculum Development.

Marzano, R. J., Warrick, P. B., Rains, C. L., & DuFour, R. (2018). *Leading a high reliability school.* Bloomington, IN: Solution Tree Press.

Marzano, R. J., Warrick, P. B., & Simms, J. A. (2014). *A handbook for high reliability schools: The next step in school reform.* Bloomington, IN: Marzano Resources.

Marzano, R. J., & Waters, T. (2009). *District leadership that works: Striking the right balance.* Bloomington, IN: Solution Tree Press.

Marzano, R. J., Waters, T., & McNulty, B. A. (2005). *School leadership that works: From research to results.* Alexandria, VA: Association for Supervision and Curriculum Development.

Marzano, R. J., Yanoski, D. C., Hoegh, J. K., & Simms, J. A. (with Heflebower, T., & Warrick, P.). (2013). *Using Common Core standards to enhance classroom instruction and assessment.* Bloomington, IN: Marzano Resources.

Marzano Academies. (n.d.). *School-level indicators.* Accessed at https://marzanoacademies.org/interventions-and-initiatives/slis/ on July 27, 2021.

Maslow, A. H. (1943). A theory of human motivation. *Psychological Review, 50*(4), 370–396.

Maslow, A. H. (1954). *Motivation and personality* (1st ed.). New York: Harper & Row.

Maslow, A. H. (1969). The farther reaches of human nature. *Journal of Transpersonal Psychology, 1*(1), 1–9.

Maslow, A. H. (1979). *The journals of A. H. Maslow* (R. J. Lowry, Ed., vols. 1 & 2). Monterey, CA: Brooks/Cole.

McGee, E. O., & Hostetler, A. L. (2014). Historicizing mathematics and mathematizing social studies for social justice: A call for integration. *Equity & Excellence in Education, 47*(2), 208–229. Accessed at http://dx.doi.org/10.1080/10665684.2014.900428 on June 15, 2022.

Möller, K. J. (2012). Developing understandings of social justice: Critical thinking in action in a literature discussion group. *Journal of Children's Literature, 38*(2), 23–36.

Muhammad, A. (2015). *Overcoming the achievement gap trap: Liberating mindsets to effect change.* Bloomington, IN: Solution Tree Press.

Nagaoka, J., Farrington, C. A., Ehrlich, S. B., & Heath, R. D. (2015). *Foundations for young adult success: A developmental framework.* Chicago: University of Chicago CCSR Publications.

National Center for Education Statistics. (2020, September). *Race and ethnicity of public school teachers and their students.* Accessed at https://nces.ed.gov/pubs2020/2020103/index.asp on May 17, 2022.

Oakley, B., Rogowsky, B., & Sejnowski, T. J. (2021). *Uncommon sense teaching: Practical insights in brain science to help students learn.* New York: TarcherPerigee.

Peale, N. V. (1952). *The power of positive thinking.* New York: Prentice-Hall.

Phan, T. (2003). Life in school: Narratives of resiliency among Vietnamese-Canadian youths. *Adolescence, 38*(151), 555–566.

Phillips, D. T. (1992). *Lincoln on leadership: Executive strategies for tough times.* New York: Warner Books.

Pierce, M., & Stapleton, D. L. (Eds.). (2003). *The 21st century principal: Current issues in leadership and policy.* Cambridge, MA: Harvard Education Press.

Poliner, R. A., & Lieber, C. M. (2004). *The advisory guide: Designing and implementing effective advisory programs in secondary schools.* Cambridge, MA: Educators for Social Responsibility.

Popham, W. J. (2001). Uses and misuses of standardized tests. *NASSP Bulletin, 85*(622), 24–31.

Portnoy, L. (2020). *Designed to learn: Using design thinking to bring purpose and passion to the classroom.* Alexandria, VA: Association for Supervision and Curriculum Development.

Prescher, T., & Werle, S. (2014). Comprehensive and sustainable? U.S. education reform from a neo-institutional perspective. *Tertium Comparationis, 20*(1), 81–110.

Preskill, H., & Catsambas, T. T. (2006). *Reframing evaluation through appreciative inquiry.* Thousand Oaks, CA: SAGE.

QuoteFancy. (n.d.). *B. C. Forbes quotes.* Accessed at https://quotefancy.com/b-c-forbes-quotes on June 9, 2022.

Rachel's Challenge. (2021). *Preventing violence and self-harm: Saving lives one heart at a time.* Accessed at https://rachelschallenge.org/our-story/our-impact/ on April 25, 2022.

Reed, L., & Johnson, L. T. (2010). Serving LGBT students: Examining the spiritual, religious, and social justice implications for an African American school administrator. *The Journal of Negro Education, 79*(3), 390–404.

Reeves, D. B. (2003). The six principles of effective accountability. In M. Pierce & D. L. Stapleton (Eds.), *The 21st century principal: Current issues in leadership and policy* (pp. 19–28). Cambridge, MA: Harvard Education Press.

Reeves, D. B. (2006). *The learning leader: How to focus school improvement for better results.* Alexandria, VA: Association for Supervision and Curriculum Development.

Reeves, D. B. (2016). *From leading to succeeding: The seven elements of effective leadership in education.* Bloomington, IN: Solution Tree Press.

Reid, D. B. (2017). U.S. principals' interpretation and implementation of teacher evaluation policies. *The Qualitative Report, 22*(5), 1457–1470.

Reivich, K., & Shatté, A. (2003). *The resilience factor: 7 keys to finding your inner strength and overcoming life's hurdles.* New York: Broadway Books.

Riser-Kositsky, M. (2022, January 7). *Education statistics: Facts about American schools.* Accessed at www.edweek.org/leadership/education-statistics-facts-about-american-schools/2019/01 on May 17, 2022.

Robertson, P. M., & Guerra, P. L. (2016). The voice of one—The power of many: Advancing social justice one individual at a time. *Multicultural Education, 23*(2), 2–12.

Rodman, A. (2019). *Personalized professional learning: A job-embedded pathway for elevating teacher voice.* Alexandria, VA: Association for Supervision and Curriculum Development.

Rollins, S. P. (2014). *Learning in the fast lane: 8 ways to put all students on the road to academic success.* Alexandria, VA: Association for Supervision and Curriculum Development.

Rosenthal, J. A. (1996). Qualitative descriptors of strength of association and effect size. *Journal of Social Service Research*, *21*(4), 37–59.

Rubin, L. B. (1996). *The transcendent child: Tales of triumph over the past*. New York: Basic Books.

Rutter, M. (1990). Psychosocial resilience and protective mechanisms. In J. Rolf, A. S. Masten, D. Cicchetti, K. H. Nuechterlein, & S. Weintraub (Eds.), *Risk and protective factors in the development of psychopathology* (pp. 181–214). New York: Cambridge University Press.

Ruyle, M., Child, L., & Dome, N. (2022). *The school wellness wheel: A framework addressing trauma, culture, and mastery to raise student achievement*. Bloomington, IN: Marzano Resources.

Salvador, K., & Kelly-McHale, J. (2017). Music teacher educator perspectives on social justice. *Journal of Research in Music Education*, *65*(4), 6–24. Accessed at https://doi.org/10.1177/0022429417690340 on June 15, 2022.

Santamaría, L. J., & Jean-Marie, G. (2014). Cross-cultural dimensions of applied, critical, and transformational leadership: Women principals advancing social justice and educational equity. *Cambridge Journal of Education*, *44*(3), 333–360.

Sarıoğlu, M., & Yıldırım, Ö. (2018). The effects of clustering new words in semantic, thematic, or unrelated sets in teaching vocabulary to EFL learners. *Abant İzzet Baysal Üniversitesi Eğitim Fakültesi Dergisi*, *18*(2), 1064–1085.

Schmoker, M. (2011). *Focus: Elevating the essentials to radically improve student learning*. Alexandria, VA: Association for Supervision and Curriculum Development.

Scott, R. (n.d.). *My ethics, my codes of life*. Accessed at www.racheljoyscott.com/rachel-s-codes on June 15, 2022.

Seligman, M. E. P. (2006). *Learned optimism: How to change your mind and your life*. New York: Vintage Books.

Sharma, P., & Pandher, J. S. (2018). Teachers' professional development through teachers' professional activities. *Journal of Workplace Learning*, *30*(8), 613–625.

Simms, J. A. (2016). *The critical concepts*. Accessed at www.marzanoresources.com/the-critical-concepts.html on April 23, 2022.

Southwick, S. M., & Charney, D. S. (2012). *Resilience: The science of mastering life's greatest challenges*. New York: Cambridge University Press.

Steinberg, M. P., & Donaldson, M. L. (2016). The new educational accountability: Understanding the landscape of teacher evaluation in the post-NCLB era. *Education Finance and Policy*, *11*(3), 340–359.

Steinberg, M. P., & Garrett, R. (2016). Classroom composition and measured teacher performance: What do teacher observation scores really measure? *Educational Evaluation and Policy Analysis*, *38*(2), 293–317.

Steinberg, M. P., & Quinn, R. (2017). Education reform in the post-NCLB era: Lessons learned for transforming urban public education. *Cityscape*, *19*(1), 191–216.

Stigler, J. W., & Hiebert, J. (1999). *The teaching gap: Best ideas from the world's teachers for improving education in the classroom*. New York: Free Press.

Stoll, C., & Giddings, G. (2012). *Reawakening the learner: Creating learner-centric, standards-driven schools*. Lanham, MD: Rowman & Littlefield Education.

Sweeney, D. (2011). *Student-centered coaching: A guide for K–8 coaches and principals*. Thousand Oaks, CA: Corwin.

Sweeney, D. (2013). *Student-centered coaching at the secondary level*. Thousand Oaks, CA: Corwin.

Tait, A., & Faulkner, D. (2019). *Dream team: A practical playbook to help innovative educators change schools*. Alexandria, VA: Association for Supervision and Curriculum Development.

ThinkImpact. (2022). *High school statistics*. Accessed at www.thinkimpact.com/high-school-statistics on April 30, 2022.

Thrash, T. M., & Elliot, A. J. (2003). Inspiration as a psychological construct. *Journal of Personality and Social Psychology*, *84*(4), 871–889.

Thrash, T. M., & Elliot, A. J. (2004). Inspiration: Core characteristics, component processes, antecedents, and function. *Journal of Personality and Social Psychology*, *87*(6), 957–973.

Thrash, T. M., Elliot, A. J., Maruskin, L. A., & Cassidy, S. E. (2010). Inspiration and the promotion of well-being: Tests of causality and mediation. *Journal of Personality and Social Psychology*, *98*(3), 488–506.

U.S. Department of Education. (2010, March). *A blueprint for reform: The reauthorization of the Elementary and Secondary Education Act*. Washington, DC: Author.

U.S. Department of Education. (2016, July). *The state of racial diversity in the educator workforce*. Accessed at www2.ed.gov/rschstat/eval/highered/racial-diversity/state-racial-diversity-workforce.pdf on May 17, 2022.

Vander Ark, T. (2015, April 21). *The role of advisory in personalizing the secondary experience*. Accessed at www.gettingsmart.com/2015/04/21/the-role-of-advisory-in-personalizing-the-secondary-experience/ on May 25, 2022.

Venables, D. R. (2014). *How teachers can turn data into action.* Alexandria, VA: Association for Supervision and Curriculum Development.

Venables, D. R. (2018). *Facilitating teacher teams and authentic PLCs: The human side of leading people, protocols, and practices.* Alexandria, VA: Association for Supervision and Curriculum Development.

West, M. (2012). Global lessons for improving U.S. education. *Issues in Science and Technology, 28*(3), 37–44.

Whitaker, T. (2012). *What great principals do differently: 18 things that matter most.* New York: Routledge.

Young, V. M. (2018). Assessing the cornerstone of U.S. education reform. *The Journal of Educational Foundations, 31*(3 & 4), 74–99.

Youth Transitions Task Force. (2006, May). *Too big to be seen: The invisible dropout crisis in Boston and America.* Boston: Boston Private Industry Council.

INDEX

A Handbook for High Reliability Schools
Robert J. Marzano, Philip B. Warrick, and Julia A. Simms
Usher in the new era of school reform. The authors help you transform your schools into organizations that take proactive steps to prevent failure and ensure student success. Using a research-based five-level hierarchy along with leading and lagging indicators, you'll learn to assess, monitor, and confirm the effectiveness of your schools. Each chapter includes what actions should be taken at each level.
BKL020

Ethical Test Preparation in the Classroom
Robert J. Marzano, Christopher W. Dodson, Julia A. Simms, and Jacob P. Wipf
Large-scale assessments—and the conclusions drawn from them—have the power to either open or close future doors for your students. Based on the latest research, this resource clearly articulates everything you need to know about ethical and effective test preparation. You'll review a first-of-its-kind study of over 8,000 assessment items and receive specific recommendations for ELA, mathematics, and science.
BKL059

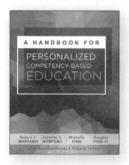

A Handbook for Personalized Competency-Based Education
Robert J. Marzano, Jennifer S. Norford, Michelle Finn, and Douglas Finn III
Ensure all students master content by designing and implementing a personalized competency-based education (PCBE) system. This handbook explores approaches, strategies, and techniques that schools and districts should consider as they begin their transition to a PCBE system. The authors share examples of how to use proficiency scales, standard operating procedures, behavior rubrics, personal tracking matrices, and other tools to aid in instruction and assessment.
BKL037

Scheduling for Personalized Competency-Based Education
Douglas Finn III and Michelle Finn
A challenge at the heart of personalized competency-based education (PCBE) is grouping and scheduling students according to their learning needs rather than their age. With this guidebook, you'll take a deep dive into the why and how of these foundational PCBE components. Gain clear guidance for gathering standards-based data and then using the results to create schedules that promote student proficiency.
BKL049

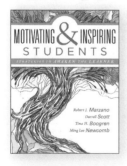

Motivating and Inspiring Students
Robert J. Marzano, Darrell Scott, Tina H. Boogren, and Ming Lee Newcomb
Bringing motivation and inspiration to the classroom is not easy. With this practical resource, you'll discover a results-driven framework—based on a six-level hierarchy of student needs and goals—that you can use to provide engaging instruction to students. The authors share comprehensive understandings of the nature of motivation and inspiration and detail specific strategies to connect with your students.
BKL025

Visit MarzanoResources.com or call 888.849.0851 to order.

Professional Development Designed for Success

Empower your staff to tap into their full potential as educators. As an all-inclusive research-into-practice resource center, we are committed to helping your school or district become highly effective at preparing every student for his or her future.

Choose from our wide range of customized professional development opportunities for teachers, administrators, and district leaders. Each session offers hands-on support, personalized answers, and accessible strategies that can be put into practice immediately.

Bring Marzano Resources experts to your school for results-oriented training on:

- ▶ Assessment & Grading
- ▶ Curriculum
- ▶ Instruction
- ▶ School Leadership

- ▶ Teacher Effectiveness
- ▶ Student Engagement
- ▶ Vocabulary
- ▶ Competency-Based Education

LEARN MORE at MarzanoResources.com/PD